The American Assembly, *Columbia University*

THE PERFORMING ARTS
AND AMERICAN SOCIETY

Prentice-Hall, Inc., *Englewood Cliffs, New Jersey*
A SPECTRUM BOOK

Library of Congress Cataloging in Publication Data
Main entry under title:

The Performing arts and American society.

(A Spectrum Book)
Edited by W. M. Lowry.
At head of title: The American Assembly, Columbia
University.
Papers prepared for the fifty-third American Assembly
at Arden House, Harriman, N.Y., Nov., 1977.
Includes index.
1. Performing arts—United States—Congresses.
I. Lowry, Wilson McNeil (date) II. American
Assembly.
PN2266.P4   790.2'0973   78-1404
ISBN 0-13-657155-7
ISBN 0-13-657148-4 pbk.

The excerpt from the letter on pp. 114-15 is used
by permission of Zelda Fichandler.

10 9 8 7 6 5 4 3 2 1

PRENTICE-HALL INTERNATIONAL, INC. (*London*)
PRENTICE-HALL OF AUSTRALIA PTY, LTD. (*Sydney*)
PRENTICE-HALL OF CANADA, LTD. (*Toronto*)
PRENTICE-HALL OF INDIA PRIVATE LIMITED (*New Delhi*)
PRENTICE-HALL OF JAPAN, INC. (*Tokyo*)
PRENTICE-HALL OF SOUTHEAST ASIA PTE., LTD. (*Singapore*)
WHITEHALL BOOKS LIMITED (*Wellington, New Zealand*)

Table of Contents

78-773   *iii*

Preface

American society over the past two decades has experienced the most rapid expansion of institutions, activities, and audiences in the performing arts in the history of this or any other nation. At the same time, the problems of maintaining this rate of growth, or even of consolidating the resources and structures attained, are clearly enormous and complex.

So stated the final report of the Fifty-third American Assembly, November 3-6, 1977, which brought together at Arden House, Harriman, New York, a group of sixty-one Americans—performers, trustees, critics, directors, managers, and teachers from the worlds of ballet, modern dance, opera, theater, and symphony—to discuss *The Future of the Performing Arts*.

In their report (obtainable directly from The American Assembly) the participants said they were encouraged by the new attention paid to American performing companies and heartened by the recently increased governmental support to the arts. Nevertheless they felt that artists and their institutions, indeed the people of the United States, needed a more clearly understood public policy concerning the arts. To that end they drew up nineteen policy recommendations designed "to protect and encourage the health of the performing arts and to reassure the American people as to the future of these important resources."

This book was put together and edited by W. McNeil Lowry as background reading for the Arden House Assembly, but it is also intended for a wider reading public, for taken together the performing arts appeal to a broad spectrum of the populace. And whether one believes in the so-called elitist view of the performing arts (i.e., support for creative excellence and activity), the so-called populist view (participation by more and more people in the arts), or whether one thinks the arts should be "popular without being popularized," the fact remains it is the public that will resolve the future role of the arts in our society. Wherefore this book—which outlines the history of the phenomenal growth of the performing arts in the last two decades and discusses some of their current problems. The expectation is that it will help us ultimately arrive at a coherent national view of the arts.

The opinions which follow belong to the authors and not to The American Assembly, a nonpartisan educational forum which takes no official position on matters it presents for public discussion. The funding of the program by the following foundations is much appreciated, but it should not be construed that they necessarily share the opinions contained herein: Andrew W. Mellon Foundation, Ford Foundation, Mary Duke Biddle Foundation, Jerome Foundation.

Clifford C. Nelson
President
The American Assembly

W. *McNeil Lowry*

Introduction

This volume deals with more than one form of art and with a variety of artists and artistic directors. (The terms of the discussion are to be found at the beginning of Chapter 1.) Therefore the bulk of its contents treat symphony, opera, theater, and dance independently rather than through an analysis of common trends and problems in the performing arts. For the sake of concreteness, even these separate chapters are focused largely, though by no means completely, on one performing company or institution. The four chosen were not chosen as the best or even the most typical (of which there may be none), but the reader can be assured that the evolution of each group reflects almost all the trends within the relevant field.

Chapter 1 covers the growth of the performing arts over the past twenty years with particular reference to the social, professional, economic, and (in the broadest sense) political factors underlying that development.

There follow then the four "case histories" in symphony, opera, theater, and ballet and a chapter dealing more comprehensively with companies in the modern dance.

W. McNeil Lowry *launched the first organized national program in the arts from The Ford Foundation in 1957 and prior to his leaving the Foundation in 1975 was responsible for its investment of some $280,000,000 in the performing arts. Under a three-year grant from the American Council of Learned Societies, he is writing a study of the development of the arts in the United States since World War II.*

The chapter on professional training and career development embraces all five fields through a symposium joining artist-teachers from all. It is not possible for one writer to deal with this subject across the performing arts if he is to do so from his own professional experience.

The volume to this point necessarily has concentrated on performing artists or the institutions which are the bridge to the public. Mr. Kirstein's chapter is a personal view of the aesthetic, philosophical, and social implications complementing what has gone before.

The conclusion treats major questions cutting across the performing arts, particularly those affecting their present and future positions in the American society, and defines the issues that must be resolved if the United States is to have a public policy in this field.

W. McNeil Lowry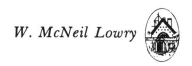

1

The Past Twenty Years

The Terms

"The performing arts" obviously constitutes a misnomer. But like that even larger substantive, "the arts," it is one buried so deeply in common usage that it cannot be discarded. It can, however, be defined for a particular context, and in the context of this volume the performing arts comprehend music (including the compound of voice and instruments that is opera), theater, and dance. Arbitrarily, discussion of these art forms has been confined to live performances before an audience. Videotape, films, and recording are not treated except through occasional references to their economic influence upon performing arts institutions using them to enlarge audiences. These media would themselves justify another volume the size of this one. This is abundantly true, of course, of cinema, an art drawing heavily for its own intrinsic uses on theater, and not a little on music and dance.

Moreover (and this is an added reason), music, opera, theater, and dance are treated less in their separate aesthetic than through the instrument—institution, company, group—by which they reach the public, by which, in effect, they become "live." In short, this volume is not a critical assessment of recent American creations in music, theater, and dance or of the repertoire of American performing groups. As significant as such a formidable task might be, it would hardly form the subject of an American Asembly. There are, fortunately, no questions of United States public policy in such an assessment. But in the importance to the society of artistic creations

3

and of the artists and institutions creating them, there is a significant issue of public policy and a timely one.

If this be true (or is at any rate the assumption underlying this volume), it can more easily be understood that the essays to be found here concentrate upon music, opera, theater, and dance in their professional aspects and upon performing artists and artistic directors and producers who strive for or have attained professional standards. The roles of the arts in education or as amateur or avocational activities in United States communities are not ignored. Quite the contrary, these uses of the arts today constitute' controversial issues of public policy directly or indirectly affecting even the professional artist and the institution that is his or her outlet. But the educational and avocational uses of the arts are herein treated tangentially; the scope of this volume does not allow for an adequate delineation of the arts at three levels of the' United States educational system or as media by which to extend avocational activities in American communities.

Finally, and perhaps logically also, much of the discussion concentrates upon music, theater, or dance as a creative *process* requiring craft, technique, and concept at increasingly professional levels, both in the development of the artist's talents and at the moment of ultimate performance before the public. It is hazarded, at least in subtext, that to make music, theater, or dance is a profession justifying strict disciplines and exertions on the part of the individual and deserving some sort of reward from the public.

Growth and Development

The expansion of performing arts institutions and companies in the United States in the past twenty years had no precedent in any similar period in any country. *How* this expansion was brought about is today better understood than *why* it began when it did. But even without the benefit of a longer historical perspective, there has been much exposition of the *why*. (The editor of this volume has frequently contributed to this, and the discussion at this point is indebted to a recent such occasion: Library of Congress Symposium, *The American Revolution: A Continuing Commitment*, "The Arts in America: Evolution and Tradition." Library of Congress, Washington, D.C., 1976.)

Many unrelated factors in the twentieth century brought a new doctrinal urgency to the arts as an ethic or aesthetic. Prior to the thirties, few of the political refugees leaving Europe for America had been noted artists. Now these came in large numbers, not only to New York but to universities, conservatories, orchestras, and dance studios across the country. The closing of the last frontiers on the American continent produced a search for new outlets for the energies released. Families only a generation or two from such antecedents sought to memorialize both the names of their fathers and the communities they had founded.

By the fifties many claims were being made for the arts in American society, largely uttered by lay patrons and community leaders. The arts were said to be:

1. important to the image of the American society abroad.
2. a means of communication and consequently of understanding between this country and others.
3. an expression of national purpose.
4. an important influence in the liberal education of the individual.
5. an important key to an American's understanding of himself, his times, and his destiny.
6. a purposeful occupation for youth.
7. in their institutional form, vital to the social, moral, and educational resources of an American community.
8. therefore good for business, especially in the new centers of population.
9. components for strengthening moral and spiritual bastions in a people whose national security might be threatened.
10. an offset to the materialism of a generally affluent society.

Note that the arguments advanced for the arts in the fifties almost totally accepted their role as a means to some other end. It is equally noteworthy that many of the proponents of these claims were busy translating their interest in the arts into buildings, a rash of cultural centers across the country. The so-called "cultural explosion" of the fifties and sixties was in great part promotional. Though on an absolute scale there was more financial support being made available for the arts, it was not always channeled into artistic enterprises meeting the criteria of quality. Artists resigned themselves to the probability that new money in the arts might first reflect itself in bigger college programs, new activities for schoolchildren, and new halls for performances. Some were bitter that the outlets for professional careers in many fields remained woefully inadequate. There were conflicting judgments among artists as to the satisfaction to be found from teaching, but there was universal discouragement over the fact that teaching remained the principal economic base for professionals in some of the important fields. (Library of Congress lecture previously noted, pp. 46-47.)

HOW THE EXPANSION WAS BROUGHT ABOUT

However complex—or even meretricious—were the social justifications for increased activity in the performing arts, the institutional, economic, and programatic strategies involved are more easily identified. Chief among these were: the increased use of the tax-exempt corporation by directors and producers, the steady rise in the proportion of Americans with college educations, the launching of the first national effort deliberately to improve and expand training and performing institutions (The Ford Foundation, 1957), and the beginning of a federal program in the arts (The National Foundation on the Humanities and the Arts, 1965).

THE NONPROFIT CORPORATION

Voluntary societies, with boards of members or patrons, had existed since the early years of the American Republic and even before. And private patronage by the very wealthy was conspicuous in a number of cities prior to the income and inheritance taxes legislated in the second decade of our own century. Two of the performing organizations treated here—symphony and opera—had already enjoyed the fruits. (Dance companies were rarely native products and remained under commercial sponsorship until the late thirties, and theater, with a few and short-lived exceptions, was regarded as commerce and entertainment.) It was only after two wars significantly increased income and inheritance tax rates that deductions for charitable giving formed any real incentive to patronage by those who did not have the luxury of living on the income of their income. A particular device now lay at hand for steadily enlarging the number of private patrons. It was underutilized by 1950, even by symphony orchestras and opera companies; one became at least a patron and more often, indeed, a trustee with an annual contribution of $1,000.

The nonprofit corporation was dramatically suited as an instrument in two other ways, moreover. In the first place, the initiative to employ it, to form a musical, theatrical, or dance group, could be taken by a would-be artistic or general director as well as by lay patrons or leaders of the community. He or she would have to draw associates into the venture, and if it were a large venture some of these would be expected to provide or to find money. But if incorporating the theater or dance company (and even in two or three cases an opera company) was the initiative of a strong director, its momentum and its direction lay chiefly under his control. The midpoint of the twentieth century witnessed a phenomenon much less familiar in the history of other nations. A society regularly assayed as devoted to materialism unwittingly provided the means by which a group of artists under the leadership of one of themselves would attempt to build the outlets for their own concepts and their own careers. ("Unwittingly"? The language of the income tax code dealt with education, science, and charity but with neither art nor culture.)

In the second and equally crucial place, the adoption of the nonprofit charter both symbolized and set apart the artistic enterprise intended. It was to be about art, hopefully or ultimately. In the artistic process, the opportunities for the artist's development and the quality of the performance were the important ends. These goals justified the tax-exempt status. They were truly philanthropic in the root sense, as much so as the goals of any college or library. And they even justified the fact that the performing group did not fail in its purpose because it could not make its way solely in revenues at the box office. To make up the difference through tax-exempt contributions appeared wholly defensible given the social and aesthetic objectives aimed at. Thus an ethical tone, not always very confidently uttered by the artistic producers themselves, came to be a subtext of the more orthodox economic analysis of the nonprofit corporation.

To make a purposeful use of the tax-exempt mechanism, the artistic or general director needed the leverage of a financial patron committed to the director's own professional objectives. In 1950 these were rare. Lay trustees dominated the policies of symphony orchestras and of all but one or two opera companies. A handful of winter stock companies in the theater were nonprofit in structure but received pathetically few contributions and struggled to survive at a semiprofessional level through only the subsidy of their own efforts. (The Fred Miller Theater in Milwaukee, founded in 1954 with $125,000 contributed by lay patrons, was an exception to the norm.) In dance, the directors of a few leading companies kept control of artistic policies but lacked the means to systematic development. And there was no way for even the most energetic and driven artistic director to join in a national effort in any field.

THE FORD FOUNDATION

The financial patron committed to the director's own professional objectives turned out to be The Ford Foundation, and the leverage on other funds it exerted between 1957 and 1975 reached many hundreds of millions of dollars. As the first national patron of the performing arts (aside from the indirect operations of the WPA in the thirties), The Ford Foundation had the choice of bringing professionals in any one field together to step by step work out planned and focused objectives for development. It made this choice in each of the performing arts between 1957 and 1966 (the year of its $80 million symphony orchestra program) and then widened its leverage in the performing arts taken together in a continuing program of cash reserve grants beginning in 1971.

This volume is not the place for an evaluation (or even a description) of The Ford Foundation's impact upon the performing arts, and the author of this chapter, who directed the program from its outset, would not in a volume for an American Assembly thrust himself into the role of an evaluator. It is helpful, however, to recapitulate the situation of each art in 1957 and to summarize some of the steps taken. These are known to the professionals in theater, music, or dance because they were heavily consulted in the planning, but more publicly they have been obscured by emphasis on the dramatic sums involved.

Theater—In 1957 the commercial theater on Broadway and on the road supported itself largely through large cast musicals and small cast popular dramas. There were, of course, exceptions to this, some of them works of art, but these two categories were the meat and potatoes of financial survival. In this decade America had a producer's theater (as opposed to an actor's, playwright's, or director's theater), but producers indirectly gave up much control to both theater owners and the agents who specialized in block sales of a popular success. (All three sometimes were asked to give the nod to a new script before it went into rehearsal.)

A new commercial theater was rising off-Broadway, at first more experimental and less conventional in repertoire, but nurtured chiefly by lower costs and the lower scales the theatrical unions allowed for audience capacities below either 200 or 300 seats. In its early years off-Broadway gave variety to the roles open to actors who worked also "uptown" and gave visibility to a number who had not yet been seen there.

The serious professional actor, dedicated to craft and wishing to develop his own, occasionally came to achieve creative moments in a long running success, frequently rehearsed a part in a play which quickly closed, and more frequently had no role at all. But the "hit or flop" economics of Broadway, the nature of its more standard fare, and the three and one-half week rehearsal periods combined to limit both the varied roles and the sustained artistic process necessary to the professional development of the actor and the director and to the most artistic representation of the work of the playwright. And opportunities to play the great roles of the classics rarely came on or off Broadway. Actors, directors, and, increasingly, playwrights sought to intensify their experience in the hidden theater of workshops like the Actor's Studio, the Neighborhood Playhouse, the Hagen-Berghoff, and many others even more hidden.

Popular hits from Broadway went out of New York in first and second road companies, by bus and truck, and to summer stock, but the road was not in a flourishing period and only rarely featured repertoire challenging the professional's craft. Scripts from Broadway went out also to about twelve to fourteen winter stock companies, mixed in a repertoire with the classics, with older American plays, and with recent European works on which Broadway had not reserved or had given up the rights.

These companies were analagous to those known in the "Little Theater" movement of the thirties (some examples of which still existed) except in their objective to reach professional status, at least as that is denoted by the possession of an Actors' Equity contract. They wanted to do new plays when they could, and one of them, the Margo Jones in Dallas, at first was limited to American premieres. In addition to their own small cadre of actors and the amateurs allowed by the Equity Z contract, they from time to time brought one or two leading players from New York or Los Angeles. The actors' agents regarded their clients' acceptance of such invitations as disasters to their careers. Playwrights' agents were even less cooperative.

In the exploratory period of its program beginning in 1957, the Ford Foundation:

1. brought artistic directors and managers of nonprofit theaters into communication with one another to share experiences and to sharpen professional and institutional objectives.
2. gave organization (The Theatre Communications Group) to the use of existing models (Alley, Arena Stage, Actor's Workshop, and others) for their further development and the development of new resident companies.
3. supported internships for on-the-job training of new administrative and managerial personnel.
4. provided technical assistance toward the building of audiences for both the existing and new companies.
5. through the Cleveland Play House, supported the training of a young company of actors who thereafter toured the United States testing the appetite for live theater in small and middle-sized communities.
6. offered funds to directors selected by theater professionals to be used at their own discretion for artistic development.
7. subsidized the performance of new plays by American playwrights who had not yet had a fully professional production.
8. supported twenty-five American poets and novelists interested in the dramatic form to live for a year within resident theater (or opera) companies.
9. by matching grants, supported annual contracts of $200 a week for ten actors to test the ensemble approach at theaters (Alley, Arena Stage, Actor's Workshop).
10. established annual auditions of young actors at the stage between university training and employment in resident companies.
11. supported architects and stage designers to collaborate with theater directors in developing models of eight new theaters.

In 1962, the trustees of The Ford Foundation announced that the arts constituted one of five areas on which the institution would concentrate for at least the next decade. In the theater the Foundation thereafter:

1. began the direct support of operating budgets (and infrequently capital plant) of selected resident professional companies.
2. continued varied forms of technical assistance to all nonprofit companies.
3. assisted directors of resident companies to work with playwrights through revision and rehearsal periods.
4. began the support of selected off-off-Broadway theaters and experimental workshops, particularly those dedicated to the new playwright.
5. helped to establish or develop black theater companies and to increase opportunities for the professional training of young blacks (Negro Ensemble Company, New Lafayette Theatre and Workshop, Inner City

Cultural Center, Free Southern Theater, New Federal Theater, and so on).

6. opened to all nonprofit companies with minimal performance seasons four-year grants to eliminate deficits and provide reserves of working capital (Cash Reserve Grants Program).

Ballet—One of the first phenomena noted by The Ford Foundation in extensive fieldwork beginning in 1957 was the enthusiasm of young students of ballet. They perforce accepted what instruction their parents could find in their own communities, and there was no organized way of going on to teachers more professionally qualified. Opportunities for performance in public came perhaps once or twice a year in recitals by so-called "civic ballets," a movement at this date spreading out of the Southeast into three other regions of the country. Only the accident of word of mouth or the hazard of a New York, or San Francisco audition could put even the most gifted on the road to a professional career, however slender and financially insecure. Between these two cities there was the small semiprofessional company of Willam Christensen in Salt Lake City and the commercially chartered company directed by Ruth Page in Chicago largely as a complement to the opera.

As a first step in testing the potentialities of a change, The Ford Foundation enabled professionals from the School of American Ballet and the San Francisco Ballet School to visit dance studios east and west of the Mississippi to select the most gifted students for advanced instruction of from one to three years and the chance to compete for a place in the corps de ballet of the New York City and San Francisco companies. Principal dancers, now household words in ballet circles, were among the young students selected in the first year. When in 1963 The Ford Foundation began a national program in ballet that eventuated in an investment of $29.8 million, it continued the program of regional scholarships but also underwrote for ten years local scholarships for the students of selected teachers in over 125 schools across the country. In three of the grants made in the same year to new companies, funds for their schools were included.

The author of Chapter 4 has noted the disposition of the first $8 million appropriated in 1963. Since that date every professional ballet company of a minimum size and performing season has been involved in The Ford Foundation's program, most for as long as twelve to fourteen years, as in the program supporting the resident theater movement. It was, indeed, the long-term dependence upon the Foundation, an unorthodox policy in organized philanthropy, which led to the device of the cash reserve grant in 1971.

Through the sixties, The Ford Foundation extended to ballet companies technical assistance in the development of subscription audiences, a technique first applied to the theater, and supported on-the-job internships to help them train new administrative and managerial personnel.

The local scholarship program of 1963–73, among other conditions, encouraged the teachers under contract to carry their auditions for students outside the studios, not only to enroll more boys, but to bring into the field young people from economic and racial minorities. A more concentrated effort in this direction was the establishment of the Harlem Dance Theatre, directed by Arthur Mitchell, as part of the Harlem School of the Arts and then as an independent corporation. The public's enthusiasm for this company of young blacks sometimes conceals the continuing importance of its very large training program. (Smaller programs aimed at the same end were from time to time supported in Boston, Newark, Los Angeles, and San Francisco.)

Opera—In 1957 American conservatories and university departments contained a wealth of young talent in the voice. There were, however, very few opportunities for their best graduates to obtain a debut on a professional stage, let alone to gain experience in a number of classical roles. Apprenticeship programs on any scale were severely limited. If they could manage it, the most ambitious young singers found outlets for modest careers in provincial European houses, occasionally to be "discovered" by American directors auditioning on the Continent. Of the four principal opera companies (Metropolitan, San Francisco, Chicago Lyric, and New York City) only the first had an extensive season and only the last gave much recognition to American singers below the star level. A number of "civic operas" in other cities put on two or three productions a year but rarely gave a new talent an important role. Frequently they drew upon the same singers who in the fall or in the spring were at the New York City Opera. Sante Fe, a new company beginning an important development, also favored Americans. But to sustain a career was almost impossible. An American might have a contract with the Metropolitan Opera without being cast within the season for more than one role.

How the opportunities for training and apprenticeship have shifted radically over the past twenty years is touched upon in Chapter 7 of this volume, the expansion of seasons and the development of new companies in Chapter 3. There are even now many American singers with reputations in Europe who are unknown at home. With few exceptions titular roles on the major operatic stages in the United States are dominated by foreigners. What has changed is that the possibility of a career in opera exists in this country, hard as it is to put it together. There have been many influences upon the process.

In one of its first grants in 1957, The Ford Foundation gave selected young singers their debut in a major operatic role at the Opera House of New Orleans. It followed with a program to subsidize the rehearsal and performance of American Guild of Musical Artists' (AGMA) "A" or "B" roles by young Americans cast by the directors of civic opera companies around the country. Thereafter it gave matching grants to such companies over a five-year period if they would guarantee to add at least one more production in a season of thirteen or more performances.

In the meantime the Foundation had embarked with the New York City Opera Company on a program to present in New York and on tour operas written by American composers. The results were questionable if judged only in terms of the size of audiences. But the Foundation nevertheless appropriated nearly a million dollars to underwrite the commissioning of new American operas and partial subsidy of their performance. Ultimately the Metropolitan chose three composers (Blitzstein[unfinished], Barber, Levy); San Francisco, two (Dello Joio, Hicks); and Chicago, one (Giannini). The New York City Opera chose many and continued to do so after successive grants from the Foundation had run their course. Only one or two of these has remained in the repertoire, but the composers assisted included, among others, Moore, Floyd, Ward, Weisgall, Kirchner, Beeson.

In the sixties the Foundation extended to opera companies on-the-job internships to train administrative and managerial personnel and gave technical assistance to the building of subscription audiences. The architect of this latter program, Danny Newman, was one of the original staff of the Chicago Lyric Opera, who had his first experience as a publicist in the theater.

Aside from the grants to expand civic opera seasons, the first general support came as a by-product of the development of the Lincoln Center for the Performing Arts. So ambitious and so taxing were the outlays for capital plant that neither the Metropolitan Opera nor the New York City Center of Music and Drama had reserves for moving to the new location and beginning expanded operations. In 1963 and in 1965 these two institutions received grants of a little more than $3 million each. The Foundation's major investment in opera came in the form of four-year cash reserve funds in the early seventies. By 1974, twenty-seven United States opera companies in one program or another shared in a total of $16 million from The Ford Foundation.

Symphony—Of all performing organizations, the symphony orchestra has been the most endemic in the United States. Indeed, for a very long time (and throughout the period under discussion here), the dominance of the orchestra over patronage in most communities intensified the struggles of other performing arts groups to develop. So accustomed is the public to both the number and the scale of symphony orchestras that it may fail to appreciate how great has been their expansion over the identical twenty-year period when theater, dance, and operatic institutions reached new peaks. That expansion came in part through the establishment of semiprofessional orchestras in the smaller cities or the movement of "community" orchestras into the ranks of the "metropolitan" (budgetary categories of the American Symphony Orchestra League). But it came chiefly from the lengthening of seasons and the inflation of costs, both pushed much more heavily by the demands of artistic personnel than by the demands of audiences. In 1957 the average annual budget even of a "major" orchestra was around $600,000. By 1971 it had moved, in constant dollars, to $2.8 million (*Finances of the Performing Arts*, The Ford Foundation, 1974).

The Ford Foundation's first interests in the symphonic field were in stimulating a repertoire of contemporary music and in improving the situation of the American conductor, and not in institutional development. Though it extended to symphony orchestras technical assistance in enlarging subscription audiences and internships for training administrators and managers, it concentrated institution building in the fields in which it appeared most timely and in which Ford Foundation funds could find the greatest impact. It was apparent that enormous sums would be required to affect the growth of even the sixty-odd principal orchestras around the country.

That these sums became available (and not at the expense of other activities in the arts) is more properly a story of The Ford Foundation's capital development and capital gains. In briefest compass, the president and trustees between 1962 and 1966 canvassed the various divisions of the Foundation for large capital expenditures that could have a national impact on institutions within its broad sphere of program interests. In the arts the two proposals made concerned museums of fine arts and symphony orchestras, and after deliberation the board of trustees appropriated $80 million for grants to symphony orchestras later to be individually negotiated and approved. The work was completed in 1966.

In that year the average orchestra with a budget above $100,000 spent 76.4 percent of it on personnel costs, 62.8 percent only on artistic personnel (*Finances of the Performing Arts*). Yet in its fieldwork leading to the new program, The Ford Foundation found that in only seven American cities did the instrumentalist in the symphony equal the salary of a public schoolteacher. The ninety-one orchestras in the sample already noted averaged fifty-two performing artists on seasonal contracts but (including the smaller orchestras) only for an average season of nineteen weeks.

The Ford Foundation's objective in committing $80 million to sixty-one major and metropolitan orchestras was not just to give them the same opportunity to struggle a decade later for the economic survival which appeared difficult enough in 1966. The grants were made to improve both the income level of the instrumentalists and the performance standards of the orchestras, ultimately raising the prestige of the player's life as a career for talented young musicians. The bulk of the Foundation's investment went into a ten-year trust in which the orchestras held varying shares to be matched in individual ratios for endowment or future operations. In addition the Foundation made contributions over five years (the period allowed for matching) to the orchestras' annual budgets in order to give them more freedom to concentrate on capital fund raising.

In 1976 and 1977 the shares in the ten-year trust were distributed to the orchestras; all but six of the sixty-one originally selected had met the conditions laid down in 1966, and a few had significantly exceeded them. As predicted, the $164.6 million in Foundation and matching funds had not brought the millennium to the symphony field though only two of the sixty-one had ceased operations during the decade. It was apparent that fiscal management best designed to capitalize on the infusion of new endowments had not been widely applied, in contrast to the results in the other performing arts of The Ford Foundation Cash Reserve Program, which not only had more stringent disciplines but in its process provided direct technical assistance in fund management and reporting. More important perhaps for the future were the unrelenting demands of the American Federation of Musicians and the sequential impact of individual contract settlements. The economic viability of the player's career has clearly been changed. In 1971 the average *low* salary was $6,958 (the average *high*, $45,650). But in 1977 the *starting* salary in the seventh highest paying orchestra (Detroit) was $20,800. (In the highest paying, Chicago, it was $26,000.) The effects of this continuing change are of course enormous throughout the education of a young musician and, taken in the abstract, characteristic of a socially important profession. It has auguries for the future, however, more complex than the obvious problem of financial resources. Some of these are touched upon in the chapter on training and career development (Chapter 7).

THE BEGINNINGS OF FEDERAL INVOLVEMENT

As the first of national scope in the field, the program of The Ford Foundation did not completely ignore the arts in general education and in social development, though here too it concentrated upon the exposure of young students to professionals (sending young composers into high schools to write for student performances, expansion of the Young Audiences program to the Midwest, enlarging the format of Affiliate Artists, Inc., testing the aesthetic perception of young children are examples). But it was clear that the Foundation could not effectively respond to the multifarious requests for funds to bring schoolchildren into theaters and concert halls and to tour performances throughout American communities. From the outset, the Foundation met such appeals with the gratuitous statement that only massive federal funds devoted to educational purposes could make any impact.

These funds came in 1965 as the result of Titles I and III of the amended National Defense Education Act administered by the Department of Health, Education, and Welfare. Performing arts institutions thus had the experience of indirect federal help to underwrite portions of their audiences for regular or special performances before any direct federal assistance to them. Prior to their rather abrupt liquidation, however, the new programs had important results as yet incompletely analyzed (Junius Eddy, *A Review of Federal Programs Supporting the Arts in Education*, The Ford Foundation, 1970). It is perhaps not absurd to say that one of the most important was the necessity forced upon state and local school systems (the direct recipients of the grants) to examine the resources and curricula in the arts available either in their own schools or in the community. At least the *expectation* was raised that schools had some responsibility for exposing young children to the arts, however little it was fulfilled in the deepening fiscal crises of the seventies. A further important result was that after 1970 a federal agency dedicated to the arts, the National Endowment for the Arts (NEA), used more and more of its funds in fulfilling some of these expectations. But this is getting ahead of the story.

BACKGROUND TO THE FEDERAL LEGISLATION OF 1965

Proposals that the federal government recognize the importance of the arts to the nation did not wait upon the promulgation of a Great Society in the sixties; an example was the bill introduced by Senator Hubert H. Humphrey in 1957. Every session of Congress saw companion bills offered, most of them *pro forma*, but through the administrations of President Eisenhower and President Kennedy federal action was limited to the appointment of a White House adviser on the arts. This post was continued by President Johnson, who also signed a National Council on the Arts into law. On the international front the State Department Advisory Commission on the Arts, at the instigation of the publisher Roy F. Larsen, for the first time used twelve professional artists and directors to set policies of the cultural presentations program. Department bureaucracy and the continuing stranglehold of a House appropriations subcommittee led to their mass resignation after three years. The Office of Education had the only sizeable funds earmarked for the arts, but for the educational purposes already noted. Congress had long felt some pressures from lobbyists for the arts, primarily from the musicians union, but these were not enough to bring any bill out of committee or even to prompt more than desultory hearings upon it.

What changed this picture in 1964 and 1965 has been frequently enough described in sporadic, ephemeral, or subjective form. Witnesses close to the scene contend really over one point: the effective weight of the arts constituency as compared to that for the humanities. In American social history the question may prove to be of little importance. At present the evidence suggests that the arts may have motivated more interest in the White House but that their being joined in the bill with the humanities (and therefore with the institutions of education) carried them through the Congress. The report of a Commission on the Humanities chaired by President Barnaby Keeney of Brown University called for a national humanities foundation, and it had the support of the powerful Representative John Fogarty of Rhode Island, as well as that of the state's Democratic Senator, Claiborne Pell. When the proponents of the arts in the House led by Representative Frank Thompson of New Jersey realized where Fogarty stood, they did not hesitate to accept a bill creating two endowments within one national foundation. Not only the American Council of Learned Societies, the Association of Graduate Schools, and Phi Beta Kappa (the constituents of the Keeney Commission), but university presidents and the nation's school teachers lobbied for both the humanities and the arts, along with the forces mobilized by Roger L. Stevens, Johnson's White House advisor on the arts.

The principal factor, however, lay in the heavy majority President Johnson wielded in the House after the election of 1964, an era in which it came to be said that legislation was "being written uptown." Johnson was personally interested in demonstrating support for cultural activities equal to or surpassing Kennedy's, and the tentative amounts involved were bargain basement in the budget of the Great Society. The dominance of the Executive in drafting the new legislation had more specific and more lasting effects. Richard Goodwin, the White House aide on the job, saw no problems in a structure with only short-term authorization and councils that were only advisory in relation to the two chairmen of the separate endowments. Thompson, Pell, and even Budget Director Kermit Gordon would have accepted continuing boards with the autonomy of that of the National Science Foundation. Roger Stevens was neutral on this point. But Goodwin was willing for the President himself to be legally the next echelon of responsibility above each chairman.

Though Stevens in 1965 began with an assemblage of generally strong personalities, the National Council of the Arts has invariably been subservient to the chairman.

THE NATIONAL ENDOWMENT FOR THE ARTS

The language of the 1965 legislation emphasized the American tradition that "encouragement and support of national progress in . . . the arts [was] primarily a matter for private and local initiative. . . ." If this principle could be stipulated, and the stipulation was obviously a *sine qua non* to passage of the bill, then national progress in the arts was "also an appropriate matter of concern to the Federal Government." To help define the limits of the government's role, Congress wrote in the principle of matching grants in two ways, one on paper and one in actuality. When using its program funds, the Endowment was not to support more than 50 percent of the project cost submitted by an applicant. In addition, a Treasury Fund was established outside the Endowment's budget which an applicant could tap by offering an equal amount from private contributions. Therefore, a $25,000 Treasury Fund grant could mean a total project budget of $100,000—$25,000 from private contributors and $50,000 in the applicant's normal share of project costs.

The First Phase—Roger L. Stevens, the first Chairman of the National Endowment, appeared to operate it on an analogy with a national foundation. Himself a professional producer, he directed the Endowment's modest funds largely through professional institutions in direct operations or as intermediaries. Only in individual fellowship programs did he use uniform grants, and he did not hesitate to make ad hoc grants of large size when he believed he was filling a gap left by other national programs or responding to a noted professional, as in large grants to the American Ballet Theatre and for an experimental workshop proposed by Jerome Robbins. Indeed, he risked putting the federal government into the role of creating new institutions and companies. The "laboratory theater" program of 1966–69, jointly sponsored by the Endowment and the Office of Education, started two new theaters—the Repertory Theater of New Orleans and the Inner City Repertory of Los Angeles —and expanded an existing company in Providence, Trinity Square. Stevens also attempted unsuccessfully to establish a national opera touring company, first through the Metropolitan Opera Association and then as an independent venture directed by Sarah Caldwell. This was during four years when federal grants to all opera companies excluding the Metropolitan totaled only $900,000. (The modest project grants of the National Opera Institute established by Stevens are not represented in this total.) In the same spirit of ad hoc direction of his funds, Stevens did not move into the support of symphony orchestras; The Ford Foundation's $80 million program was formally approved a week after President Johnson signed the 1965 legislation.

In its first phase the National Endowment employed a small program staff, some of whom were more nearly full-time consultants, freely involved members of the National Council even in grantee affairs and relied very little on panels within the various fields of the arts. Its focus was national rather than community or state, and education, though an accepted objective, was subordinate to professional development and performance. This was undoubtedly made easier by the continuing presence of some funds for the arts in the Office of Education.

Professional performing arts groups with budgets over $100,000 a year between 1965 and 1970 received about $6.4 million in federal grants. These sums increased markedly in later years, but in the period concerned represented a very large proportion of Stevens' total funds for activities in the performing arts.

Evaluation—The impact of the National Endowment on growth and development in theater, dance, symphony, and opera would be easier to analyze if the NEA had ever set forth clearly defined strategic aims in these fields. Instead the Endowment came to use three broad and general objectives coupled with "guidelines" for (by 1977) 115 separate funding programs to which organizations, artists, states, cities, schools, colleges, and private or voluntary agencies might apply. These overlapping networks have carried money far beyond artists and arts institutions and into a steadily expanding multiplicity of services. "Availability" of the arts became as important as "the development of cultural resources" and "enhancing the quality of life" was equated with supporting the creativity of artists. If we are to abstract in the context of this discussion some less general strategies, we need to look at the *structure* and the *procedures* from which they emerge. Both the strong proponents and the critics of the Endowment's course agree that this is the only way one can safely deduce its policies.

Structure and Procedure—The National Foundation on the Arts and the Humanities Act of 1965 provided that every year the National Endowment for the Arts make at least 20 percent of its program funds available to state arts councils or agencies, with three-fourths of the total disseminated in equal amounts to all and the rest at NEA's discretion. For a time federal and state programs developed more or less independently though serving together the broad objectives of the national legislation. But as the Endowment's appropriations increased and the discretionary funds were enlarged, the intermingling of federal and state initiatives became much harder to distinguish. During fiscal 1977, some $11.8 million was given to the state agencies in bloc grants but another $5.9 million at NEA's discretion. For example, the Endowment pays salaries and travel expenses of additional staff for the state councils, funds regional programs and their coordinators, provides consultants, and through the states (as well as directly) helps to support community arts programs, artists in schools, and dance touring. Nongovernmental organizations which provide services to state and community arts agencies also receive support. "City Spirit," one of NEA's special projects designed to create community forums for discussing the arts in the same 1977 funding period spent about $500,000 in 180 cities and towns.

In short, Federal-State Partnership and Special Projects (the latter spent in all $4 million in fiscal 1977) have separate staffs on the same basis as Dance, Theater, and Music. So do Expansion Arts ($6.3 million) and Education ($5 million). These and five other major program areas accounted for 100 of the staff of 218 on board in Washington, with nine regional coordinators in the field. Each program also has its own separate advisory panel appointed by the Chairman of the NEA, whose own advisers are the members of the National Council on the Arts.

The staff, with the approval of the chairman, puts both the guidelines for the 110 funding categories and the grants to be made within each to the panels for discussion and preliminary recommendations. The staff's own final recommendations are made to the chairman. They may be discussed individually or en bloc with the National Council, but the decision remains with the chairman.

Given the structure and the procedures, it may be difficult to quantify the impact on the four fields treated in this volume, but it is not hard to understand why performers, directors, and managers by 1977 felt the presence, however perceived, of the National Endowment. Though the NEA says officially that its guidelines are set up to respond to needs, the arts constituency has a very large and diverse number of these guidelines to examine to determine what these needs are and how they were arrived at.

During fiscal 1977 symphony orchstras with budgets above $100,000 received federal funds of $16.3 million. Opera companies large and small received $3.4 million. Taken together these grants represented 74 percent of expenditures in music. In the same period nonprofit theater companies of all sizes were given about $4.9 million of a total of $5.9 million dispersed in that program area. The program in dance is a little more difficult to recapitulate in the same manner. Resident professional dance companies received only about $465,000 in direct grants. In the NEA touring program, the three larger companies were involved in grants totalling $1 million, far below the $2 million given to the small companies. Production grants to companies of all sizes were about $800,000. It is difficult to derive exact proportions, but within total 1977 federal funds in dance of close to $6 million, perhaps $2.5 million involved the larger professional companies in ballet and modern dance.

Taken together federal funds which went directly to professional performing institutions in symphony, opera, theater, and dance represented $19 million out of total fiscal 1977 federal funds of $85 million. (An additional $6 million assisted other aspects of these fields.) The arts fields outside the performing arts (architecture, media arts, literature, museums, and the visual arts) accounted for another $26 million. The total of funds through the state councils was $16 million.

An addition to annual program funds in the performing arts came in 1977 with the NEA "Challenge Program" of grants to be matched over one to three years. In July the Endowment announced grants of $27 million in this program, of which $16.3 million affected performing groups in theater, opera, symphony, and dance.

Policy—The most objective answer about the impact of the National Endowment clearly lies in the issue of proportions and presumably therefore of priorities. From the summary quantifications noted there are obviously two ways of analyzing priorities. The first is in the proportion of total expenditures devoted to "the development of cultural resources" and to grants to individuals in the program areas of symphony, opera, theater, and dance, *as further proportioned* with the expenditures of NEA outside these (and the literary and plastic) arts fields (p. 17). Debate over these relative priorities has been, of course, the burden of most public discussion of the National Endowment during the two terms of Chairman Nancy Hanks and in her second term began to get some attention in congressional hearings on NEA authorization and appropriations bills.

The second way of analyzing these priorities, while sticking strictly to quantitative data, is to examine the grants for the "development of cultural resources" in proportion to the operating budgets (the crudest measure of "needs") in performing arts institutions. This subject too in the mid-seventies began to characterize some public discussion of the NEA, with more immediacy and perspective than in the broadside advocacy formulae of the sixties, one of which asked the federal government to assume 10 percent of operating budgets and thus appeared to deprive the National Endowment of control over many of its choices.

In the 1977 period being taken for illustrative purposes, $3.4 million, as has been noted, went to opera companies of all sizes. The largest grant was $700,000 to the Metropolitan, or 2.21 percent of that company's annual operating budget. Grants of $155,000 to the New York City Opera and of $195,000 to the Chicago Lyric accounted for 2 and 3 percent of budget, respectively. Grants to small budget companies, however, represented greater percentages of operating budgets, 5 percent for the Milwaukee Florentine and a little more than 6 percent to Cincinnati.

The Theatre Communications Group (TCG) made a survey of forty-nine nonprofit theaters in the period 1975–76 and found that federal grants accounted for 6.4 percent of expenditures. Variations between theater companies of larger or smaller budgets were less noticeable than in opera companies.

From this purely quantitative analysis two important facts emerge. One is that the advent of the federal government as a new source of regular funds has had impact on a large number of performing companies in each field, though primarily on those with small operations. The other is that the proportionate weight of this new funding source is out of scale to both inflation and growth. Perhaps it requires a decade to assimilate and accommodate to a new source of funding institutions in the arts, particularly one not traditional in American society. But this new funding source developed in the period of the most sweeping expansion of performing arts institutions in our history. Growth came not only in the number of such institutions but in the increasing scale of operations of those already in existence. In short, they were doing more each year and not just paying higher costs for what they had previously done. If then the increasing federal source of funds rather quickly put a ceiling on regular grants to performing arts groups, the effect was dynamic rather than static since expectations about the potential proportions of public funding influenced not only the institutions themselves but their other patrons. By the mid-seventies these effects figured largely in the recurring talk of chronic economic "crisis" in the performing arts and castigations of the scale of federal support even when (until 1976) the overall budget of the NEA was going up.

That opera companies received $3.4 million in one year, for example, was impressive and theoretically an auspicious sign of future stability in that field. But that $155,000 was (outside the Metropolitan) the ceiling among such grants forced a different perspective. It was not alleviated by advocacy of a larger budget for the NEA, though Opera America and other spokesmen in the field joined in that activity. The large increases in the annual budgets of the Endowment had not radically changed the proportions going toward "developing cultural resources" as against the other objectives it had assumed.

In an analysis of the last twenty years of the performing arts, therefore, it was not merely academic to conclude that maintenance of NEA priorities current in 1977 could inhibit continued growth. This is true despite the crucial fact that government's willingness to make annually recurring grants in the arts was a watershed in American social history.

The Corporations—No source of support for the performing arts is more frequently questioned and less accurately defined than the corporate sector. The Business Committee for the Arts (BCA), after a mail survey in 1976, estimated $221 million, of which at least half came out of business expenses for public relations and goodwill.

There was not universal agreement on this estimate. The 1975–76 TCG survey referred to, reports that forty-nine nonprofit theaters received from business and corporate sources a total of $988,000 or 2.2 percent of their operating budgets. BCA says that this represented seven cents of each corporate dollar to the arts in 1975. Symphony orchestras received twelve cents; opera and dance, three cents each. The arts constituency takes note of the fact that corporations making the largest disbursements in the arts are first, those in need of an improved public image; and second, those which favor television and other media over performing arts companies. In 1976 Mobil Oil spent $4 million on the commercial networks and $2 million on public television, and included in these totals were the sums earmarked for promoting the programs in publicity. Only $500,000 went to arts institutions, including museums, directly. A similar sum to these institutions came from the Mobil Foundation.

Some directors and managers of performing arts groups believe there are long-term, if ill-defined, values from airing performances on television. But they think the net *financial* reward to the company under current contracts is derisory, and they believe that some day corporations must be educated to see direct support in this field as in their own self-interest, if only as institutional advertising.

POSTSCRIPT: THE ECONOMIC MODEL

This continuing emphasis on "unearned income" sources is, of course, a characteristic of the nonprofit corporation in the performing arts which, as this chapter has shown, was the chosen instrument for expansion over the past twenty years of symphony, opera, theater, and dance in the United States. There were two reasons. The first lay in the realm of *objective*. To reach the highest qualitative standards in each art field and to provide an outlet for training and developing individual talents, in other words the concentration on the artistic *process*, the performing group had to justify its importance to the society as an object of philanthropy and not rely upon short-term commercial appeal as entertainment. The second lay in the realm of *economics*. Like colleges and hospitals, a performing arts enterprise is labor both intensive and limited in one way or another in the mass distribution of its products. Salaries and fees average over 70 percent of all expenditures; in any one field they are over 50 percent. And earned income ranges between 50 and 75 percent among the four performing arts fields, with an average of about 52 percent if they are all taken together.

The most basic feature of the economic model is the pattern of expenditures, which within each art form does not change regardless of the scale of operations. Performing arts managers have some degree of control in fixing the overall limits of a budget, but once this is done the expenditure patterns are fixed. Patterns of earned income over the past twenty years have had noticeable variations, particularly in the increased ratio of subscription to single-ticket income pushed in theater, opera, and ballet and in the use of contract or services income for special performances by modern dance, symphony, and ballet. Patterns of unearned (or contributed) income change, as one of the important themes in this chapter has abundantly shown, though in the mid-seventies these changes are only proportional. The one constancy in unearned income patterns is the paramount position of private local patronage.

Joseph Roddy

2

The Symphony

In the early 1960s, a century after the Union armies marching through Georgia put it to the torch, Atlanta offered towering glass and concrete proofs that it had passed beyond full recovery and started on its aggrandizement. Its resident boosters with large business interests were promising to make it the world's next great city. To fit it first with the essentials of a big American city, they found a major league baseball franchise they could buy in Milwaukee where the National League's Braves had played their home games ever since they left Boston in 1953. But even before the mayor of Atlanta threw out his first major league pitch to the Atlanta Braves in the spring of 1966, the boosters had decided that a major league symphony orchestra was another adornment the city needed to measure up to their ambitions for it.

Building the Atlanta Symphony

If major league symphony orchestras, like baseball teams, could be bought on the outside and moved in, the acquisitive Atlantians might well have abandoned their own undersized and unrenowned ensemble and tried buying Boston's, Philadelphia's, New York's, Cleveland's, Chicago's, or Los Angeles'—the country's Big Six

JOSEPH RODDY, *now a freelance writer finishing a major book on* Sol Hurok, *was formerly a Senior Editor of* Life *magazine and a Senior Editor of* Look *magazine.*

and quite arguably the world's six best. Since not a one of them was on the sales block, however, the boosters demanded that their own orchestra be rebuilt into one they could regard as a kind of expansion team in some new symphonic Big Ten. For that overhaul they needed a new conductor, and members of the city's search committee sized up all the likeliest candidates. When they had finished looking and listening, they did not select one of the illustrious foreign-born maestri on the international guest-conducting circuit. They chose instead Robert Shaw, the California-born associate conductor of the Cleveland Orchestra when its music director was the martinet George Szell and it had no peer in performances of the Mozart to Brahms repertoire.

THE NEW CONDUCTOR

For his first job in music Shaw had been the director of Fred Waring's glee club. Between broadcasts and road tours he had assembled about 150 enthusiastic amateurs around New York—this writer was one of them—into a troupe called the Collegiate Chorale. Arturo Toscanini used it, or smaller vocal forces assembled and rehearsed by Shaw, just about every time he needed a choral group for his weekly NBC Symphony Orchestra broadcasts. The old Italian tyrant showed his gratitude by turning over his orchestra to Shaw at times to get the country's most successful choral conductor well launched as a conductor of instrumentalists. After Toscanini's retirement, Shaw went to study and work with Szell in Cleveland where he was the associate conductor until he agreed to be the new music director in Atlanta.

For its incoming music director and the orchestra he would rebuild there would be, of course, a new hall. Cultural centers were becoming an urban fashion then throughout the country. Plans for Atlanta's Memorial Arts Center were settled in 1965 by a new administrative combine calling itself the Atlanta Arts Alliance. The city's High Museum, its School of Art, and the symphony orchestra then dissolved fiscally into the Alliance. Through its board of directors the Alliance became the city's ministry of culture that left its three constituents with all the artistic autonomy they could hold onto, while it held tight control of their budgets and dunned Atlanta corporations to help support them. In a show of fealty to the

Alliance, the orchestra's board of directors renamed themselves a less sovereign sounding board of sponsors, whose role from then on was to hover diplomatically between the Alliance and the orchestra or between commerce and art—a very storm-ridden space.

THE FORD FOUNDATION

Atlanta had its big plans well underway before the fall of 1965 when a great gust of good fortune blew in from the Northeast. The Ford Foundation in New York had decided to commit over $80 million to what it described quietly as a program of assistance to sixty-one United States orchestras. The assistance reached Atlanta as a $750,000 grant delivered in $150,000 payments for five years that helped cover the orchestra's increased operating expenses and as a $1 million grant made to the orchestra's endowment fund that arrived ten years later. During that time, the Ford million was held in a New York bank trust though its dividends were sent to Atlanta. There the orchestra was required to raise a matching million for its endowment fund within five years and then to hold what it raised in an inviolable trust for another five. In the fall of 1976, the Ford grant was sent to Atlanta where, for the first time in its history, the orchestra had a $2 million capital asset. But during that ten-year period under Shaw, the orchestra's annual expenditures had risen from about $300,000 to just under $3 million.

RISING COSTS

According to the definition makers and data collectors at the American Symphony Orchestra League, there are thirty-one major symphony orchestras in the country, "major" because they spend more than a million dollars each year on their music making. At the end of its 1976 season, Atlanta ranked nineteenth in expenditures on the League's list. At its top was Boston which spent over $10 million that year. It was followed by Chicago with close to $8 million, New York with $7.3 million, Cleveland with $6.2 million, Los Angeles with about $6 million, and—the sixth of the Big Six—Philadelphia with $5.5 million. The thirty-first and last of the majors, Kansas City, paid out $1.3 million that year for its own symphonic music.

SPENDING THE FORD FUNDS

From their performances, the Big Six earned back from 55 to 75 percent of what they paid out. Atlanta earned back just over 52 percent. Like all the others, it counted on the interest and dividend earnings of its endowment funds; the generosity of its contributors; and local, state, federal, or private foundation grants to make up the difference. In Atlanta they did. In other cities where they did not, the Ford endowment funds are already being converted to cash deposits in checking accounts to pay bills and meet payrolls.

THE CHANGING ROLE OF MUSICIANS

When Shaw came to Atlanta, he took over an orchestra of seventy-five musicians who regarded it as their part-time employment. The better players held music teaching jobs in either the public schools or the state colleges, and the others were escapees from an assortment of professions and trades in the city with an unaccountably large representation from insurance businesses. "All of them used the orchestra here the way you and the others in New York used the Collegiate Chorale," Shaw told me as we talked in the studio of his Atlanta home. "It was their way of loving music."

The orchestra had started as a city high school group twenty years before Shaw took it over. In his first two seasons, it moved from being a marginally professional orchestra with rehearsals after school and office hours to a fully professional one with rehearsals during the day for concerts three nights a week and some Sunday matinées. With that change many of the public school teachers left the orchestra to hold onto their pension benefits; the avocationists left to hold their jobs, and others withdrew because they were unable to measure up to the musicianship Shaw had become accustomed to in Cleveland. Most of their replacements were not from Juilliard or Eastman or Curtis in the Northeast but were recent graduates from the music departments of North Texas State University, Florida State, Michigan, or Indiana. They were, Shaw soon realized, widely inexperienced in the repertoire, but that meant that they were unspoiled by professionalism. In his first year in Atlanta, the orchestra played sixty-eight concerts in a thirty-week season, and in his tenth they played two hundred in a forty-eight-week season. Their weekly minimum pay when he took over was $135, and it was

$270 ten years later. For Shaw's second season in Atlanta the orchestra moved from the acoustic vasts of the city's municipal auditorium to its new Memorial Arts Center hall that is now regarded as too small. The cost of building and furnishing the Center that year was $13 million, a figure that was pondered on with some bitterness by most of the orchestra's musicians. They were earning less than $7,000 that year for playing in it.

MORALE OF THE PLAYERS

All over the country in the late 1960s symphony members were pointing out that The Ford Foundation had specified that its grants were to be used to help raise incomes throughout what it termed "one of the most underpaid professional groups in American society." That was a useful quotation to cite at union contract bargaining sessions that may have cost some of the orchestras more than the subsidies coming to them from the Foundation.

Although they still trail the nearby New Orleans, Houston, and Dallas orchestras in their minimum wage scales, the young musicians in Atlanta can now place some compensating value on the estimates circulating through the Southeast that they play better than those who earn more. That self-esteem was solidly reinforced during their Kennedy Center performances at the inauguration ceremonies for their fellow Georgian, Jimmy Carter. The Washington performances were followed by a series of Beethoven performances in Carnegie Hall that left some New York critics writing notices that made excellent reading for some of the orchestra's sponsors back at the Memorial Arts Center. "Right now," Shaw said when we talked, "I don't think there is an orchestra in the United States that can play Beethoven as well as this one." It would, he adds craftily, play a more sonorous Beethoven if it had twenty more players, or as many as the best orchestras regard as their regular complements. "We're an 87-member team playing what amounts to a year-round schedule in a 105-member league," he said. Shaw wants to add pairs of first and second violins, violas, cellos, and double basses, as well as co-principal or associate principal winds. He points out that Atlanta's winds may be bearing up under a performance load no other major orchestra in the United States carries. With co-principals, the first plays one half of the program, and the second plays the other half. "But not here," Shaw said. "Here they play the whole program. So we're beginning to lose them to the bigger orchestras where they will play less and earn more."

THE BOARD OF SPONSORS

The conductor complains that way, not just to any solicitous visitor or to the press who see to it that his dissatisfactions get into print, but regularly and sometimes abrasively to the members of the orchestra's board of sponsors. Many of them have not felt instructed by his lectures, nor stirred to find the money that is needed to bring the orchestra to the size he wants it. He thinks it should tour overseas, make recordings, perform more on television, and have a fifty-two week season. The public pressure he puts on the sponsors for those changes produces a counter-pressure against the conductor. It takes a variety of forms, and one of the harshest is to attribute any empty seats in the hall either to his performance or to his programs.

THE BOARD AND HENRY SOPKIN

It is, of course, the easiest case to make against a music director. The conductor who preceded Shaw in Atlanta was Henry Sopkin, who left a $9,000 a year college teaching job in 1945 to become the $3,000 a year music director of the Atlanta Symphony in 1945 when its entire budget was $5,000. That had risen to $55,000 by 1949, and the fifty-member orchestra was over $18,000 in debt when one member of its board of directors told the conductor that his programs did not provide what most Atlantians wanted to hear. The complaint bearer wanted to hear more Rudolf Friml, Victor Herbert, George Gershwin, and other "tuneful" composers. In her master's thesis, *The Sopkin Years*, Anne Arant McFarland, a former member of the orchestra, described the conflict:

> It was an understood premise that the board of directors should not dictate artistic standards to the musical director; but since they did hold the purse strings, they did in fact have an influence on the programming.

In the following seasons, that influence moved Sopkin to make his programs tuneful with selections from *South Pacific* and *Carousel* by Richard Rodgers and *Showboat* by Jerome Kern, along with a cluster of Irving Berlin songs and George Gershwin tunes, but not a note of Friml or Herbert.

THE BOARD AND SHAW

Shaw's first serious trouble with his board of sponsors broke out five years after he arrived. For his 1971–72 season he set out to give a continuity to its fourteen programs by contrasting the eighteenth century works of the Austrian classicist Josef Haydn with the twentieth century works of the American iconoclast Charles Ives. Ives, who lived until 1954 in Danbury, Connecticut, was the crusty Yankee who thought concert-goers' ears should be regularly stretched or they would grow flabby. Before the series was finished the conductor had a call from the president of the orchestra's board of sponsors who told him that its ten-member executive committee had decided not to renew his contract at the end of the season. Why? Shaw asked. Because his programming had become too astringent, was the answer. Possibly so, Shaw allowed, but as he recounted the incident when we talked he could suggest another source of some local dissatisfaction with him. He had not been playing the social game in Atlanta because it took up time he needed for studying scores. Those who were making sizeable cash contributions to close the gap between what his orchestra earned and what it had to spend to keep performing liked to think of themselves as social intimates of the conductor, even when they did not like what he conducted. In their view he would have no orchestra to conduct if they did not cover the debts he was running up. "I was not going out to their receptions," Shaw said. "I wasn't going to their dinners."

THE CRISIS IN RELATIONS

But the charge they made against him was that Atlantians were not going to his Ives concerts because they did not want to hear unfamiliar music. The empty seats were the case for Shaw's dismissal. When the full board's fifty members learned of it from their morning papers, some were annoyed because they had no part in the vote, but it was what the voters decided that left a few of the other sponsors indignant. They placed a half-page public notice in Atlanta's leading newspaper urging all those who were renewing their symphony subscriptions to make their checks payable to Robert Shaw as the music director of the Atlanta Symphony Orchestra.

It was a hastily devised tactic to outflank the executive committee, and it produced more checks for subscription sales than the box office had ever had before. While the conductor was endorsing the checks, the sponsors were withdrawing his dismissal and renewing his contract. "They had to ask me to stay," he said. "I can sort of laugh about it five years later, but I really am still dealing with a board on which 20 or 40 percent of the members hate my guts."

The Current Scene

Shaw seems not to mind having detractors working against him. The simple fact is that he likes what he is doing in Atlanta and thinks it is where he belongs. Said Shaw:

> It is a little mysterious and difficult to prove, but I am very sure that there is a sort of climate that all people are borne along by. It's as natural to me that Szell should have asked me to come to Cleveland at the time he did as that I should have been asked to come to Atlanta at the time I did. I'm not saying anything like God works in mysterious ways. But as this orchestra's music director, my commitment was to the classical repertoire that builds technical discipline and finesse instead of exploiting color and obfuscating detail. And that comes out of my association with Szell more than my association with Toscanini. Toscanini sort of went "wham" over the whole thing and said, "This is what the piece sounds like." Szell's extraordinary genius was to find a way to put a piece together from the inside and then put a cover over it. Maybe I learned that. But anyway, I had to deal with my own strengths when I came here. I had not really had much experience in the romantic repertory. Mahler just simply didn't interest me then. Psychologically I was sort of repelled by it. And I'd had enough experience in show business to think I could somehow tell posture from integrity.

THE JOB OF MUSICAL DIRECTOR

> And there was one other thing. Beginning at about the time I came here, the podium soloist as a traveling phenomenon reached the point where one conductor might have two orchestras or three. And that was partly in self-protection because there's just no way a conductor can handle a forty-week season by himself and give his audience something new each week. Because he could handle only so much repertoire, it was necessary for the podium soloist to do his act in San Francisco and then repeat it, say, in Berlin. But it also meant that many of our major orchestras were left without anybody minding them. Here I've stayed in full charge because I'm not trying to make a career as a guest conductor.

Shaw paused for a spell then before backing away from the speech he seemed to be starting.

> This sort of self-analysis is a little embarrassing. It's just that I'm really not interested in getting up in front of a new public or a new orchestra every few weeks. I've had about as much success in a limited field as is good for a person and any more would only rot me. So I'd rather stay where I am and work harder.

A few days later the Atlanta papers were speculating that Shaw might leave at the end of the season if the board of sponsors did not provide him with a new orchestra manager he could work with more agreeably. The conductor Shaw was clearly the source of the stories. They set off a flurry of hope in some of the sponsors and apprehension in others. A few days later the board renewed the manager's contract for one year, Shaw's for three, and left the antagonisms unchanged.

QUALITY VERSUS MONEY

The tension between Shaw and his board of sponsors in Atlanta wells up between just about all symphony boards and the music directors they engage. Money, of course, is the root of all that alienates them. The orchestras and their endowment funds do not earn the amounts of it their music directors feel they should have for solid musical reasons, and the boards say they cannot raise it from contributors, the foundations, and government sources. But without it, or without higher wage scales for their instrumentalists (*ergo* better orchestras), more overtime rehearsals (better performances), more celebrated guest soloists (celebrity by association), and new audiences won over in other cities or countries (conquering heroship), many music directors feel their artistic aims stifled.

Shaw is one of them. David Goldwasser, the retiring president of the Atlanta orchestra's board of sponsors, is well aware of his feelings. Explained Goldwasser:

> The picture here is that we are one of a handful of major symphonies that have no deficits, and that is attributable to our very close management of the expenditures of the orchestra. That close management sometimes results in the music director not getting the additional players, new instruments, foreign bookings, and all the trappings that musicians look for. But we've played it with fiscal responsibility, and we are not putting up the dollars. So Mr. Shaw says, "If I had a more cooperative manager, I'd get some of those things."

But in such a prospering place as Atlanta with its ambitions to be the world's next great city, is it really not possible to raise the money Shaw feels he needs?

THE BOARD'S VIEW

According to Goldwasser:

Well, you know, it's difficult for someone to say it's not possible. When people don't want to do something they say it's not possible, and I'm afraid that's Mr. Shaw's position. But you know that artistic demands can be very flexible. They'll take you as far as you're going to let them. But income is not that flexible. There's so much, and when that's gone there is no more. So we have to live within our income. That's just our nature. We feel that we have done extremely well to have financed the growth that we have already experienced, and that to push us too fast would be disastrous because we don't believe we could match up to it. Our fund raising is limited by the Atlanta Arts Alliance. It has to approve our budget, and it will not approve a deficit budget, nor will it give us a free hand to go out and raise money. So we have certain limitations. We can only get individual personal gifts. We cannot get corporate or foundation or institutional gifts, and since the Alliance makes up our deficit, it carefully approves or disapproves our budget line by line.

And are the Alliance people making artistic decisions then, line by line?" In a sense they are," Goldwasser allowed, "because they are saying that there are only so many dollars and that the orchestra must learn to live on them."

THE ISSUE OF PUBLIC SUPPORT

And if your music director cannot live on them, and retain his artistic self-respect, where should he turn for support?

We've taken private support almost as far as we can. We're getting to the point now where we're at the mercy of government assistance. We have to get it or we'll just fold. The cost of what we are already doing is just getting completely out of hand.

Between 65 and 70 percent of all the money the orchestra spends each year in Atlanta goes to its musicians in salaries or in fees to its guest artists. With two of the Big Six orchestras (Cleveland and Boston) that proportion is much lower. With the others (Chicago, New York, Philadelphia, Los Angeles) it ranges between 58 and 63 percent. But, again, Kansas City is close to 70 percent. In Atlanta

Mr. Goldwasser was worrying about his mounting payroll. "We employ artistic people," he said, "and they are all woefully underpaid." He sounded almost anguished about that for a moment, but he recovered and continued in his best board room manner.

Now no one is forcing these people into these fields. No one told them they must be artists or musicians. But they have a right to expect their wages to be adjusted up to something comparable to their abilities. So when we have exploited the public to its fullest degree as far as fund raising is concerned, where are we going to turn in order to provide the pay for those musicians?

He waited for my answer, but I outwaited him.

A LAST RESORT

Said Goldwasser with just a trace of contempt:

The government. Everybody's looking to the government now. We all use the example of what they do in Europe. Well, it's a pretty poor example in many respects because all those people are on the government payroll and they get pretty lackadaisical and pretty sour in their performances and in their attitudes. So I hope we don't come to that. Yet we have no other place to go to except to the government if the performing arts are to flourish.

HOW MUCH DOES THE PUBLIC CARE?

The performing art of the symphony orchestra is already flourishing in its fashion, of course. The ninety-one orchestras assisting in The Ford Foundation's study, *The Finances of the Performing Arts,* published in 1974, gave 5,587 concerts in their 1970–71 seasons. According to the assisting computers, there were 9,911,808 available seats at them, and 7,379,299 (or about 74 percent) were filled with ticket buyers. If not one of them returned during the season, it could be contended that close to 4 percent of the country's population of 200 million went to *one* symphony concert that year. But since the computers disclosed that almost half a million of those attending held subscription tickets for from five to twenty concerts, and since bi-weekly symphony concert goers are about as habit-bound as weekly church goers, the far more credible possibility is that less than 1 percent of the population attended a symphony concert during that season, or during any subsequent one.

In Atlanta, on its principal concert series in 1976–77, the orchestra gave eighty performances in the Memorial Arts Center where there are 1,762 seats, or places at the concerts for 140,960 ticket-holders. By its box office count, 88 percent of the seats were occupied by 5,989 subscribers, each of whom attended from six to twenty-four concerts, and by 38,340 single-ticket buyers. If half of the single-ticket buyers went to two or more performances and the subscription-ticket buyers did not share their tickets, a valiant and foolhardy guesser can rush in where no statistician would risk being found with the surmise that not more than 25,000 Atlantians attended some of their orchestra's symphony concerts that season. And since Atlanta's metropolitan population that year was 1,820,000, then less than 1.5 percent of them cared enough about Shaw's orchestra to buy a ticket costing from three to eight dollars to a performance.

SHAW'S VIEW

Whether the regular audience for symphony concerts anywhere is even less than 1 percent or more than 3 percent of the population is arguable. What is not arguable is that it is an elitist activity for the financially advantaged. That raises the persisting ethical question about the use of public tax money for a performing art that is not of any wide public interest. Shaw has thought about why the use of that money seems justified, perhaps even to the point of being a civil obligation. "I suppose you ask, first of all, do you want to live in a community where there are no schoolrooms, libraries, universities, and museums?" Shaw slipped into the role of Atlanta's most resistant taxpayer then and answered his own question. "I want to be where there's a school," he said, "but I don't give a goddam about an orchestra. And particularly I don't want any goddam ballet around screwing up my kids." He reverted then to his music director persona: "You'd probably have to marshal statistics that show that dollars follow the flag, and that if you build a society which is not necessarily attractive to yourself, but is to others who may have slightly different tastes than yours, it's good for the economy generally."

BASES FOR POLICY

We agreed that the economy—the nation's, his, mine, or one of his second violinists'—was not what we wanted any art to serve because it surely had far higher purposes. I reminded him that the

New York State Arts Council was spreading its money into all of its assembly districts to be certain that every legislator voting for its appropriations could justify them to his constituents. As a result, the money was supporting local quilt-making clubs of little artistic intent with funds that the New York City Ballet might put to exalting artistic uses. I said that I found that appalling, and that the ballet's managing director, Lincoln Kirstein, probably found it immoral if not uncivilizing, and possibly even criminal. Since Shaw had played the role of a hard-pressed Atlanta taxpayer quite convincingly, I proposed that he slip into the role of head money distributor at the New York State Arts Council, or even at the National Endowment for the Arts in Washington. He said:

> People like you become devils' advocates because the devils have no advocates. Look, nobody's ever written me a letter saying, "You son-of-a-bitch, I'm being taxed for your orchestra, and I don't like it." Certainly Nancy Hanks must be sensitive to that. Yet when we get any tax grants here it's to give concerts in rural areas so that the politicians are protected. So Kirstein's position seems to me a pretty brave one intellectually. I guess that would have been George Szell's position too. Elitist. Very elitist. If people didn't wear tuxedos to his concerts in Cleveland, he thought probably he wasn't conducting well enough. He thought he was attracting the wrong class of people. But that's a very difficult thing to do. I'm not sure I can rationalize it, or make a reasonable apology for it, but intuitively I sort of feel that unless symphonic music reaches the people, the general populace, it's going to atrophy. So I think that in the long run, not in my generation, and not in my particular institution here, something has to be done so that symphonic music gets into the mulch of Carl Sandburg's *The People*. I think what must be created in them is the desire to create. In that sense art isn't importable or even observable. Either people make it themselves or it isn't made. You've got to begin somewhere, and participation is more important than observation. A great teacher, like Paul Hindemith when he was at Yale, could walk into a room and soon have the students writing their own songs. Maybe that can only happen on a one-to-one relationship, and I'm not sure how bureaucratically it can function, but I think the principle is true and that given the right leader and the right teacher, it can happen.

STANDARD SETTING VERSUS DISPERSAL

Then you would distribute tax money widely? Shaw would, and he went on. "Now the two questions for Nancy Hanks are, one, how much should she use to set standards, and, two, how much

should she use to stimulate interest?" I asked him to answer the
questions he had for her.

If I were the National Endowment, I'd pick the institutions that are
setting standards and I'd give them a hundred percent. But here, for
me, it's not that simple. I think our position is to set standards too, but
I'm afraid that if we don't involve the people we also lose our way. The
quandary goes back to Thomas Jefferson from that speech that men
are created equal in opportunity but not yet in intelligence and taste.
And the vitality of the arts depends upon their reaching the people
without losing their own integrity.

THE UNIONS

Were the musicians' unions helping with that? Shaw answered:

I wrote some harsher sentences about that the other day than I've ever
written before. But maybe they were sort of evasive too because they
said that if the musicians' principal interests are monetary, then the
whole heart goes out of music. In a sense, unions and art are a little
incompatible and self-negating. The artist essentially is the guy who
is driven in upon himself. So I think the unions have obviously helped
his family more than they've helped him. But I don't think they've
done much for the arts. There's the Musicians' Performance Fund that
works very handsomely in this community because there are nice guys
in the union and all of a sudden you find performances with small
orchestras at churches of repertoire which couldn't be done by the
symphony. And their support goes in many directions. It goes, for instance, into putting string quartets in the schools. The end makes the
means reasonable, sort of. Makes the means acceptable. And also, it
forestalls criticism to be able to say, "Look, we're spending all this
money in good works," and that helps a little bit. But, in general, when
the union becomes so big that the good which is sought is no longer
common, then it's trouble.

THE BOARD AGAIN

His orchestra's board of sponsors seemed hardly more idealistic
to him. Do they think you should set standards or involve the
people? He replied:

They're so desperate for any help they can get, they get the support
first and then try justifying it by principles. But I think this is generally
true of anybody, of any institution. They look for the money and then
try to rationalize it some way. I wish they would recognize that the greatest untapped natural resource for the arts in the United States is the
vitality and creative managerial capacity of the performers. In the

London Symphony and the Berlin Philharmonic and in European opera houses, somehow the managerial and production and promotion staffs come out of the performance pool. And we just simply haven't done it in the United States. We've talked about it for years, but in Atlanta we don't have a single player representative who's welcome at board meetings. It's absolutely preposterous. The board should be able to pick five or six of our players, if only as a political maneuver and ploy, who could talk with them. That's simply got to change if there's going to be a change in management.

BREAKING OUT OF THE HALL

Shaw would like the board to make Atlanta unique in American music by having it get away a little bit from the rigidity of the symphony orchestra and the rigidity of its audience and create what he would call a Musical Arts Association. The association would serve the community with symphony, opera, choral, and ballet performances and chamber music "so that the players got their soloistic opportunities to preserve their sanity." Shaw had seen a plan like it working in Leningrad where the symphony orchestra was touring in the United States, another was playing operas in the Kirov Theatre.

That's important, not only for the purposes of education, but to keep the symphony guys honest and involved and to help them remember the reason they got into the arts in the first place. Because the pressures of professionalism are very, very real. I mean the psychological pressures of having to play only under somebody's dictation are severe enough. But the pressures of financial parity—the Chicago Orchestra against New York Philharmonic against the Metropolitan Opera against Philadelphia and so on; who's on top and who's getting the money and who has the lowest standard of living—those hagglings just kill, kill, kill human dignity. And they are terribly bad for music. The thing that keeps music vital is the thing that made the Collegiate Chorale so extraordinary. Do you remember how those poor people got whipped by me? And I don't like whipping people. I was whipping myself too, I guess. And somehow when everybody is doing it for love, you can take all sorts of slaps. It's an extraordinary event in my life to have gone through that, suffered through that, and belonged to it at that time, and it's the thing that keeps music pure.

THE INFLUENCE OF PRIVATE SUPPORT

Would he feel untainted if he had all of the financial support he needed from government sources?

It seems to me that the combination of support from government and private sectors—a terrible word—is important for shortening the chain of command, to have some close financial responsibility, which means some sort of cost supervision and criticism. If it all comes from Washington, if it all comes by mail, then it's spent more simply than if somebody's there watching; and it's spent more impersonally and without pressure and stimulus. You'd almost have no audience in a sense. You wouldn't have to keep convincing people that this is worthwhile. The present system forces you to redefine your own objectives constantly, to decide whether you're in the audience education business or just going onward and upward with the arts for art's sake.

But would that choice be any different, I asked him, if the money just came, as he said, in the mail?

MOTIVATION: THE FINAL ANSWER

Maybe my point is too abstract. But unless there's a flow of tension and counter-insurgency or whatever between an artist and his audience, he just can't keep being straight with himself. I think in my own case that if I hadn't been savaged by the board here, I wouldn't be as difficult to bite the next time.

Shaw is one of the world's more approachable sorts a few hours after he has been approached. So it seemed time to ask him if he had settled into Atlanta to lift up music's faithful or to work out his own salvation. His answer:

I'm not stupid enough to think that I can save them without saving myself at the same time. I said the other day that it was important for me to be here, and today I don't think it's quite so important, but I also think it's an awful lot more important than anything anybody else is doing.

Martin Mayer

3

The Opera

Introduction

Opera is the big business of the performing arts. Even after the considerable truncation of its own season and the expansion of theirs, the Metropolitan Opera still takes in more money at the box office than all the Big Four Symphony orchestras together. And in everything nonfinancial that counts, opera in America is enjoying unprecedented and unanticipated good health. Its intellectual standing as an art form has never been higher, and its popularity as a way to spend an evening has been growing at an accelerating rate. The success of the televised *La Bohème* live from the Met—the biggest audience public television had ever drawn—was the coronation of a full-grown trend, not the birth of a new phenomenon.

But it takes more people to produce a minute's live operatic entertainment than to produce a minute in any other performing enterprise—conductor and musicians, solo and choral singers, solo and ensemble dancers, stage director and assistants, scene designers, builders and movers, costume and make-up and wig and prop peo-

MARTIN MAYER *has long been a regular critic and reporter of symphonic and opera performances and of musical recordings. He has directed many studies of performing arts subjects, including one supported by the Twentieth Century Fund on development and influence of performing arts centers in the United States. He is also the author of a number of books on subjects other than the arts, including a recent one on housing.*

ple, lighting designers and technicians, and very large crews front of the house and upstairs to handle the labors associated with operating a large theater. The Metropolitan Opera meets a payroll of 1,500 people, more than 700 of them all year, full-time. Something like 80 percent of an opera company's budget goes to paying for the people.

The burden per salable seat has been rising more rapidly than the cost-of-living index, and thus more rapidly than a rational marketing policy can raise the price of tickets to what is, after all, a discretionary, luxury item in anybody's budget. To the extent that tickets are sold by subscription—and in most successful opera companies three-quarters of the seats are sold in advance by subscription—the numbers are already very large. A pair of orchestra seats for a ten-performance Metropolitan Opera subscription runs $500, to be shelled out in one lump in the spring. A 10 percent increase is the food budget for a week.

Thus it has been extremely difficult to increase box-office receipts for opera even in the recent bull market for the art form. The Metropolitan took in $11.7 million in 1966–67, and $13.6 million in 1974–75, an increase of only 16 percent over a time when the general price level rose almost 70 percent. (Later figures are not precisely comparable because the season was shortened.) Opera America, the trade association of opera companies, predicts that between 1977 and 1982 the share of expenditures of the nation's forty-two larger opera companies covered by earned income will decline from 53 percent to 45 percent.

Opera was not always a money-losing activity. Before World War I the extraordinary disparity between the discretionary income of the wealthy and the wage level of semiskilled workers permitted ticket prices high enough to pay soloists 50 percent of the gross receipts and still leave something over for the impresario. In the years before World War I when the Metropolitan Opera and Oscar Hammerstein were throwing broadsides at each other in New York, an orchestra seat cost five dollars, an orchestral musician was well paid at seventy dollars a week, choristers and ballet dancers averaged about twenty-five dollars a week, and stagehands considered themselves fortunate to make twenty dollars a week. And production standards were much lower, requiring fewer people on stage, behind stage, and in the pit.

Moreover, opera in those days was distinctly a high society entertainment. The basic income for both the Metropolitan and Hammerstein came from the sale of boxes for the entire season to the socially prominent or socially ambitious; and in theory the people stood guarantee for the enterprise. Outside New York, opera was most frequently offered by touring companies, usually to an audience that had bought its tickets well in advance from a local promoter or committee who guaranteed payment of a certain minimum to the company. (Nevertheless, the receipts in the lesser cities were sufficiently uncertain to establish a tradition by which singers are paid before rather than after they perform. When Maria Callas came to the Metropolitan Opera in the 1950s, Rudolf Bing remembered in his memoirs, she insisted on being paid before each performance in cash dollars; the Metropolitan's check wasn't good enough.)

In the 1920s Giulio Gatti-Casazza and Wall Street banker Otto Kahn ran the Metropolitan Opera (and apparently made money at it, though they never said so); utilities holding company operator Samuel Insull formed a permanent opera company for Chicago (and distinctly did not make money at it: an arriviste both socially and artistically, he had to pay maximum prices for everything he presented). Either would have been astonished at the idea that an opera manager would have to solicit contributions from the public or (much worse) grants from the government. Kahn in 1924 turned down an offer of an endowment grant from the Juilliard Foundation.

But Insull's opera company went out of business in the Great Crash (closely followed by Insull's holding companies), and the Met would certainly have gone under in the late 1930s without the extraordinary organizing and fund-raising efforts of Mrs. August Belmont, a former actress of great accomplishment, who established the Metropolitan Opera Guild as a supporting arm for a reorganized company. This general solicitation was not expected to become a regular feature, however. When prosperity returned, opera would pay its way again, with perhaps occasional help from dedicated wealthy board members.

Only the Metropolitan and the San Francisco Opera, housed in a War Memorial auditorium that gave the city a stake in its continuance, were institutionalized through the fires of the Depression. The other presumably permanent American opera companies—Philadelphia, Boston, Chicago, St. Louis, New Orleans—simply disappeared. Chicago's was the saddest case, because it had been the most ambitious artistically (the great singing actress Mary Garden had been its manager at one point), and because the plans for its permanence had been so ingeniously laid. The home of the Chicago Civic Opera had been placed in a block-long skyscraper office building under an arrangement by which the profits from the building would be a source of steady support for the production of opera (and of drama at a Chicago Civic Theatre at the opposite end of the building). The gala opening was a week before Black Monday in 1929. Less than three years later, the whole shebang—office building and opera company, complete with accumulated sets, costumes, and props and the warehouse that held them—had been sold in bankruptcy court to its creditors, and there was no opera in Chicago.

The Civic Opera House did not suffer the indignities of Chicago's splendid Auditorium which was converted to bowling alleys, but it did undergo a variety of miscellaneous uses, including adaptation to a movie theater, which required drilling holes in the stage to anchor a giant screen. (At one point it was proposed to replace the wood frame of the pit with concrete walls to cut maintenance costs, a disaster averted only at the last moment by the intervention of the original architect of the theater.) Touring companies appeared occasionally in the theater, and during the war a new attempt was made to establish a permanent opera producing company, using the resources of sets and costumes still in the warehouse; in 1946 this venture, too, collapsed.

The revival of opera in Chicago is very much the story of one woman, Carol Fox, who grew up in the 1940s as the theatrically dedicated daughter of one of the city's leading families. She found her way backstage during the wartime revival of the opera company as president of the junior auxiliary of the women's league that was helping the house, and not long after finishing high school, she went off to study professionally—acting with Max Reinhardt at the Pasadena Playhouse, singing with Giovanni Martinelli and Fausto Cleva (who had been the director of the Chicago Opera in the 1940s) in New York, and then in Italy. She was back in New York in early 1952, coaching repertory with the young conductor Nicola Rescigno when Rescigno got a call from Fortune Gallo, an entrepreneur of touring opera companies who was hoping to establish a regular season in Chicago and wanted Rescigno's services for it. Knowing Miss Fox was from Chicago, Rescigno asked her advice, and she urged against it. There were too many people who remembered the glamor of Insull's company for a *sauve-qui-peut* touring group to give satisfaction in Chicago; besides, her native city deserved better. During the course of her exposition, it occurred to her for the first time that maybe she—with Rescigno and some help from old friends—could do it herself.

The friend she had most in mind was Larry Kelly, once an aspiring pianist good enough to have studied with Artur Schnabel, then a young executive running his late father's real estate enterprises because his widowed mother had no one else to ask. Kelly was intrigued. He and Miss Fox got together with their respective family lawyers and explored the possibilities. Kemper Insurance, owners of the skyscraper opera house building, were not actually obliged by the terms of their purchase to help restore the stage to opera, but there were tax benefits for them if they did so. Fox and Kelly paid a call on the Kemper management, and were rebuffed; there were plans to restore opera to the Civic stage—with mature, experienced, practical people in charge. Like Fortune Gallo. But Kemper could scarcely refuse Fox and Kelly the right to rent the facilities on the same terms as the local schools, who used the auditorium for graduation ceremonies. Fox and Kelly decided to begin their careers as impresarios with a "calling card" production that would demonstrate their qualifications to run an opera season in Chicago.

Lyric Opera of Chicago

The "Lyric Theatre" (later Lyric Opera) of Chicago was incorporated in fall 1952, together with a guild of sponsors who would help raise money for the fledgling. (The guild was needed because until Lyric Theatre demonstrated that it couldn't make money producing opera, the Internal Revenue Service would not issue it a certificate as a nonprofit charitable entity that could receive tax-deductible contributions. A guild, having no source of income, *was* demonstrably nonprofit and automatically qualified.) Advertising men Fairfax Cone and Clint Frank, local boosters, were active in the early promotion and fund-raising efforts. Because the claim was that the new company would bring Chicago the best, the "calling card" production, in February 1954, was Mozart's *Don Giovanni,* with a cast including Eleanor Steber, then the leading American dramatic soprano; Nicola Rossi-Lemeni from Italy; the young Canadian tenor Leopold Simoneau; John Brownlee; Bidu Sayao; and Irene Jordan. Rescigno conducted. The sets and costumes were lent from the warehouse. The theater was virtually sold out, paying $31,000 of the $42,000 cost, and Claudia Cassidy of The *Chicago Tribune* described the performance as "a kind of miracle." Kemper okayed a three-week season that fall.

In 1954 it was still possible to sign up singers on less than six months' notice. Miss Fox went to Italy and brought back Maria Callas, already the reigning Queen of La Scala, to make her American professional debut in Chicago with an opening night *Norma*. The price was $2,000 per performance plus expenses, very high for those days (the Metropolitan's top fee was then $1,500); but the six Callas performances—two each of Norma, Violetta in *La Traviata*, and Lucia di Lammermoor—gave the new company national recognition. Among the others Miss Fox signed for the first season on her Italian voyage were Giulietta Simionato, Giuseppe diStefano, Tito Gobbi, and Gian Giacomon Guelfi. Rescigno conducted six of the eight productions (a prodigious feat in three weeks), and the other two were led by Jonel Perlea. The orchestra was drawn in part from personnel of the Chicago Symphony. One of the productions, with sets and costumes adapted from earlier use in other operas, was a world premiere of *The Taming of the Shrew* by the American composer Vittorio Giannini.

The second season established Chicago in the major leagues once and for all, adding Renata Tebaldi to Miss Callas as equal prima donna (somewhat to the discomfort of both), Jussi Bjoerling and Carlo Bergonzi (making his American debut) to diStefano in the cast of tenors, Ettore Bastianini to Gobbi on the baritone roster, and Ebe Stignani, the greatest modern Italian mezzo-soprano, near the end of her career but making her American stage debut for the Lyric. Vera Zorina and Alicia Markova were among the solo dancers. Tullio Serafin, making a triumphant return to America more than twenty years after he had been the leading conductor at the Metropolitan, shared the podium with Rescigno.

The names are listed because they were important. No other opera company in the world presented in five weeks such a concentration of world class operatic talent. Despite the presence of a contemporary opera (Raffaello de Banfields' *Lord Byron's Love Letter*) and a seventeenth century piece (a staging of Monteverdi's *Il Ballo delle Ingrate*), the house was sold to 88 percent of capacity.

Box-office receipts were more than $415,000. Unfortunately, costs were almost $620,000, and the gap between the two was greater than could be raised by young Miss Fox, young Mr. Kelly, and their young friends.

Lyric Theatre came out of its second season more than $50,000 in debt, and Miss Fox told her colleagues that there was no way the company could continue without the recruitment of older, richer, more eminent Chicagoans to the board. Kelly and Rescigno, fearing instant ossification and the loss of artistic control, rebelled and took Miss Fox to court when she began suiting action to words. If the beginnings had not been so brilliant and so apparently advantageous to the city (Mayor Richard Daley was joining the board, too, as honorary chairman), the well-publicized squabble among the founders would have doomed the Lyric.

Instead, Kelly and Rescigno were in effect bought off (they went away to Dallas with the proceeds to launch the Dallas Opera), and for the five-week 1956 season (which saw debuts with the company by sopranos Birgit Nilsson and Inge Borkh, tenors Mario del Monaco and Richard Tucker, and baritone Paul Schoeffler), the new board in fact raised $30,000 more than the gap between receipts and costs, restoring fiscal health to the company. This season also brought four new conductors: Dmitri Mitropoulos, the American Emerson Buckley, Georg Solti in his American opera debut, and the young Italian Bruno Bartoletti, who would subsequently become and remain musical director of the company.

In the early years, the Chicago Lyric benefited considerably from the use of volunteer help (Miss Fox herself took no salary; she observed recently that her father's largest contribution was not cash but his daughter's support), from the willingness of Kemper in effect to split the value of its tax exemption by charging low rent and permitting the use of the warehouse sets and costumes, and from the subscription development expertise of Danny Newman, who pioneered the intensive use of mail-order promotion to sell series of opera tickets. (In theory, receipts from subscription sales should not be taken into income until the performance is delivered; in fact, for struggling performing arts companies, subscriptions provide working capital that could not otherwise be raised.) From the beginning, too, the subscription lists were used as tools in soliciting contributions, a process now computerized.

Accounting practices for opera companies require that expenses associated with new productions be charged entirely against the season in which the production is first mounted; unlike a business, an opera cannot capitalize its sunk costs and amortize them over future presentation. Thus the existence of the old productions in the warehouse released significant funds to pay performance fees to the stellar casts Miss Fox assembled in Europe. When the contents of the warehouse became unsatisfactory, Miss Fox found an ingenious substitute in the form of productions borrowed from opera houses elsewhere in the world. The first was a *Traviata* from the Teatro Massimo in Palermo in 1956. By 1959 Lyric was borrowing no fewer than six productions—Rossini's *La Cenerentola*, Verdi's *Simon Boccanegra*, and Wagner's *Der Fliegende Holländer* from Rome; Puccini's *Turandot* and Mozart's *Cosi Fan Tutte* from San Francisco; and Janacek's *Jenufa* from Covent Garden in London. Later, Chicago would work out "co-productions," planned with other American opera companies to make sure the scenery was usable on the several stages. (The *La Bohème* production televised from the Metropolitan Opera had first been performed in Chicago.)

In New York, Rudolf Bing had struck a bargain with the board of the Metropolitan Opera that he would not call upon the company's resources for new productions, and the board would allow him all the productions he could finance through special contributions for this purpose. Miss Fox followed, slowly of necessity, with increasing success in the company's second decade. The death of two of the regular donors of new productions, however, forced Chicago to abandon this approach to opera financing. In the 1977 season, new productions were part of the regular budget, forcing a considerable extension of the annual fund-raising effort. Part of the purpose of the shift may have been to assure Lyric's qualification for a challenge grant from the National Endowment for the Arts: the added contributions to the general fund qualify as "new money" to be matched at a rate of one for three by the federal government.

After twenty-three years, Lyric's operation is relatively routine. At this writing the season is twelve weeks long; the budget approaches $7 million, half of which must be raised in the form of contributions. Miss Fox, described on the program as "Founder and General Manager," still runs the company, helped (but obviously not very closely controlled) by a board of directors that numbers no fewer than seventy souls. As one of her assistants put it, "They know she's not going to do anything to wreck the company." The market for the product is spectacularly strong—for 1977, Lyric sold 24,000 subscriptions (up from only 10,000 in 1972), representing more than 85 percent of the seating capacity for all performances. In recent years, Lyric has sold more than 100 percent of its capacity, through a system by which ticketholders unable to attend take a chit for a tax-deductible contribution in lieu of a refund and permit their seats to be resold by the box office.

Sales success gives Miss Fox her margin for contingencies, which are never remote in opera. She and her business staff budget eighteen months in advance—firmly for the upcoming season, more tentatively for its successor—on the assumption that the company will sell to 90 percent of capacity, permitting the first $250,000 of cost overruns to be met from income overruns. The size of the planned operating deficit before contributions is essentially a function of the repertory for the year: an *Aïda* (requiring five world-class singers and a huge assemblage of choristers, dancers, and costumed supers) may cost twice as much per performance as an *Orfeo* (requiring three singers of no extraordinary vocal range, a small chorus that need not be visible, and a few dancers). The planning language in Chicago refers to "x" operas and "x + y" operas; part of the planning task of the business and production staffs is to balance them out. Production is always happy to do one "x" for every "x + y"; business wants three "x" for every "x + y." Miss Fox mediates and decides.

In the end she makes the artistic decisions, too (opera productions are collaborations, but opera houses are not run by committees). Over the years, however, Miss Fox had allowed her artistic judgments to be strongly influenced by advisers—from 1958 until his death in 1975, by Pino Donati, a veteran administrator in Italian houses; and since the latter 1960s by conductor Bruno Bartoletti. The time lag between artistic decision and performance is now greater than the lag between budgetary decision and performance—these days, conductors, singers, directors, and designers must be engaged three years before the audience sees the opera—which means that the boundaries of the budget are roughly fixed before budget matters per se appear on the table, a situation no less worrisome in Chicago than elsewhere. Once, in 1967, the Civic Opera was darkened for a year by a pair of miscalculations—by the company as to the money that would be necessary to get the musicians' union to sign a contract, and by the union as to the raise actually available for its members. Special contributions of $300,000 tided the Lyric over its cancelled season, and for a while the lost year gave Miss Fox better control over her budget than any other opera manager in the country.

The one decision Miss Fox cannot make herself is the total amount of money that can safely be budgeted for receipts from contributions; she and her fund-raising staff can make a presentation, but the collective judgment of the board must control. The figure the board adopts is then ratified by a procedure unique to Chicago —the annual meeting of "voting members" which takes place at the opera house itself. Until 1977 every contributor of $100 or more was a voting member of the Lyric Opera (starting in 1978 the minimum contribution for this distinction is $250). Once the figures are announced and approved at the annual meeting, the constituency is more or less committed to seeing that they will be met.

Nevertheless, Chicago has usually gone over the top through the "matching grant" device, by which one very large contributor or a foundation (in 1972–75, The Ford Foundation; in 1976, the Chicago Community Trust) has made a large gift contingent on matching contributions from the public. The requirement has usually been two or three more dollars from the public for every dollar from the challenger. This device has now been adopted as public policy for a portion of the grants awarded by the National Endowment for the Arts (NEA), which is fine for arts organizations that have not solicited challenge grants in the past, but perilous for Chicago. In 1977 the Lyric not very enthusiastically accepted NEA challenge grants of $300,000 a year for two years. But NEA insisted on considering as basic support the very large contributions raised in previous years by private challenge grants, and these do not arrive again without special stimulus. This bucket may go to the well only once a year; and with NEA's challenge in being, others will be far less likely to make similar offers even if you can take the bucket twice. Given the widespread support the Lyric Opera enjoys—and the budgetary decision that moved contributions for new productions to the "new money" category for NEA purposes—Miss Fox and her board can probably survive the government's generosity; but the fact is that in Chicago a carelessly thought program could destroy the financial stability of the opera company. It is a very serious weakness of such programs that they reward fund-raising skills rather than artistic performance; the Arts Council of Great Britain's approach of supporting "exemplary institutions" (in large part by reference to ticket sales) would clearly be preferable.

The threat on the horizon for the Lyric as for other opera companies is the continuing increase in labor costs. Early in 1977, the Lyric signed a three-year contract with the musicians' union which guaranteed a 48.6 percent increase in musicians' income from 1976 to 1979—a raise from $390 to $500 a week in the minimum salary, an increase from $440 to $850 in vacation allowance, and an extension from fifteen to seventeen weeks of assured employment. It is hard to see how Lyric's future budgets can be kept under $9 million, or how box office receipts can be raised above $3.5 million (which would be a 40 percent increase over the 1976 receipts). Thus at least $5.5 million has to be raised from various sources in 1979—65 percent more than the maximum Lyric has yet raised in one year from gifts, opening night galas, opera balls, restricted contributions for productions, etc. The other side of the coin is that in the last year of the contract, 1979, the players who make possible the musical quality of the Lyric's performances still receive, including overtime after twenty-two hours, perhaps $11,000 a man for their labors. An opera company can easily become dangerously poor without making any of its employees comfortably rich.

Lyric's present situation is still very much a function of the circumstances of its founding. It is an essentially Italian theater in the major American city with the smallest representation of Italo-American population, because that was Miss Fox's taste and training. The great economy in the operation of the company is the house itself, rented by Kemper Insurance (complete with the warehouse and its contents which include, for example, complete armories of stage weapons for armies of almost any era) at a price of about $1,500 per performance. The great continuing asset is the increasing age, authority, and prominence of Miss Fox's friends—the "kids" of 1952 who put up a few thousand dollars each to get the company started and can now contribute for themselves and their corporations in very much larger amounts. An investment has been made, moreover, in persuading future generations to share the enthusiasm. Half a million dollars of Miss Fox's annual budget goes to an opera school which gives low-priced spring performances of chamber opera and may—improbably but possibly—be training the next Carol Fox. In 1977, under the direction of the great dancer

Maria Tallchief (married to an eminent Chicagoan), a new ballet
school was launched by the Lyric in collaboration with the School of
American Ballet of George Balanchine.

Nevertheless, it is clear that no replacements wait ready in the
wings for Carol Fox as impresario and manager or Danny Newman
as subscription magician and promoter. The Lyric Opera is dependent to a degree almost unknown to museums or symphony
orchestras on the personal qualities and characteristics of the only
leaders it has ever had. What keeps people from being upset is that
this vulnerability, unknown to the commercial world or most other
kinds of arts enterprise, is a commonplace of opera companies.

The Boston Opera is Sarah Caldwell—ex-violinist turned stage
director, conductor, and fund raiser extraordinary. The Santa Fe
exists only because conductor John Crosby's family had a hacienda
there; the theater was built in his back yard. The ambitiousness of
the Seattle Opera is clearly that of Glynn Ross. Houston is perhaps
the most spectacular case. Formerly a garish and occasional ex-
travaganza, the Houston Grand Opera has become the largest continuing feature of that city's cultural life, with subsidiary companies to produce outdoor opera in the spring and to tour across
the state. Each of the six operas offered in Jones Hall, the center-
piece of the city's urban renewal program, receives six performances,
and 87 percent of the 1976–77 season was sold in advance by
subscription. Houston's director David Gockley was a singer and a
conductor before going to business school to train himself as an
administrator. Little of what Houston has accomplished could have
happened without him.

Most of these companies are so new as major factors that no
changing of the guard has been required. The New York City Opera
did survive the death of its founder Morton Baum, largely because
the creative "diumvirate" of Julius Rudel and John White had
deeply involved themselves in the financial and budgeting operations. This was a remarkable accomplishment, because Baum essentially kept the affairs of the institution under his hat; and his
successors in the leadership of the City Center board had much
less capacious hats. Though they have not always been as cost conscious as their best friends might wish, working artists *can* run the
opera houses they have founded, as John Crosby and Sarah Caldwell
have demonstrated (Carol Fox has never been a working artist at
the Lyric: one of her conditions for starting it was that she would

never sing on its stage). But when the institution has been structured to be run by a lawyer-politician like Baum, it is difficult for artists to assume control. At the City Opera, there are signs that direction of financial and business management by artists has come to an impasse; and no one has yet spied the sail of a new Morton Baum on the horizon.

In Dallas, an opera company left rudderless by the death of Larry Kelly decided to look in the other direction, hiring a general manager whose experience was mostly in the business end of the arts. An exceedingly able and likeable young executive, the second Dallas general manager was treasurer of a nonprofit enterprise forwarding the careers of young musicians and was entirely untested in areas of artistic decision.

In the two cities where opera has been growing most rapidly during the past few years—San Diego and Miami—the general managers (Tito Capobianco and Robert Herman, respectively) appear to have been hired as employees of a committed board, much as a general manager might be hired by the Metropolitan. In Washington, the board of the Opera Society organized a switch from Ian Strasfogel to George London without causing a missed beat in any part of the planning. But expanding what had been a weak opera company in a booming metropolitan area is not by any means the same problem as maintaining levels of quality previously established by a dedicated, specialized—and clever—leadership in a stable or declining city. And there is no way any opera company, however inspiringly led, can win them all, every year.

Conclusion

The case for making an opera company securely permanent is not entirely clear cut. The major European opera houses have their ups and downs—the improvement in Covent Garden and the decline of La Scala from 1954 to 1965 were lessons this critic will not forget. If it had not been a government bureaucracy, La Scala would probably have changed managements much more quickly than it did. The practical significance of institutionalized opera, with the bills paid by the state, may be that the company and its leaders survive the years when what is presented on the stage is not worth the price the audience pays for its tickets. Archbishop Temple once noted that it was not true that any religion was better than no religion at all, and the long, sad story of opera in Philadelphia can be taken as a demonstration that the dictum applies to more than churches. Still, there are usually good deeds that shine in the naughtiest of opera worlds. Even in the days when its routine productions were disastrous beyond American imaginings, the Paris Opera could come up with a *Tosca* directed by Franco Zeffirelli for Maria Callas. The revival of quality in an extant musical theater is considerably more likely than the revival of a dead theater; coming back from the dead takes luck as well as faith. The seven years from 1946 to 1953, when Chicago had no opera at all, could have been extended for many more without the accidents that brought Carol Fox back home.

The task that confronts national and local governments is the construction of support systems that will sustain a popular institution that cannot pay its way, without enthroning a bureaucratized management that loses touch with its public. The patchwork of clever grants being sewed together by the National Endowment for the Arts, while welcome enough to boards and managers that might otherwise find themselves naked, will not accomplish this task. Chicago is perhaps the test case: a first-class performing company demonstrably well managed and accepted to the hilt by its own community, which has handled its own problems admirably and uncomplainingly—but cannot seriously hope to make viable plans for the 1980s without assurances of major and continuing support from the tax revenues of some government.

There are new reasons—and reinforcements for old reasons—to worry about increasing reliance on tax revenues for the support of the performing arts. As appropriations rise, more and more legislators feel the need to grab a piece of this money for their constituents, regardless of the quality of local talent. A preference for Caruso over Elvis Presley, to speak only of the dead, is portrayed as a sure sign of vicious elitism. Moreover, several appointments—among them the chairmen of the New York State Council on the Arts in 1975 and the National Endowment for the Humanities in 1977—have raised once again the fears of politicization in grants programs that over time may shape artistic effort in America. But there is no choice—the numbers have got out of hand. Two centuries have passed since Sam Johnson defined opera as an expensive and irrational entertainment, and many more critics would now defend its rationality; the expense is worse than ever.

Ideally, opera and all the arts should live by revenues received for services rendered—which includes for these purposes donations by those who can afford to pay more for their pleasures. The established American system of government support—matching and more-than-matching federal grants, through deductions from taxable income—has served opera well in the past but is now overloaded. An ambitious broadcasting service that could spread some form of performance to a larger audience—and pay for the privilege of doing so—would be far preferable to a system of government appropriations; but it is not going to happen on anything like a large enough scale. Assuming the substance of the argument—that opera needs and will receive grants from tax revenues—a much harder look must now be given to the multiform questions of procedure that have been passed by in the rush to the gold mines.

George Gelles

4

The Ballet

Introduction

> The problem of the provinces is delicate. . . . Provincial ballet direc-
> tors are always being betrayed in their selfless efforts to bring national
> or local companies into being. . . . The smaller troupe at its best is
> usually in a state of hopeful evolution, interesting to those responsible,
> and to a very small, if passionate, portion of the local public. . . . To
> persist, the managers of provincial companies must always ignore the
> true state of their place's history, geography, and economy.

This precise if fastidious assessment was offered by Lincoln
Kirstein in his 1959 disquisition "What Ballet is About." Aimed at
the vast American public whose appreciation of classical dancing
could be characterized charitably as moot, Kirstein's appraisal
seemed apt at the time. While well aware of the efforts being made
by choreographers and dancers to establish their art around the
world—"provincial" activity in Kirstein's purview embraces "Argen-
tine, Australian, Danish, Dutch, Swedish, and South African ballet,"
as well as that found in the American outbacks—he was equally
alert to the manifold difficulties connected with any such venture.
Indeed, few patrons of the performing arts can ever have built upon
less hospitable ground than did Kirstein in 1934 when he began to
nurture the genius of George Balanchine on an alien terrain.

GEORGE GELLES, *a freelance writer, was formerly a critic and reporter on*
The Washington Star *and was Project Director for the Bicentennial grants*
program of the National Endowment for the Arts.

His view of 1959 remains valid. Kirstein's keen judgment, however, had to be modified shortly after its publication, at least as it applied to dance in America, for by the middle of the 1960s there was considerable cause for hope: professionalism clearly had increased, the audience had grown, and national and government foundations had begun to realize their responsibilities toward the most evanescent of the arts. Despite these gains, which have continued until today, ballet directors outside New York are still faced with formidable challenges. Indeed, the question well might be asked whether the challenges to the major companies based *in* New York are any less severe.

The profile of these issues can be traced in an account of the Pennsylvania Ballet and its director, Barbara Weisberger. Brought into existence in 1962–63 with the assistance of The Ford Foundation, the troupe has an enviable record of growth. It is administratively well-managed and artistically well-defined, but problems persist and many of them are the identical ailments to which Kirstein referred.

The Thirties and Forties

If the Pennsylvanians provide a balletic bellwether to the field of native dance for the last fifteen years, they necessarily tell us little about the discipline's history in the thirty years that fell between the dissolution of the Ballets Russes on the death of Serge Diaghilev in 1929 and the appearance of Kirstein's primer. Although the importance of the era is often ignored in the story of American dance, there was a wealth of activity on the country's stages.

Dominant throughout the 1930s were performances given by foreign ensembles, most notably by the heirs to the Diaghilev patrimony, the Ballet Russe de Monte Carlo and the Original Ballet Russe, commanded respectively by Leonide Massine and Colonel Wassily de Basil. But there were scores of performances, too, by companies whose thrust was more frankly American—the American Ballet, the Ballet Caravan, the Ruth Page-Bentley Stone Ballet, and the Philadelphia Ballet.

A somewhat more precise measure of this activity is provided by the issue of *Dance Magazine* for May 1939. An article entitled "The Ballet Unionizes" reports that during the season of 1938–39 the

major ballet companies in the country gave a total of 397 performances in which 142 American dancers participated for a total of
6,428 "man-performances." While slight by present standards, the
figures are worthy of notice, for they show us the field in its infancy.

If the 1930s was a time for expansion, the 1940s was a period to
trim and solidify. The American Ballet Theatre consolidated and
built on the Mordkin Ballet, and the New York City Ballet evolved
from and clarified the Ballet Society. Yet there also were ventures
whose interest lay in their idiosyncrasy and not in their lasting importance, such as the Dance Players—"an all-American company
offering dance plays on American themes"—and the Foxhole Ballet,
a response to the need for entertainment of a wartime population.

Beginnings of Change

The most significant aspect of the subsequent decade was not
its entrepreneurial initiative—only the ensemble founded in 1954
by Robert Joffrey would finally prove able to survive—but the ubi-
quitous rise of the "civic" ballet (which is also referred to as "community" ballet and "regional" ballet). The reasons for this development must be many, but three factors can be quickly perceived:
one is the incipient awareness of classical dance that resulted from
the nationwide touring of celebrated ensembles in the prior two
decades; another is the fact that the teenage population, a prime
source of students, was cresting in the late 1950s as a result of the
"baby boom" triggered by World War II; and still another is the
wider availability of competent teachers who could be found
throughout the country, many of them former dancers whose effective stage lives had ended.

THE CIVIC BALLET

Although the civic ballet can trace its history back to 1929 when
Dorothy Alexander founded a company in Atlanta, it did not co-
alesce as a movement until 1956. In that year the Southeastern
Regional Ballet Festival Association was established. Two years later
a Northeast arm was formed, and the rest of the country was sub-
sequently organized. Quantitative growth was uniformly impressive;
in the Southeastern regional alone, for example, there was a five-fold
increase in the number of companies between 1955 and 1970. In

fact, by the start of the 1970s there were more than 300 civic ballets to be found throughout the country.

If an interest in ballet was incontrovertible, the quality of these groups was open to question. Essentially they were annual or semi-annual recitals of the students of one or more dance teachers in the community. Despite three decades of dedicated civic activities, no ballet of artistic dimensions was able to take root in the heartland of America by the end of the 1950s. New York and San Francisco were consistently hospitable to professional ventures, but excellence elsewhere was rare.

The critical issue that faced the ballet community at the start of the 1960s clearly can be imagined: how could companies of merit be supported in cities that had experienced and enjoyed the classical dance but had been unable to build a tradition of their own? Put in another fashion: how might you alter the conventional equation so that a provincial center might become endowed with an artistic magnetism as potent as that of a metropolis?

THE FORD FOUNDATION

In 1957 these questions were addressed by The Ford Foundation which undertook a five-year study that investigated the state of the country's performing organizations and training institutions. Its findings were translated into immediate action. Starting in 1959 gifted students throughout the country began to receive scholarships for advanced schooling in New York and San Francisco, and in December 1963, the Foundation announced awards totaling $7,756,750 to assist the classical dance in America.

This massive program of grants, which at that point represented the largest sum ever allotted by a foundation to a single art form, methodically set about to stabilize the field by supporting a series of resident professional companies and schools throughout the country, ensembles that would transcend the community ballets. In addition, the program underwrote for a decade an integrated system of local scholarships in selected studios around the country.

The Foundation focused first on two companies that already had attained professional status. The New York City Ballet received $200,000 a year for ten years and the San Francisco Ballet, which in 1957 had outgrown its symbiotic relationship with the local opera company, a relationship that stretched back to 1933, received

$644,000 over a ten-year period. (Money was also appropriated to give an independent status to the Joffrey Ballet, which received an initial grant of $155,000 in 1964.)

Attention then was turned to three companies whose achievements were more modest. The Utah Ballet (now Ballet West), established by Willam Christensen in 1952 as a civic ensemble, received $175,000 to support performances and provide scholarships for promising local dancers; the Houston Ballet, organized in 1955, received $173,750 to bolster its training activities and lay the groundwork for development of an independent company; and the National Ballet in Washington, founded at the start of 1963, received $400,000 to strengthen its school and lengthen its season.

Two companies, additionally, were in effect brought to life by The Ford Foundation grants. The Boston Ballet, directed by Virginia Williams, received $144,000 to ease the transition to professional status, and the Pennsylvania Ballet, which had without Ford Foundation assistance given its premiere performance in 1963, was awarded $295,000 to aid in establishing itself as a company.

THE GRANT TO THE PENNSYLVANIA BALLET

As one well might imagine, The Ford Foundation's largesse inspired reactions ranging widely from profound gratitude to pique. One of the six grants, however, aroused a special attention—the one to the Pennsylvania Ballet. The *New York Times*, for instance, called it "the most curious of all" the awards and noted that it would be

> making possible the establishment of a company where none has existed and where the need or great desire for one has not manifested itself . . . it does seem strange that the hoped-for success of [this] project should take precedence over the demonstrated accomplishments of people who have worked for years elsewhere.

DANCE IN PHILADELPHIA

Yet reasons for the grant were ample. Among American cities Philadelphia had shown an interest in the dance that was second to none. In 1734 it was the site of the discipline's colonial debut, an exhibition of that part of "the theater of marvels" known as rope dancing, and by the late eighteenth century it was the young republic's center of theatrical and social dancing, a distinction it could continue to claim throughout most of the nineteenth century, as English, French, and Italian artists settled into the city's cultural life, entertaining and instructing its populace.

More germane, perhaps, to the establishment of Weisberger's Pennsylvania Ballet was the founding in 1935 by Catherine Littlefield of the Philadelphia Ballet (which was originally called the Littlefield Ballet). This was the first company to be organized, directed, and staffed by Americans, no mean achievement in a field so heavily indebted to foreign artists. When wartime service claimed most of its men in 1942, the troupe was forced to disband.

A Company and Its Director

The establishment of the Pennsylvania Ballet had, of course, a marginal relationship to these earlier ventures. Its impetus was derived not from an undue respect for history but rather from the ambitions and energies of Barbara Weisberger, whom The *New York Times*, while wary of the support she had won, conceded was "a brilliant, gifted, and sincere woman."

Before starting her company at the age of thirty-six, Weisberger had built a reputation and a fund of good will as a ballet teacher in Wilkes-Barre, Pennsylvania. Yet her history intersects with Philadelphia's past. While a teenager living with her family in Wilmington, Delaware, she commuted afternoons to study with the Littlefields, Catherine and her sister Dorothie. Earlier, when the family still lived in Brooklyn, her birthplace, she had been accepted at the age of eight for training at the School of American Ballet, and this tangible link with George Balanchine would figure prominently when she chose to form a troupe of her own.

THE TIMING NATIONALLY

In making the decision to start an ensemble, Weisberger was influenced by a fortuitous confluence of circumstances:

> It was timing and for some reason it became a certain madness. It is relevant, however, that the Pennsylvania Ballet began when it did. It happened at just that significant period when there was a large amount of money available for the development of existing professional companies of merit and for burgeoning professional companies. It was a big amount and it allowed us growth which we needed; the company couldn't just come into being at a certain level of strength, either artistically or economically.

THE TIMING FOR WEISBERGER

Just why I started the company I can answer only from retrospect. These reasons may not have been so specifically in my mind but they have become apparent to me as the years have gone by. I had a little regional company when I had been teaching in Wilkes-Barre and had done some choreography; I had the desire to do it, obviously, since I built a company to give myself the outlet for it. I adored teaching but I was also aware of the fact that as the years went on there was no place for my dancers to go. There were so few companies, all with so many people coming into them. If there were alternatives in their lives I could not in all good conscience pressure them to take the chance on becoming a dancer because the professional world was so limited. They could go to the New York City Ballet or to Ballet Theatre, and in the East that was about it in the 1950s. And there were some beauties that were lost, real beauties, and that bothered me.

THE SAFEGUARD OF CONTINUITY

So we started. We had $3,300, some from a few kind angels and most of which I borrowed. We rented a studio that cost $500 a month and we were always being locked out. But the point is that we did something which was absolutely necessary that we never could have done had it not been for The Ford Foundation: we held a company together for a long period of time even when it was not performing. Our point of view was, keep them together; do something, but keep them together. We certainly did not justify this course by the income we were getting. We would have 29 percent earned income, maybe 33 percent in better years, though always meeting the challenge of the matching money. And without that it never could have happened.

WILL IT COME AGAIN?

I have great stubbornness and drive and the capability of communicating enthusiasm and going out and getting help, but with all that, it still could not have happened without The Ford Foundation grants. And it could not happen today. That's why I worry so about others. It is a very tough business and it is very sad. When people ask me for advice in starting up a company I want to tell them, don't. But of course some people you are not going to stop.

PHILADELPHIA AS HOST

Probably the best thing, the luckiest thing, was that I was not a Philadelphian, because I didn't know what to be cautious about and what to be afraid of. I went in head-first; I didn't really understand the personality of Philadelphia, its intimidating aspects. In the past twenty-five or thirty years there had not been a major cultural institution that had been able to begin and persist.

It was impossible at first for us, too. It was close to Wilkes-Barre, where I still live, so I could practically commute. And it had a dance heritage and there was a sentimental attachment on my part, since I had studied with the Littlefields. The strangest thing about Philadelphia is its mixture of feelings about being so close to New York. And there is a sort of lethargy, a lack of motivation that comes about because of an unwillingness to acknowledge a competitive spirit with New York.

I also think it is quite remarkable that although in most large cities you can quickly identify the movers and shakers in the arts, in Philadelphia this is not so. So it was very hard for us to open up the door. We had no sizeable audience at first. But in fact there was not an audience when the Littlefields were here, either. Nobody even thought about the heritage.

THE PLACE OF REPERTOIRE

Artistically we have always had a very strong point of view, and we get criticized for it. We're told, you don't listen to us in the audience; we want full-length classical ballets and you are doing all these contemporary things. We have a point of view and we have integrity about that point of view. Yet we cannot be so foolish as to turn our back on what is sellable. We are eclectic in our repertoire, as all ballet companies have to be with the exception of the New York City Ballet. Their repertoire is built around Balanchine, but we have to do a little bit of everything. Not all of the pieces have to be important choreography, but if they are well-danced then we are still a good company. I look very realistically at what is happening creatively in dance and my hope is that one day I will find a man or a woman who has some choreographic inspiration. Then I will be happy to build the company around that individual. But until that happens, it is continued happy hunting elsewhere.

THE SUPREMACY OF THE ENSEMBLE

You don't try to fool the public. Say what you are, move ahead as what you are, and don't fool yourselves or them. Don't think you are going to bring in guest artists to snare the public and then do all the things you really want to do. It doesn't happen that way. Your audience feels cheated after that or they get mentally set to expect guests all the time. And what have you done? You've defeated your most important purpose, which is to perpetuate, to continue. You've also hurt the morale of the dancers, who, except in very specific instances, don't want to work all year and then have the goodies given away.

Anyway, it is a myth that you sell a million tickets because you have a guest artist. First of all, it is stupid to bring in somebody whose talent is way up here while the rest of your company is way down there. Get your dancers built up to the level where they are so good that they are going to be asked to be guest artists. Secondly, who sells all those tickets? Two people: Nureyev and Baryshnikov. Maybe Makarova. So what's the point?

FUNDING IN THE ARTS

I think we are good. But to get funding we have been begging, demeaning ourselves, and often presenting ourselves as everything but what we are. We are not a community service organization. Primarily we exist to perform and to be the conduit for creative and performing artists. Of course an important offshoot of that purpose is to serve the community with community programs and educational programs, because we don't exist for our own self-glorification. But we almost always have been accommodating our talents to fit the needs of our funding sources rather than vice versa. They are not coming to us, or very rarely, and saying "What do you need?" We are going to them and saying "How can we serve you?" Many of us have become very strong at grantsmanship, but what have we done? Often we have created programs which we never would have wanted to do, simply to fit a set of guidelines. That happens all the time, except for a few notable exceptions such as The Ford Foundation and several other private foundations. Admittedly, the public funding sources face many political and populist pressures. Now some programs of the National Endowment and of state arts councils are concerning themselves with quality and responding to the needs of the field, a hopeful sign which needs fostering.

I feel that the only way this whole problem of funding in the arts will ever improve is when there is a forthright, honest statement of public policy which will finally affect long-term attitudes and understanding.

THE PENALTIES OF GROWTH

Starting around 1969 we reached a plateau and there was an identity crisis that involved me and my role with the company, and most importantly, the role of the company itself. Any director of a company whose choreography is not the nucleus of the repertoire will at some point go through this hell of trying to find the reasons for the company's existence. We were close to a one-woman operation but growing like Topsy; there was my own difficulty in coping with the Jewish-mother syndrome; there were love-hate relationships all around. All these circumstances were necessary when we started, but as we developed they began to create all sorts of problems.

Things were slipping artistically. There was no consistency in the teaching and no focus to the ensemble. I did not feel I was giving support to the dancers or choreographers or teachers because I was constantly being drawn away to do administrative chores that needed tending to. The company was weakening in the quality of the dancing, in the level of the dancers, in the interest of the choreography.

I knew that something had to be done. Someone had to help us. It was not an easy situation for me because if I chose somebody I really wanted, it would have to be a strong person and that would only mean that I would be doing still less. I could not expect that someone would join us who did not have ideas of his own and the desire to proceed with them.

THE HARKARVY PERIOD

So along came Ben Harkarvy, whom I invited to join the company in 1972. It was an undefined relationship at first. We would sort of see how we lived together. He was an associate artistic director along with Robert Rodham, and he was very capable, so I was able—it was almost a relief to me—to entrust much artistic responsibility to him.

A prolific choreographer and respected teacher, Harkarvy had been artistic director of the Royal Winnipeg Ballet, the National Ballet of Holland, and the Harkness Ballet, as well as founder of the Netherlands Dance Theatre, before joining the Pennsylvanians at the age of forty-three.

Right away the look on the stage became more polished than it ever had been, but possibly less gutsy. Perhaps I'm not seeing things very clearly; perhaps what I'm now calling gutsy was really a lack of polish, though actually one would not have expected enormous polish from a young company; there are other attributes that you want to capitalize on. I think I would have taken the company in a slightly different direction had I been in complete control, or stressed a different emphasis. That's inevitable, because if you work with the dancers every day, part of you comes through. I don't even mean your judgments; I mean your personality. Not that Ben is rigid; its just that he's another personality and that shows itself. There used to be a great deal of verve and life, and of course there still is; I'm sure it hasn't gone. But it now comes through in the discipline. It's not that the individual dancers were undisciplined before he arrived; they worked very hard. But discipline was not the overriding effect. Nevertheless, there was a lovely spirit.

However, after Harkarvy's first year we attained even greater public success and critical approval. But by its second year an identification crisis arose. He could not deal with being associate artistic director on the same level with Bobby Rodham. Nor could he deal with the still rather unclarified relationship to me. After much painful soul-searching, I assumed the title of executive artistic director and named Harkarvy artistic director.

ROBERT RODHAM

Welcome though Harkarvy's arrival must have been in 1972, it was the cause of considerable disruption in other areas. For Weisberger, it would mean relinquishing much of the artistic control with which she had molded her company since its inception. For Robert Rodham, the new appointment would prove even more decisive.

A student of Weisberger's in Wilkes-Barre, Rodham had gone on to the School of American Ballet, danced with the New York City Ballet, and then followed his former teacher to Philadelphia. He was by Weisberger's side almost from the start of the company, as dancer, choreographer, and ballet master. It is he, in fact, whom she credits for the exemplary style that the company brings to its performances of works by George Balanchine, performances that to many are the company's glory. By 1969 he had risen to the rank of principal ballet master under Weisberger's artistic direction. In the season of 1973–74 he was one of two associate artistic directors, the other being Harkarvy. The next season he was named *régisseur*, with Harkarvy artistic director and Weisberger executive artistic director. His title then reverted to ballet master, and with two of his junior colleagues he shared that role from the fall of 1975 through the spring of 1976. In the 1976–77 season he was on the faculty of the School of the Pennsylvania Ballet. In the summer of 1977 he left the company altogether.

ASSUMPTION OF CONTROL

According to Barbara Weisberger:

> Perhaps the most traumatic dilemma about being a director of a company is to accept with grace the amount of time that we spend administering and managing, away from doing what we really want to do. It is not at all satisfactory, but I don't know what my options are. I made the decision to do it, and the further away I was taken from the studio, from teaching and coaching and choreographing, the less confidence I had about myself in those particular roles. But I saw that there were things in these administrative areas that other people would not, could not do as well. At some point I accepted that that was my role, perhaps by default. Even now I'm the bane of my staff because there I am with my nose in everything. I'm sure I relay a great many mixed messages.

Weisberger's role was more undefined, even to herself, from 1972 to the 1976 season. With presidents and general managers assuming administrative functions and responsibilities on the one hand and Harkarvy taking the artistic prerogatives on the other, Weisberger seemed to fall in some nebulous area in between. After weighing her alternative courses of action through a good part of the 1976–77 season, Weisberger assumed the position of director with operating control of the company under revised organizational structure; and with the managing director, Timothy Duncan, one one side and the artistic director, Harkarvy, on the other, she was now responsible directly to the president and the board of trustees. As the 1977–78 year began, this definition of roles also indicated Weisberger's intention of balancing her time to allow for greater involvement in the artistic area. "I'm not going to change titles because it is so confusing to the public, and who cares? But I am going to start going to more rehearsals and having more frequent communication with the dancers."

FINANCIAL GROWTH AND NEEDS

If one sets aside this interplay of personalities almost *sui generis* in the development of a performing company, the progress of the Pennsylvania Ballet is seen to have been sure when measured by conventional parameters. In the six seasons following that of 1965–66, for example, the annual budget of the company quintupled to approximately $1,500,000, mainly because of the influx of Ford Foundation funds, which to date has totalled $4,870,000, in comparison to $4,600,000 granted the Joffrey and $4,200,000 to the New York City Ballet. For the season of 1976–77, the total operating expenditures stood at approximately $2,375,000, lower than the budget of the San Francisco Ballet ($2,500,000) and the Joffrey ($3,448,000), but significantly higher than the others: Ballet West ($1,180,000), the Boston Ballet ($1,380,000), and the Houston Ballet ($1,375,000).

IN PERSPECTIVE WITH OTHERS

A further comparison can be made by examining a single season, that of 1970–71, which was analyzed in a Ford Foundation report published in 1974, *The Finances of the Performing Arts*. In it, nine ballet companies throughout the country reported government and national foundation grants that equalled an average of 54 percent of their annual budgets; the Pennsylvania Ballet that season raised 52.2 percent of its budget from these sources. Where the company average for state and local contributions to annual budgets totalled 9 percent and 4 percent respectively, the Pennsylvania Ballet, under Weisberger's energetic management, raised 17 percent of its budget from state and 11 percent from local sources. Earned income, however, was disappointing; while the nine companies raised an average of 53 percent of their total operating expenditures by earned income, the Pennsylvanians raised only 36 percent. A significant increase would not occur until the season of 1975–76, when earned income equalled 49 percent of total operating expenditures.

The length of the company's season compared favorably, as well, with the average reported by the other ballets. Compared to a mean season of thirty-eight weeks, the Pennsylvanians worked forty-five. Since the season of 1970–71 the duration of the company's average season has stabilized at forty weeks, a period that includes both rehearsal time and the all-important tours.

THE AUDIENCE

As do virtually all other companies throughout the country, the Pennsylvania cultivates a multiple constituency. There is of course the local Philadelphia audience, which in the season of 1976–77 was catered to with four series that comprised forty performances; in addition, there were sixteen performances of "The Nutcracker." The aggregate audience for these fifty-six performances was approximately 93,500. Weisberger estimates that 4 percent of the population of the city, the fourth largest in America, is annually exposed to at least one of the company's performances, and this figure is consistent with the finding supplied in an additional survey that complemented The Ford Foundation report.

A second constituency is formed by an audience that resides throughout Pennsylvania. Since it began touring the state extensively in 1965, the troupe has been to approximately seventy smaller towns; its visits have become a strand in the fabric of these cities' cultural lives, which strengthens the case for continued state support. Another constituency is found in towns throughout the nation and reached with a series of residencies. In a five-week period in the spring of 1977, for example, the ballet played Wichita, Kansas;

Lincoln, Nebraska; Tulsa, Oklahoma; Kansas City and St. Louis, Missouri; Carbondale, Illinois; Seattle, Washington; Portland, Oregon; and Cincinnati, Columbus, Cleveland, and Akron, Ohio. Although such tours are often taxing, they are a valuable stimulant to the national interest in dance. Much in the manner of the "Russian" ballets in the 1930s and the American Ballet Theatre in the ensuing two decades, the Pennsylvania, as well as its sister ensembles, is enabling a broad swath of the population to experience live performances of unquestioned quality.

NEW YORK

Most crucial, perhaps, are those tours made by the company to its fourth constituency in New York City. Since 1974 the Pennsylvania Ballet has been the "resident ballet company" at the Brooklyn Academy of Music, though the residency usually lasts but a fortnight each season. New York, however, has been considered vital to the company's fortunes since 1968 when the troupe first performed in the City Center of Music and Drama on West Fifty-fifth Street.

Few debuts can have been more auspicious. Gracing the program was a statement signed by George Balanchine and Lincoln Kirstein:

> It is a pleasure to welcome the Pennsylvania Ballet. . . . We have watched the growth of this young ballet organization since its start. Barbara Weisberger has used courage and intelligence in building an ensemble and repertory. New York welcomes her company and her dancers.

And the accolades after the opening night were resounding. Although the compliments offered by The *New York Times* were somewhat coy and oblique—a performance was "still raw, yet not unexciting" and gave a "coltish pleasure, with its glint of anxious eagerness in every eye"—the paper's critic clearly attempted to boost the company into the public's awareness. Mistakes admittedly were made. The repertory of eleven works was overly ambitious for a one-week stand, and musicians and stage hands were found to be uncommonly expensive. But the ballet proved its point: after its successful New York showing even Philadelphians would have to admit that the company was an estimable and serious endeavor.

THE ECLECTIC REPERTOIRE

Yet with most other companies whose repertoires are not predominantly reflective of the gifts of a single individual, the Pennsylvania has an arduous search for works that are substantial and varied. To many eyes the roster of dances has been decidedly uneven. In a brief essay published in 1976, Harkarvy drew a three-fold distinction among the thirty-two works that the company then presented. First, he wrote, there were pieces "in the classical idiom of the nineteenth and twentieth centuries." Second, there were "ballets created elsewhere by contemporary choreographers [that] enrich our repertory as the classics of our time." And third, there were works created for the company specifically.

Seven ballets by Balanchine formed the cores of the initial category in the active repertoire of the company—"Allegro Brillante," "Concerto Barocco," "The Four Temperaments," "Raymonda Variations," "Scotch Symphony," "Serenade," and "Symphony in C"—and in the 1977–78 season the "Divertimento No. 15" was added to the list. There is little question about the eminence of these works —any company would be proud to be entrusted with their care— and little question, as well, that the Pennsylvanians dance them with distinction. Also in this category was a version of Fokine's "Les Sylphides."

More troublesome to cognoscenti were Harkarvy's second and third groups. The second included "After Eden" and "Carmina Burana" by John Butler; "Concerto Grosso" by Charles Czarny; "The Moor's Pavane" by Jose Limon; "Jardin aux Lilas" by Antony Tudor; five ballets by the Dutch choreographer Hans van Manen, with whom Harkarvy worked closely in Holland—"Adagio Hammerklavier," "Grosse Fugue," "Opera Lemaître," "Septet Extra," and "Solo for Voice I"—and three ballets by Harkarvy himself— "Grand Pas Espagnol," "Madrigalesco," and "Recital for Cello and Eight Dancers."

The third group of works made for the Pennsylvanians expressly included pieces by Robert Rodham ("An American Rhapsody" and "In Retrospect"), Rodney Griffin ("Eakin's View"), Margo Sappington ("Under the Sun"), and of course Benjamin Harkarvy ("Continuum," "Time Past Summer," and "From Gentle Circles").

In a class by itself must be "The Nutcracker."

Dance historians and aficionados would probably agree that only the works by Limon and Tudor are of more than passing interest among the twenty-three pieces in Harkarvy's categories two and three. Some of the others are wonderfully serviceable and show the dancers in a flattering light; this is surely true of Harkarvy's earlier works, which are superbly crafted and ingratiating entertainments. Conspicuously missing were large-scale full-length story ballets, the traditional bedrock of repertoires. Among companies of its class the Pennsylvania is alone in avoiding these works. Other troupes embrace them; Ballet West, for example, mounted an opulent eveing-long "Don Quixote" in the season of 1975–76, and in that same season the San Francisco Ballet performed "Romeo and Juliet," while both the Ballets of Houston and Boston presented "Cinderella." Overly ambitious though these productions might have been, it still can be argued that their demands forced the companies to expand their dimensions, and some of this growth was most surely beneficial.

THE FOCUS ON THE ENSEMBLE

The situation in which the Pennsylvanians found themselves at the close of the season of 1976–77 can be seen to have resulted in part from Weisberger's commendable philosophy, akin to that of her mentor, George Balanchine, which stresses the primacy of the corps de ballet before the importance of any single dancer. Despite the presence of fine artists in its ranks, it is the ensemble itself that Weisberger hopes will be acknowledged as the "prima ballerina assoluta." Given this predilection and the size of the troupe—it normally numbers thirty members and never has exceeded thirty-six—the repertoire through the years has emphasized what might be called chamber ballets.

CONTRASTING EXAMPLES

Two contrary approaches were illustrated during the period of the Pennsylvania Ballet's development. One was taken by the National Ballet, which was founded contemporaneously with the Pennsylvania and dissolved in 1973. Similar to the Pennsylvania in size, the National, under the artistic direction of Frederic Franklin and Ben Stevenson, tried to build a repertoire that mixed recensions of full-length classics such as "Giselle," freshly choreographed versions of large-scale works such as "Cinderella," and selected works by Franklin and Stevenson that were especially tailored for a handful of dancers. It was an attractive mix that seemed to work in winning both critical and popular acclaim. That the company was forced to disband at its moment of optimum strength was not solely of its own fault but also the result of the opening of the Kennedy Center for the Performing Arts, an organization which favored other companies over the local species.

Another approach was that of the American Ballet Theatre, the most venerable of American ensembles devoted to the classical dance. For more than thirty-five years the company has built its repute on the fame of transient stars who lend a season luster as they shoot through the balletic firmament. The corps de ballet inevitably has suffered in morale and expertise, while the company itself has no audience it truly can call its own. Its following is predictably fickle, responding to names with a glamorous cachet, ignoring the less well-known. In reorganizing responsibilities in 1977, Weisberger hoped to steer her dancers on a course that avoided both commercialism and the near anonymity of individual members of the company. The image of her dancers would be heightened in the public eye. As she freely admitted, "It might be possible in our public relations to be more human in our presentation of the dancers, to make them more identifiable to the public."

COMMUNITY PREFERENCES

Audience surveys in Philadelphia in the spring of 1977 showed that something more is wanted in the way of theatricality. Weisberger's public longs to taste the opulence of the "classical" ballet, even as represented by the Pennsylvanians' production of "The Sleeping Beauty," a show that was dropped from the repertoire in 1967. It was this same piece, as set by Ben Stevenson on the National Ballet, that won the Washington company critical applause and an additional measure of public support, deficient though it might have been in particulars of style and in scope.

There are reasons, of course, that prevent a more flamboyant approach. Visual excitement costs money to create, and while the Pennsylvania Ballet has been generally well managed through the years, it never has enjoyed the sort of lavish patronage earmarked for luxury productions. Community support has been generous.

Local private sources contributed $850,000 in the 1977 fiscal year. There have, however, been not more than one or two patrons in the company's brief existence to begin to compare to Edward Bok or Mary Louise Bok, great names in the history of the Philadelphia Orchestra and the Curtis Institute. Fundamentally, however, the company has purposefully avoided story ballets and the ornate decors with which they are dressed, a policy that directly reflects Weisberger's determination to build an ensemble of broad and even strengths. Given such a goal, story ballets have been anathema, built as they are on dramatic stratifications and scenic effects.

AN ESTABLISHED NATIONAL COMPANY

The Pennsylvania Ballet can be justly proud of its past. It has earned an honored place in the history of American dance through its tenacity and resourcefulness. With ballet companies everywhere. it shares certain problems that must be resolved in a manner that facilitates its favorable growth. It is not merely a matter of economic expansion, but of growth that allows the dancers to deepen in personal character, the repertoire to widen in choreographic excellence, the administration to strengthen in financial integrity.

Above all is the imperative need to survive, as Weisberger has always realized. Her persistence in the face of adversity calls to mind the words that Arnold Schoenberg sent to the National Institute of Arts and Letters when he was elected to that body in 1947. Recalling the struggle for acceptance among his fellow composers and the concert-going public, he tried in his imperfect English to describe his fight for artistic existence:

> Personally I had the feeling as if I had fallen into an ocean of boiling water, and not knowing how to swim or to get out in another manner, I tried with my arms and legs as best as I could. I did not know what saved me; why I was not drowned or cooked alive . . . I have perhaps only one merit: I never gave up. . . .

Joseph H. Mazo

5

Modern Dance

If there were a muse of modern dance her name would have to be Polymorphos, and she would be the most frenetic of goddesses. Imagine the bemused deity (in traditional guise, dressed in black leotards and tights, her feet bare, straight hair coerced into a strict bun) forced to preside simultaneously over the full theatrical apparatus of Martha Graham's heroic quests, the virtuosity of Merce Cunningham's Einsteinian investigations, the arduous rituals of Kei Takei, the grotesqueries of Pilobolus, the minimalism of Lucinda Childs, and the luminous environments of Alwin Nikolais.

The Idiosyncratic Art

Modern dance is the most idiosyncratic of the performing arts. It is the product of no school; it is not merely the most recent generation of a long genealogy of art. American modern dance was created by rebels who devised new choreographic languages to give kinetic form to their opinions. It is the art form of individualists. It is said that if you ask five socialists, you get six opinions; if you ask five modern dancers, you get eight.

JOSEPH H. MAZO *is dance critic of* Women's Wear Daily *and the author of* Dance Is a Contact Sport *and* Prime Movers: The Makers of Modern Dance in America. *He has studied theater at New York University and the University of Washington and has professional experience in that field.*

CONSTANT REAPPRAISAL

Aficionados of ballet have maintained from time to time that without the long tradition and academic code of movement of their preferred form, modern dance is at a disadvantage, that it does not have a sufficiently secure foundation on which to erect its structures. The codified techniques of Martha Graham, Merce Cunningham, and others have, of course, provided modern dance with such a foundation. However, what may well be more important is that recent generations of choreographers have disdained to build on it. Instead, they have started digging all over again, seeking new ways to express contemporary ideas. This insistence on beginning afresh every fifteen or twenty years is perhaps one of the greatest virtues of modern dance. Constant reappraisal, the eternal distrust of the eternal, creates an art that reflects the chief concerns of each succeeding generation.

Guarding Against Decay—The architects of American Modern dance—Loie Fuller, Isadora Duncan, Ruth St. Denis, and Ted Shawn—and their successors—Doris Humphrey, Charles Weidman, and Martha Graham—despised ballet because the ballet they encountered was sadly shopworn. It was a triumph of debased form over abandoned content, rather like a sixth-grade performance of *Hamlet* in which the actors remember their lines rather well but are unable to comprehend Shakespeare's words or the ideas and emotions they carry.

Contemporary modern dance choreographers offer their predecessors great respect, but are always on guard against the threat of being trapped in an outmoded form or an antiquated conceit. At times this iconoclasm results (in the immortal words of Lyndon B. Johnson) in "throwing the baby out with the dirty dishes." Fortunately, there is sufficient respect for the past to permit the rescue of important theories and works. Techniques of notation and video recording are helping dance change its position as the most ephemeral of arts. The late 1970s brought to dance great interest in recreating the works of the past: The Joyce Trisler Danscompany with "The Spirit of Denishawn," which returned to the stage works by Ruth St. Denis and Ted Shawn; Anabelle Gamson with her recreations of the dances of Isadora Duncan; the restaging by several companies of important pieces made by Doris Humphrey. An interest in reconstructing past masterpieces often characterizes a period of artistic transition; logically enough, the re-creators of great dances are not those who have achieved the first rank in original work. Gamson's own pieces are of less interest than her studies of Duncan; Trisler's vision of Denishawn was her greatest critical success.

The Abstracts of the Time—More important than reverence for the past is a reflection of the present. Modern dance, which demands no equipment beyond space and bodies and which often reveres no technique other than the one under development, often is able to respond to contemporary thought more quickly than other arts. Modern dancers ride the intellectual and emotional currents of their time like gulls on updraughts. That is one reason that many of the greatest modern dance choreographers have worked for years before achieving wide recognition among the public. They often appear to scent a change in the societal winds long before the rest of us.

A Time of Growth

The period that began in July 1962 with the first dance concert at Judson Memorial Church in New York and continued for nearly a decade brought a virtual explosion of creativity to modern dance. The following decade brought an equivalent increase in popularity, a spurt of growth unparalleled in the history of the art. In 1977 David White, director of Dance Theatre Workshop (DTW) said, "The 1970s can be characterized as an era of prolific growth in modern dance, in terms of both companies and audiences."

SIGNS OF OVERABUNDANCE

Even so, in 1977 the rate of growth of the dance audience, especially in New York City, was clearly slowing. The Martha Graham Company's Broadway season that year did not draw nearly so well as it had during previous engagements, and other companies also found more empty seats than they had come to expect.

One reason for the beginning of a decline in attendance was the abundance of performances offered to New York dance fans. Four major companies appeared in the city at the same time during the spring of 1977, and many other important performances were being held in small theaters and lofts. Ballet pulled people away from modern dance; modern dance lured some of the audience from ballet; and companies of all persuasions attracted customers away from one another. The audience for dance, large though it is, is finite, and it is being divided among many more companies than in the past. There were approximately 200 modern dance companies in the United States early in 1977, according to figures compiled by the Association of American Dance Companies. Slightly more than half made their headquarters in New York.

A NEW WAY TO GROW

That nearly 50 percent of the nation's modern dance troupes in 1977 made their homes outside New York is indicative of the intense changes in the art since the early 1960s. Sybil Shearer was a pioneer when she left New York and took her talents to Chicago in the 1940s, and Lester Horton founded a company and a style in Los Angeles in 1932. Bella Lewitzky, an alumna of the Horton company, has done important work in Southern California since the mid-1960s, and Anna Halprin established herself in San Francisco even earlier.

The migration of choreographers beyond New York and the establishment of resident companies in other cities began early in the 1960s and continued during the next fifteen years. Young choreographers left their places as dancers with companies based in New York to found ensembles elsewhere. By the late 1970s there were about ten modern dance companies in Boston, and the Metropolitan Cultural Alliance (encompassing several arts) was functioning there. The Bay Area Dance Coalition was in operation in California. These groups seek to build audiences and to provide services for their artist members, using techniques similar to those employed by DTW in New York. DTW provides its artist members (204 of them) with such services as a computerized mail operation, the use of a bulk mailing permit, a list of booking sponsors, and its expertise as an advertising agency. It also serves as a producing organization.

Cooperative Ventures—Explains David White:

> Conventional arts management is unfeasible for many of the smaller companies, in New York and elsewhere. They can't afford it. Companies will have to rely more and more on cooperative activities in business. And companies in other cities still need to draw on the ex-

perience and expertise we have in New York in management and building audiences.

REPERTORY COMPANIES

Historically, modern dance companies have been created to perform the works of a single choreographer, and this method of organization continues to dominate the art. But many companies, particularly outside New York, now constitute themselves as repertory troupes performing the works of several dance-makers. Some of these pieces are created on the performing company; some are taken from the repertoires of other groups; some are revivals of classic pieces of modern dance. Concert Dance Company of Boston, for example, performs Doris Humphrey's "Day on Earth." One of the war cries of the 1960s was "Participatory Democracy," and dance companies, affected by the political climate, chose to glorify themselves as groups rather than as followers of a dominant artist. (Perhaps they recalled Bertolt Brecht's poetic dialogue: "Young Alexander conquered India. All alone?") Instead of such names as The Jose Limon Dance Company, one began to read such composite billings as Meredith Monk/The House and Jennifer Muller and The Works. Even less individualistic nomenclature has been used: The Grand Union, Pilobolus, Repertory Dance Theatre. The latter group, of Salt Lake City, proudly notes in its program that its affairs are conducted by committee, not by a single artistic director. Unfortunately, the trademark of committee management—the lack of a dominant, individual character—is imprinted on the troupe's performances.

Flattening of Style—When the Repertory Dance Theatre appeared in New York, critics noted unhappily that dances by different choreographers were performed without variations of style. It is becoming clear that a repertory group cannot perform the work of a choreographer with the same nuances and shades of movement as a company trained by that choreographer to do his work. The entire repertoire may take on the bland sameness of meals eaten in fast-food restaurants. However, the repertory system does bring choreographers and their work to communities outside New York; it does help to build an audience for dance; and it does provide the possibility of reviving classic works that might otherwise be lost.

Visiting Choreographers—One of the grants offered by the National Endowment for the Arts (NEA) is given to allow dance companies to enjoy the services of visiting choreographers. The NEA's program for 1977 called for such grants to bring Douglas Dunn, an important avant-garde artist, to the Repertory Dance Theatre; to allow Merce Cunningham to make a work for the 5 x 2 Dance Company; and to permit other companies to work with experienced choreographers such as Viola Farber, Kathryn Posin, and Don Redlich. The grant gives the choreographer $5,000 and expenses.

The work of visiting resident choreographers can greatly enrich a company. New England Dinosaur, Boston, performs works by its artistic director, Toby Armour, and by a former artistic director, the late James Waring, as well as works by Carolyn Brown and Trisha Brown. Waring's residence with the company not only permitted the preservation of his whimsical and beautiful dances after his death, but allowed audiences to see those works as the choreographer wanted them performed.

A Hope of Permanence—There is hope that visiting choreographers may eventually develop permanent alliances with companies outside New York. This could contribute greatly to the development of troupes throughout the United States, many of which have not yet attained the artistic standards prevalent in New York. Viola Farber, a highly important choreographer and teacher, was forced to disband her company in 1977 for lack of funds. New York, overpopulated with modern dance companies, may not be able to support Farber, but she undoubtedly could build a company in another city into a major artistic force by teaching its dancers her techniques and making works for them. This could also lead to the development of new choreographic talent and the establishment of a style.

The Tyrone Guthrie Theater in Minneapolis, American Conservatory Theatre in San Francisco, and several other dramatic companies exemplify the superior artistry that can be established in communities throughout the country with the aid of directors of genius. The growth of such companies began not too long before modern dance began to move beyond New York, and there are enough gifted choreographers to allow the development of parallel troupes in modern dance.

Alliance with Ballet

At a press conference in 1975, Martha Graham referred to her works as "ballets," a term she certainly would not have employed forty years earlier. Twyla Tharp has said, "Ballet technique is the technique most worth investing your time in. It is the most thorough, the most versatile, the most logical, rigorous, and elegant. . . ." Modern dancers have developed great respect for the older art, and both have benefited from the alliance. Choreographers such as John Butler and Glen Tetley, trained in both disciplines, have contributed to a process of cross-fertilization.

Recently, ballet companies have been commissioning works from modern dance choreographers and transferring dances from the companies of modern artists into their own. Lar Lubovitch, who leads his own modern company, has mounted dances on several ballet troupes including American Ballet Theatre (ABT) and the Pennsylvania Ballet. Kathryn Posin's "Waves," made on her own company in 1975, was taken into the repertory of the Eliot Feld Ballet two years later. Twyla Tharp has staged three dances for the Joffrey Ballet and one, "Push Comes to Shove," on ABT. (Paradoxically, her rise to popular fame grew largely from the publicity surrounding "Push.")

Posin's "Waves" is rather bland, and some of Lubovitch's balletic efforts, such as "Scherzo for Massa Jack," rank as unmitigated disasters. But this cannot be attributed to the medium of a ballet company by those who know the choreographer's work for his own troupe. Lubovitch and Posin are members of the middle class of modern dance: each has a following and has received some respectable reviews, but neither can be ranked as a major artist. Those choreographers whose dances have sat well on ballet companies— Tharp, Taylor, Cunningham—are among the finest artists in their own milieu. They are precisely the artists who most desire and need to work with their own companies.

NOT ALWAYS FULFILLING

Much contemporary ballet employs methods derived from modern dance, and many modern dance choreographers draw on the techniques and traditions of ballet. However, major artists of modern dance find that ballet companies are not the best showcases for their works. Paul Taylor's "Aureole" is in the repertory of The Royal Danish Ballet. The lyricism of the work would seem to suit it for balletic interpretation, but Taylor has said, "It is hard to teach 'Aureole' to ballet people. It requires a very different way of moving." Modern dance works performed by a ballet company look different from the same works danced by the company of the creating choreographer, just as they do when performed by a modern dance repertory company.

Need for Individuation

Modern dance encompasses many techniques of movement, and a choreographer's work can be performed properly only by a company conversant with his individual style. Furthermore, a choreographer almost always makes his best works on dancers he has trained for the purpose. If they do not understand the nuances of his way of moving, he must work with them until they do. The most important work in modern dance continues to be accomplished by choreographers who can assemble companies to act as their instruments. Dancers often contribute to the development of a work, and these contributions come most easily when dancers know one another and the choreographer, when mutual respect has developed among the members of a company. For these reasons, because modern dance continues to be an idiosyncratic art, we must look for further growth to individual choreographers and individuated companies.

DEVELOPMENT OF GENERATIONS

The history of modern dance is largely one of disciples who left their teachers to experiment on their own, and that history is continuing. Martha Graham, Doris Humphrey, and Charles Weidman broke with their mentors, Ruth St. Denis and Ted Shawn. Graham, in turn, recruited for her company Erick Hawkins, Merce Cunningham, and Paul Taylor, all of whom went on to create their own styles of dance. Douglas Dunn, Carolyn Brown, Viola Farber, and Gus Solomons, Jr. all studied or danced with Cunningham then went their ways. Taylor can list among his alumni Twyla Tharp, Laura Dean, and Senta Driver, each of whom takes a different approach to dance.

During the winter–spring season of 1977, audiences in New York could see performances by the companies of Graham, Cunningham, and Taylor—the three greatest living choreographers of American modern dance—and by those who broke with them, along with the works of dance-makers who derive from other houses. This learning from individuals by individuals, and the presentation to an audience of the results of inspired rebellion, is the sap of modern dance.

NO SINGLE STYLE

Modern dance in the 1970s is not a unified art, although definite trends can be recognized. Classicism opposes romanticism; cool formalism vies with emotional theatricality; pedestrian movement faces off against virtuosity. A minimalist such as Laura Dean reduces dance to its essentials, while Meredith Monk constructs elaborate dance-theater-music pieces that use a developing series of symbols to create an emotional effect. Kei Takei's slow fascinating rituals test the endurance of the dancers and amplify the meaning of each movement. Trisha Brown moves dance beyond its normal setting, as when she had her company move on the walls and ceiling of a space with the aid of machinery and hand-grips. Several artists, including Senta Driver, seek to eliminate sex roles from dance, using men and women as performers without regard to gender. Many, following Merce Cunningham, eliminate drama and role-playing, making dance its own subject.

At the same time, such established choreographers as Graham, Taylor, Cunningham, Alwin Nikolais, Murray Louis, and Alvin Ailey continue to make dances in the techniques and styles they have developed. This richness is sustained by choreographers working independently with their own companies.

THE QUESTION OF QUALITY

Paul Taylor, considering the deluge of dance pouring out of SoHo lofts in 1976, remarked, "There are a lot of closet choreographers around. They're working for themselves and maybe a small coterie of their friends; they're not really involved." About the same time, Merce Cunningham commented on the loss in attention given to many of the young choreographers of the 1960s who had seemed to take their principles from his. "Maybe they limited themselves too much," he said in his gentle, unreproachful manner. "You can't ever limit yourself."

There are major choreographers like Cunningham and Martha Graham who employ relatively large companies and others like Twyla Tharp who work with more limited groups. Economics has a great deal to do with it, but so does artistic need. A modern dance choreographer cannot be measured by the size of his company or even by the number of performances he gives a year. Meredith Monk designs her works specifically for the spaces in which they are to be performed and asks why "theater always has to happen at 8 P.M.? Why can't it be at 10 Saturday morning, when the audience has the whole day afterwards?" Monk does not want to give a New York season every year; she needs the time to prepare her work and rehearse with her company, The House.

Style No Guarantee—In such an individual art, one cannot measure achievement by choice of style. Laura Dean and Lucinda Childs are minimalists of dance, deliberately working with limited kinetic materials, but their repeated production of provocative, striking dances does not set a cachet on minimalism—there are plenty of bad stark choreographers around.

A reputation for being part of the avant-garde is no surety either. Anna Halprin came to New York in the early 1970s with the reputation of a pioneer of nude dance. The critical reception accorded her season was not the kind to invite a return engagement, even with clothes on. However, Kei Takei, an equally unconventional choreographer, is a subtle and eloquent artist who deserves her high reputation even though her work probably will never suit—and may often disturb—much of the general public.

If iconoclasm has no intrinsic value, neither does the attempt to carry on an established tradition. In modern dance, the originator of a method often is its greatest exponent. Pearl Lang, who works in the manner of Martha Graham, is merely a good choreographer; Graham is one of the century's great artists.

Modern dance, like any other endeavor, has its share of incompetent practitioners; most of its workers are what might be termed solid professionals, possessing skills and talent comparable to those of the average author of popular entertainments. Choreographers such as Louis Falco, Rudy Perez, and Paul Sansardo please their personal constituencies and turn out work that is sometimes interesting or amusing, sometimes dreadful, but nearly always workmanlike.

The Happy Few—The great contributions to the art have been and still are made by a few individuals of genius. They go beyond the childlike enthusiasms of many of the repertory companies; the tinkering with technique, resurrection of old works, and echoes of popular sentiment of the avant-garde and middle class; the echoes of a master's work that defines the disciples of schools. They can be measured only by the canons of their works and the impressions made by those works on the educated sensitivities of the time. Most of the choreographers mentioned in this chapter—Lewitzky, Monk, Tharp, Douglas Dunn, Trisha Brown, Dean, Takei, Nikolais, and Louis—for one reason or another belong in that company, although the degree of genius and skill of course differs even among them. Senta Driver and Pilobolus are innovators of importance, although Driver is still too young as an artist to be fairly judged. Graham, Cunningham, and Taylor represent greatness. Apart from their devotion to dance, these artists share little; their purposes, their methods, their outputs vary with their personalities and artistic needs. They represent, however, a fair sample of the important work being done in modern dance, which is why they have been selected to stand as examples within this survey.

Seeking New Techniques

Yvonne Ranier, one of the rebels of the 1960s, proclaimed a credo: "No to spectacle, no to virtuosity . . . no to the involvement of the performer or the spectator . . . no to moving or being moved." Ranier and other dancers of her time sought to concentrate on movement alone, and many incorporated pedestrian movement in their work and choreographed pieces for nondancers. At a seminar at American University in Washington in the summer of 1976, critic George Jackson remarked, "It is no longer a question of ballet versus modern dance, but of technique versus non technique." By following Ranier's dicta, a group of adventurous iconoclasts—angry young dancers—freed themselves from old forms and restraints only to bind themselves with new ones.

TRAINING NEW DANCERS

The schools of Martha Graham and Merce Cunningham continue to train dancers, as do such institutions as Juilliard. Many colleges offer dance programs, which often are under the direction of working choreographers. Laura Foreman and the members of her company teach at The New School, New York, and Gus Solomons, Jr. and his dancers spend twenty-eight weeks a year in residence at The California Institute of the Arts. However, truly major choreographers are almost never involved in such ventures; they cannot take the time away from their own companies and creations. Foreman, for example, is far more important as an organizer of showcases for young talent than as a choreographer. As a result, choreographers of the younger generation find that dancers from most schools are about fifteen years behind the times. Some established choreographers, such as Alwin Nikolais and Paul Taylor, draw dancers from colleges and train them in their personal styles. Meredith Monk, whose beautifully subtle, involved works require much interaction, looks for "performers who can sing, dance, and act. I am most strict about singing skills, although recently I have started to pay more attention to dancing." Such performers are not easy to find.

A Need for New Techniques—The investigative, innovative work of the best avant-garde modern choreographers was hampered during the 1970s by a lack of new training grounds for dancers. A large percentage of New York's professional modern dancers could be found in ballet classes every morning, not because they wanted to dance ballet, but because those classes provided the only dance discipline suited to them, the techniques taught by Graham and Cunningham being too specialized for their purposes.

Senta Driver complained in 1977 that no teacher could be found who was developing and imparting to dancers the methods needed to perform the works of contemporary choreographers. "We're not renewing the process Martha [Graham] started," she said. "We're cutting off our own feet." Driver, whose work requires great strength, has her dancers do push-ups, as does Twyla Tharp, while admitting that this is no substitute for codifying a technique as Martha Graham did.

One contemporary and highly personal technique has been developed by Pilobolus Dance Theater. The original members of the group, all trained at Dartmouth, used gymnastic disciplines, along with yoga, to form the basis of the company's unique method. Other artists could almost certainly gain from studying this technique, although it must be remarked that at times the content of Pilobolus' dances seems to derive from the technique, rather than the other way around. The works tend to be cool and underemotional, colored with a charmingly grotesque humor, and based in a deep concern for natural relationships. Pilobolus has produced brilliant works, but some of its dances are far more interesting in the method of their presentation than in their content.

The example of Pilobolus does give hope that the search for new techniques is being pursued. Grants are needed, not merely for choreographers, but for teachers capable of working with contemporary dance-makers to develop new forms of technique. The establishment of schools that will revise technique to suit new dancers and stimulate young choreographers, that carry on the process developed by Graham, Jose Limon, Cunningham, and others of the earlier generations of modern dancers, is an urgent need.

Touring

Since Ruth St. Denis took to vaudeville stage before World War I, touring has been the salvation of modern dance. "No modern company can make money on Broadway," said David White, "but they can make money on a tightly booked tour." Touring has helped build an audience for modern dance, although some of the credit must go to television. "I've been around long enough so people got used to looking at me," said Merce Cunningham in 1977. "People aren't disturbed any more because we don't dance to the music." At the same time, Meredith Monk explained that her avant-garde work was warmly received in Austin, Texas, and in upstate New York.

DANCE TOURING PROGRAM

The National Endowment for the Arts has helped make modern dance available throughout the country with its Dance Touring Program which began in 1967–68 with a budget of $25,000; four companies toured for a total of five weeks in two states. The projected program for 1977–78 called for 117 companies to tour for a total of 440 weeks in fifty states and jurisdictions on a budget of $1.9 million. Suzanne Weil, head of the dance program of NEA said in 1977, "The program has made all the difference in spreading dance and giving companies a chance to work. Back in 1968–69, everybody was doing one-night stands."

Community Services—Companies on tour do more than give performances. They offer lecture-demonstrations in schools, helping students to understand dance. Members of the visiting company work with local dance schools and companies and, when the sponsor is a college, with the dance department. Master classes are given by members of the company for students in the community or for members of local companies. The standard touring contract for a company makes provision for these services and they are included in the company's fee. (A medium-sized company's fee for one week is about $7,500.) In short, a company operating under the Dance Touring Program is providing a residency in the community, not merely a series of performances.

Method of Operation—The Dance Touring Program distributes its money—generally through state and local agencies—to sponsors who wish to hire a company. NEA pays thirty percent of the fees of two companies for half-week residencies or of one company for a full week. The program operates on a "first-come, first-served basis"; when the budget for a year has been spent, the program is closed. "In 1977 the money closed out on February 23," Weil said, "and as a result some companies had incomplete tours. There simply was not enough money to fill out the schedules—we couldn't keep up with the demand."

Controversy Over Standards—In 1972–73 qualitative requirements for companies participating in the touring program were abandoned, but by 1977, Weil said, the NEA was considering reinstating them. Some observers strongly oppose standards, but others point out that some communities had turned against dance completely because a company of low quality did a residency there. Companies seeking to perform at major showcases in New York—The New York Dance Festival, the Dance Umbrella, or the Clark Center series—are selected by a committee of outside professionals. Such programs could also be implemented by NEA. Senta Driver suggested in 1977 that, should standards be avoided, videotapes of various companies should be made available to potential sponsors to help them select a company that would suit them.

Further Development—Some companies, Weil said,

> were redirecting their artistic goals to get into the program because it provides such a cachet. We have not provided enough alternatives, but we're going to. We want to try tiered tours, where companies work primarily in their own regions of the country. Companies like to develop a regional base, and we can't afford to send every company to every town in the United States.

An amplification of the Dance Touring Program came with the adoption of NEA's Long-Term Residency Program, under which a sponsor may apply for as much as half the cost of a residency of two weeks or more. As a result, The Alvin Ailey American Dance Theater spent four weeks in Atlanta in the summer of 1977, and the Merce Cunningham company was booked for a month in Boston. "This program creates a second home for companies," Weil said, "and means that they don't have to spend all their money on air fare."

State and local bodies and foundations also help to support residencies, and large companies continue to book theatrical tours, as they have in the past. The enthusiasm of many cities for dance has increased, and residencies permit companies to give premieres in many cities other than New York. In 1976, for example, Minneapolis saw the first performance of Laura Dean's "Dream." This was an important occasion; Dean's sparse minimalism will never be a hit on Broadway, but she is an original and brilliant artist and the premiere of one of her works is an event in dance.

The Problems of Growth

In the early days of modern dance a relatively small number of individual companies gave a relatively small number of performances each year. In the words of Judith A. Jedlicka, executive director of The National Corporate Fund for Dance, "They had no boards, no management, no support. It is no longer possible to work that way. The proliferation of companies, the need to perform, the higher costs of performing make management a necessity." The higher costs of performing also make financial aid a necessity. In

1976 Alwin Nikolais said that he often found foreign tours more feasible financially than seasons in New York because of the high cost of union theatrical labor in the city. That complaint has been echoed by other artists of similar importance who find the rising cost of labor a major threat.

The study compiled by The Association of American Dance Companies in May 1977 reported that fifty-one modern dance companies (about 25 percent of the nation's total) had combined budgets for 1975–76 of $8,659,134. They employed 462 dancers. Touring fees and income from ticket sales accounted for 57 percent of the income of those companies. Professional troupes with annual budgets of more than $500,000 (four reporting) gained 74 percent of their income in this fashion. Organizations with annual budgets of less than $25,000 (eight reporting) earned only 37 percent of their income through fees and tickets. In general, modern dance companies averaged a higher percentage of income from touring and ticket sales than did ballet companies included in the survey. It is clear that no dance company can survive without assistance from governments, grants, gifts, and the personal purses of the artists.

THE HIGH COST OF DANCING

During 1976–77 DTW produced short seasons (usually weekends) for fourteen modern dance companies showing the work of eighteen choreographers. The cost of this venture was $8,000 although both budget and amenities were limited.

In November 1974 Senta Driver, a young member of Paul Taylor's company, left to form her own dance organization, which she called Harry. Harry gave its first concert in March 1975; Driver found a theater and paid the costs of performance, about $2,600. The budget for her company's first fiscal year was $4,000, which included the salaries of two dancers, each of whom earned $140 a week for ten weeks of the year. (It is not usual for companies to pay dancers during the first season of operation.)

Not until June 1976 did Harry receive its first paid booking—an engagement to perform at Ohio State University in March 1977. The company received five reviews from prestigious publications at its first concert, yet five of its seasons between November 1974 and June 1977 were self-produced, which means that Driver paid about 90 percent of the cost of the performance. At the same time, the budget grew from $4,000 the first fiscal year to $8,000 in the second and $12,000 in the third.

"I Have Not Had It Hard . . ."—Driver and her company were selected to appear in The New York Dance Festival in the fall of 1976, which brought her the services of a management company. The following spring the company danced at a matinee of the Dance Umbrella. Driver's work was consistently reviewed; her reputation grew, but attendance came nowhere near meeting the company's budget. In addition to some help from private contributors, Harry raised fifty dollars during a fund-raising campaign in Greenwich, Connecticut, and pulled in thirteen contributions of ten dollars and twenty-five dollars each during a fund-raising campaign in 1976–77. By the end of Harry's third season, the company. was receiving prestigious engagements, and Driver was still paying the rent with free-lance typing. "I have not had it hard," she said in June 1977. "The company is moving as quickly as it is possible to move. . . . I start with far more oportunities than Paul [Taylor] did."

CORPORATE AID

Paul Taylor nearly disbanded his company in September 1976; he could not afford to continue. A rescue operation was mounted by the National Endowment for the Arts and The National Corporate Fund for Dance and the company survived. However, explained Judith Jedlicka of the Corporate Fund, "We had to make sure that Paul restructured his entire board of directors and took on people who knew about management and could help him." One member of the reconstituted board sold $9,000 worth of tickets to Taylor's benefit performance the following spring. Manufacturers Hanover Trust Company donated its suite at the Waldorf-Astoria for the party after the performance. The same corporation paid for printing a fund-raising circular for a Taylor company tour that helped bring in $10,000.

More important, executives of several corporations who became interested in the company (and in other companies) devoted their time to insure proper management. Jedlicka said,

> There is a need for business people on these boards, a need for fund-raisers, and a need for guidance in financial matters. Modern dance

companies have lived from day to day, and only recently have the big ones had boards giving them proper financial management.

The Corporate Fund helps to support eight dance companies of which four are modern troupes and one—The Alvin Ailey American Dance Theater—is a hybrid. It also gives aid to several smaller but important modern groups. The Fund seeks to convince corporations to make some of their contributions to dance. As bait, executives of the Corporate Fund take executives of corporations to performances and rehearsals.

FOUNDATION AID

A grant of $370,000 was extended in May 1966 by the Rockefeller Foundation to the University of Utah in Salt Lake City for the purpose of establishing a modern dance company, which developed to be the Repertory Dance Theatre. Grants for the continuation of the project totaling $415,000 were added in 1968 and in 1972.

In 1968 The Ford Foundation gave grants totaling $485,000 to help produce a total of twenty-five weeks of modern dance performances in New York. Among those performances were those of the historic festival of avant-garde dance at the Billy Rose Theater, an event which helped make the general public aware of the new forms being developed in modern dance.

In 1974 The Ford Foundation provided an eight-month grant of $25,000 to Connecticut College to help support the presentation of six to eight new modern dance companies at that year's American Dance Festival in New London.

Twyla Tharp has been the recipient of a Mellon grant, and other choreographers and companies have been aided by Guggenheim and Rockefeller fellowships. It is not necessary to list them, simply to point out that a decline in aid from foundations almost certainly must result in a decline in production and creativity.

SELF-HELP

During the 1976–77 season in New York, Merce Cunningham, Martha Graham, Paul Taylor, and Alwin Nikolais and Murray Louis (paired) had seasons on Broadway. Alvin Ailey presented his regular performances at City Center, and Twyla Tharp had a two-week run at the Brooklyn Academy of Music. Nearly all of those seasons included a benefit performance and some had more than one. Benefits, with high-priced tickets entitling the holders to attend a party after the performance, are not beloved of choreographers or dancers. Benefit audiences are not the most appreciative on earth and their members seldom show up during the remainder of the season. However, benefit performances do make money for dance companies, as ballet troupes have known for some time. Modern dance companies are beginning to learn the financial value of benefits. However, they generally succeed only for large companies with established names, those sufficiently chic to attract the rich and fashionable.

GOVERNMENTAL AID

State, local, and federal governments are a major source of funds for modern dance companies, and must continue to be. In addition to the touring programs already noted, the National Endowment for the Arts provides grants in a number of categories: production grants for the creation of new works, grants to allow choreographers rehearsal time with their companies, workshop fellowships ($1,800 in 1977) for young choreographers.

NEA also provides grants of up to $10,000 for major choreographers who have no companies—important artists such as Anna Sokolow and Pearl Primus—to allow them to work.

Production grants of as much as $100,000, which must be matched by other contributions, are also available. These, needless to say, are designed for the major companies.

To qualify for the smaller production grants, a company must be professional, have been in existence for three years, and must give twenty weeks of performances a year. In the mid-1970s it sometimes appeared as if too many of those grants were going to companies which could be styled the middle class of modern dance—solid, with a personal constituency, but not particularly adventurous. Too few, it seemed, were going to the major troupes or to the young, innovative artists who might constitute the next generation of modern dance.

However, the list of grant recipients for 1978 included such major artists as Laura Dean, Trisha Brown, and Kei Takei, along with choreographers outside New York such as Bill Evans, who left the Repertory Dance Theatre to start a company in Seattle.

A Time of Consolidation

Toward the end of the 1970s, it was clear that the rebellion that had characterized the 1960s was over, and that the phenomenal growth of the modern dance audience of the earlier part of the decade was reaching a plateau. It was also terribly clear that modern dance was becoming more and more expensive to produce. It was a period of consolidating gains, of learning to select among the choices developed during the 1960s, of spreading dance companies throughout the country, of seeking new techniques, and of reviving works of the past and reexamining the history of the art.

Modern dance had at last become an accepted segment of American life and had achieved a wide following among young people. Corporations, foundations, private individuals, and governments were slowly accepting at least part of their responsibility to support the art, although a great deal more support clearly was required. Perhaps most important, dancers and choreographers continued to seek new methods of movement and theatrical presentation. Artists discovered a need to root themselves in new techniques, having discarded some of the older ones; and the giants of modern dance, who had invented the older methods, continued to create and perform, giving continuity to a very young art. Finally, modern dance continued to reflect the image of its era, for was not the decade of the 1970s largely a time of consolidation?

Julius Novick

6

The Theater

Prologue

Not long ago, it was generally assumed in the United States that Broadway was the professional theater and the professional theater was Broadway. Period. And as recently as the late 1940s this assumption was essentially true. Aside from Broadway and its transcontinental extension "the road," there were a number of summer stock companies and a smaller number of winter stock companies, mostly surviving by serving up old Broadway hits. As far as professional theater was concerned, there was virtually nothing else.

Even in the late forties and the early fifties, not everyone was happy with this situation. It was generally conceded that Broadway did certain things well: realistic dramas, light comedies, musicals. Looking back, we can see the late forties and the fifties as a sort of Broadway golden age, the age of *A Streetcar Named Desire* and *Death of a Salesman* and *Long Day's Journey into Night* and *Guys and Dolls*, achievements that in their varying ways the American theater has never surpassed.

JULIUS NOVICK *is a theater critic for* The Village Voice, *author of* Beyond Broadway: The Quest for Permanent Theaters, *and Associate Professor of Literature at the College at Purchase of the State University of New York. He is now devoting himself to a book on the theater in the United States since World War II with the help of a grant from the Guggenheim Foundation.*

But Broadway was and is a commercial institution. It devotes itself as best it can to making money, and it is a well-known fact that the imperatives of commerce and of art are not always the same. Many people felt the limitations of Broadway and chafed under them. It became a cliché to attack the commercial theater for timidity, lack of integrity, meretriciousness, surrender to the bourgeois audience. (The complainers, of course, were another bourgeois audience. The civil war between the bourgeoisie and the bourgeoisie has been going on for a long time; but that is another matter.)

Meanwhile the live theater was faced with competition from movies and radio, and increasingly from television as well; theaters in New York and elsewhere gave up the ghost and became movie houses and parking lots. What had been the American theater was visibly disappearing. And as matters got worse economically, they did not improve artistically. It was not only radicals, avant-gardists, and high-brows who complained. Brooks Atkinson of The *New York Times*, then dean of American theater critics, was moved to write:

> The Broadway theater has been slowly becoming a neurotic ordeal. The cost of production and operation has become so high that successes have to be fantastically successful and failures have become catastrophes. . . . It is not art, but an unsuccessful form of high-pressure huckstering. There is almost no continuity of employment among actors, playwrights, and allied artists and craftsmen. The whole business is conducted in an atmosphere of crises, strain, and emergency.

It became clear that there were certain things that Broadway could not or would not do adequately: classical revivals; revivals even of those modern classics that had originated on Broadway; new American plays too delicate or esoteric for the Broadway audience; certain kinds of European drama; experimental theater generally.

OFF-BROADWAY

Long before the war, of course, groups of professional theater people had struggled to establish and maintain alternatives to Broadway; very few of these attempts prospered for long, but in the late forties and fifties, the struggle began again. People who could not or would not work on Broadway began putting on plays in converted night clubs, movie houses, and meeting halls in various parts of Manhattan, and off-Broadway was born. Some off-Broadway productions transferred to Broadway without much success, but off-Broadway prospered in its own place for several fruitful and stimulating years. Low rents, low salaries, and low production budgets made it possible to survive while playing in small theaters to small audiences.

But the low rents, low salaries, and low production budgets crept inexorably higher and higher. It became harder and harder for off-Broadway productions, which were mainly financed by private investors, to make money or even to break even. Commercial pressures impeded artistic intentions. It was like Broadway all over again only worse, in a way, since it was even harder to make back your investment off-Broadway than on, so far did rising costs outpace the limited seating capacity of the off-Broadway houses. By the early seventies, off-Broadway was withering on the vine, a victim of economic unviability.

PERMANENT, NONPROFIT THEATERS

By the late 50s it had become evident that the future of the American theater depended on a kind of theatrical organization unfamiliar in America though standard and traditional in Europe.

Both Broadway and, for the most part, off-Broadway are organized on an ad hoc basis. A producer secures a "property," raises money, hires a director, designers, actors, rents a theater, puts on his production; when it closes, everyone disperses. We needed theaters that would break the cycle of constantly beginning from scratch, that would have a life beyond the individual production, that would make the word "theater" mean an institution, not a piece of real estate for rent to all comers. (Many off-Broadway groups attempted to become theaters of this sort. A few—notably the Circle in the Square—succeeded. By doing so, they transcended off-Broadway and became something else.)

Furthermore, in order to do what they could do, what they needed to do, these theaters would ultimately have to be organized on a nonprofit basis. The economists Baumol and Bowen have shown that the performing arts, as a handicraft industry in a technological world, can only become more and more uneconomical. In order to be free of an abject slavery to the box office, theaters would either have to embrace poverty as a way of life, with all the limitations (as well as the liberations) that poverty entails, or else seek support from private patrons, from foundations, and from the government. Or do both.

Permanent, nonprofit theaters. We needed them, and now—amazingly, to anyone who remembers what things were like a quarter of a century ago—we have them. Big ones, small ones, white ones, black ones, popular, esoteric, radical, conservative. In 1976 Theatre Communications Group (TCG), "the national service organization for the nonprofit professional theater in the United States," counted a total of 176 such theaters. Of these, the 151 theaters that responded to TCG's request for information reported a combined annual budget of nearly $80 million and a combined annual attendance of nearly 12 million. (During the 1976–77 season, by comparison, 8.6 million people attended the Broadway theater.) Clearly it is no longer true that in America the professional theater and the Broadway theater are the same thing.

OFF-OFF-BROADWAY

There are all kinds of nonprofit professional theaters, but there are two *main* kinds. Since by the early sixties off-Broadway was no longer receptive to most experimental work, avant-garde actors and directors moved into coffeehouses and lofts and churches, and off-off-Broadway began. Off-off-Broadway embraced poverty: the actors worked for carfare or for love, and production expenses were met by passing the hat. Today there are dozens of off-off-Broadway theaters; nobody knows exactly how many, because even while you count, one or two may die and two or three others may spring up. The goal is usually to be a theater, not just to put on this production or that; but the goal is not always attainable.

Off-off-Broadway is open and fluid; if you and your friends wish to call yourselves off-off-Broadway theater, there is no one to say you nay. At one end of its spectrum, off-off-Broadway is what we used to call "amateur." At the other end, it is composed of dedicated, trained, skilled professionals; some of them are thinking of moving on to other things, some of them are Broadway actors between engagements; while others expect to work all their professional lives in the off-off-Broadway community that centers around the East Village in New York. Many off-off-Broadway groups are still struggling and marginal; one winner of a 1977 Obie Award (given for achievement in o-B and o-o-B theater) could not be at the ceremonies because he was standing on line at the unemployment office; and one announced that she was appearing in a porno movie to support her Theater for the New City.

A few off-off-Broadway theaters are large and well-established. Ellen Stewart founded the Café La Mama in a basement in the East Village in 1962; Ellen Stewart still presides over the La Mama Experimental Theatre Club (still located in the East Village), which occupies three buildings and has received support from several foundations and from the state and federal governments.

But off-off-Broadway, like off-Broadway, is essentially a small-scale operation. Working often at a far experimental edge, it performs mainly for small audiences. And though there are off-off-Broadway outposts in a number of cities, the movement is centered mainly in New York. Theater in this country is a minority art, reaching only a small percentage of the population; off-off-Broadway reaches only a tiny minority of that small minority.

RESIDENT THEATERS

Most of the permanent nonprofit theaters have a different objective. They produce a variety of plays: classics, Broadway and off-Broadway successes and failures, new plays of various descriptions. They are actively seeking to enlarge their audiences. And they are to be found in all parts of the country. These theaters have been variously called regional theaters or repertory theaters or resident theaters. "Regional," the most common term, is somewhat of a misnomer, since these theaters reflect the personalities of their leaders far more than they reflect their "regions"; anyway, "regional" tends to mean "outside New York," and there are such theaters in New York as well as in the "regions." "Repertory" can also be misleading, for reasons that will appear below. Let us stick to "resident."

Off-off-Broadway theaters and resident theaters are alike in being nonprofit and, in intention at least, permanent. But with certain anomalous exceptions, they are easier to tell apart in practice than in theory. Off-off-Broadway theaters are, on the whole, poor, small, irregular in their performing schedules, experimental in their work, bohemian in their attitudes, rough, shaggy, funky. And they want to stay that way, in order to keep their freedom. For the resident theaters, on the other hand, poverty and smallness are generally conditions to be grown out of as soon as possible; their development is toward institutionalization, toward taking a stable place in the community alongside libraries, art museums, symphony orchestras. Resident theaters are trying to preserve, develop, extend the traditions that off-off-Broadway wants to bust out of. They complement each other.

But the resident theaters reach a much larger public. Off-off-Broadway serves the larger community by staying far on its periphery, which enables it to be independent of the community's tastes and assumptions as they are right now. Resident theater meets the community more directly, trying to stay in touch with it (or with a larger minority of it) while helping it to move forward. Off-off-Broadway by its very nature cannot (and would not want to) be at the center of the theater; the avant-garde is by definition not the main body. Resident theater, on the other hand, is the model by which the American theater will, in the main, be organized in the latter part of the twentieth century. Therefore the rest of this chapter will be devoted to a study of one such theater.

ARENA STAGE

Arena Stage in Washington, D.C., started very small in 1950. Today it is one of the largest of the resident theaters, as well as one of the oldest. There is no consensus as to which is the best—very few people have seen enough productions in enough theaters in enough cities to be able to venture an absolute opinion—but Arena is on everyone's list of the best half-dozen. And there is a general sense in the resident theater movement (it *is* a movement now, after some lonely early years) that Arena is somehow central, prototypical.

In 1976, on the recommendation of the American Theater Critics Association, Arena received the first Tony Award ever given to a theater outside New York—not for any particular production, but for its general stature and achievement. It seemed only natural that the Arena should be the first theater so honored. As much as any other resident theater—and without losing its own particular identity—it stands for all of them.

Act One: The Hippodrome

BEGINNINGS

In the years after World War II, whatever was wrong with Broadway was even more wrong on the road. Since the thirties, when stars like the Lunts and Katharine Cornell used to tour all across the country on principles of *noblesse oblige*, the road had been largely a matter of tired, undistinguished casts performing an even more restricted range of plays than was available on Broadway itself. "Road-company" was a slang term meaning a second-rate copy. Audiences diminished; theaters closed. In Washington, D.C., in 1948 the National Theater closed its doors because Actor's Equity refused to allow its members to perform before segregated audiences and the theater owner refused to integrate. And so for a couple of years there was no professional theater at all in the nation's capital unless, of course, you counted the Gayety Burlesque.

It was around this time that Edward Mangum and Zelda Fichandler began talking about starting a theater in Washington. Mangum was a professor of drama at George Washington University; Ms. Fichandler was one of his graduate students. For a while, they had their eye on an old hulk on the Potomac that they were going to turn into a showboat; then they took an option on an old movie house called the Hippodrome, in a shabby part of downtown Washington.

Tom Fichandler was working full time for the Twentieth Century Fund but managed to serve as the theater's business manager from the very beginning. He points out that Arena was organized

> not as a nonprofit organization, but as a business organization. . . . In 1949, who would give us money to start a theater? Everybody thought, you make a fortune in the theater, so they were willing to invest as stockholders.

Mangum and the Fichandlers raised $15,000 by selling stock in the new organization at $50 a share. But though in its early years the Arena made money in order to exist, it never existed in order to make money.

THEATER-IN-THE-ROUND

The founders held auditions in Washington and signed up a resident company of eight actors. The Hippodrome was converted into an arena theater or theater-in-the-round, a living-room-size stage, sixteen feet by twenty feet, surrounded on all four sides by the audience. But the District of Columbia was very reluctant to grant the remodelled Hippodrome a license as a theater; it thought a theater was supposed to have a proscenium and an asbestos fire curtain separating the audience from the stage. Who ever heard of a theater with the stage in the middle of the audience? When Ms. Fichandler pointed out, in an eloquent and scholarly letter, that night clubs and sports arenas and circuses managed very well with the audience surrounding the action, the authorities grudgingly granted the license, but only on condition that the new theater not call itself a theater. And so it was named Arena Stage.

At that time, a number of theater people were rather messianic about theater-in-the-round, which made virtually any space usable as a theater, saved money on sets, and brought the spectators into a new intimacy with the performers. Margo Jones in Dallas, Nina Vance in Houston, Glenn Hughes at the University of Washington all had promoted it. This form of staging has not prevailed, though Arena and others are still loyal to it. The commercial theater continues to function on old-fashioned proscenium stages; and in the resident theater the thrust stage, inspired by the Elizabethan stages on which Shakespeare's plays were performed, with the spectators surrounding the action on three sides instead of four, is more popular than the full four-sided arena. But the near monopoly of the proscenium arch and the picture frame stage has been decisively broken; in both thrust-stage theaters and theaters-in-the-round, actors and audience, after hundreds of years of separation, are once again in the same room.

THE EARLY YEARS

Arena Stage opened its doors on August 17, 1950 with a performance of *She Stoops to Conquer* by Oliver Goldsmith. During that first season the new Company did an astonishing seventeen productions, including plays by Shakespeare, Shaw, Synge, Molière, Gogol, Wilde, John Steinbeck, Elmer Rice, and Tennessee Williams. The second season was somewhat less onerous: only ten productions, including three repeated from the first year.

In April 1952 Ed Mangum resigned to take a post at a theater in Honolulu, and Zelda Fichandler was left to run Arena Stage single-handedly. She has been running it ever since. She was twenty-five when the theatre opened, twenty-seven when she took sole charge. She had no conventional credentials for running a theater. She had never (has never) worked in any professional theater except her own. She earned the right to run a large, prosperous, well-known theater—Arena Stage—by years spent running a small, struggling, obscure theater—also Arena Stage, in earlier days. Somehow, as the theater grew, she managed to grow with it.

Today she says:

> . . . that vague, and yet grounded idea that started in 1949, it's still essentially what we are. It always seemed to me that it would work. I thought that people wanted it, and I thought that it should be. And would be. . . . And even when people didn't come and we'd play to thirty or forty people in the 247-seat house, I thought, in time, they will come. . . . The idea was . . . why should there be ten or twelve blocks in one city [*i.e.*, Broadway] which gathered and presented and fostered the art of theater when people live everywhere? Why should it be that forces for creating theater are assembled and then when that singular episode is over, the forces are disassembled, when theater is a collective art? It's almost an architectural principle, that form follows function. The function is to continually examine human experience, so you must have an institution that allows you to do that.

During those early years, the company included George Grizzard, Pernell Roberts, Lester Rawlins, Frances Sternhagen, Michael Higgins, and others, young actors then who have since made reputations for themselves. Alan Schneider came to direct *The Glass Menagerie* in 1951 and has been returning ever since. New plays were not popular with Arena's audience in those days; one exception was *All Summer Long* by Robert Anderson. Alan Schneider staged it at Arena in 1953, and staged it on Broadway the following season, where it had a moderate *succès d'estime* and perhaps suggested to a few people in New York that some theatrical activity worth noticing was going on at some distance from the Main Stem.

But it wasn't easy. Ms. Fichandler remembers:

> We did a play every two weeks, and sometimes every three. We slept on the floor of the theater, got two or three hours of sleep a night. We

survived by the skin of our teeth. And we did seventeen plays in one season without really an organization. I mean, we just *did everything* there was to do. You designed mailing pieces and did ads and directed and read scripts and scurried for actors. And you just scrambled. There were no laws, there were no rules, there was no order, there were no system. You just watched what was happening and changed from day to day. You put one play in rehearsal, it didn't sound good, you took it out. Put another one in. And counted on the fact that more of your decisions would be right than wrong. And somehow, in that economy, when the tickets were $1.90, there was a lot of room for that kind of haphazard formulation of day-to-day life. Now, anyone starting a theater has got to have a better *ship,* or it'll go down. And we almost went down a couple of times. *Room Service* [the famous American farce by Murray and Boretz] saved us once. Something always saved us. We'd be down to no money, you know, like $28.00, and then a play would pull us out.

Tom Fichandler remembers:

. . . by golly, we paid dividends [to the stockholders] a large part of the time. But they were coming out of the hides of the people who were working there—like me, who was working for zero money. And other people were working for practically nothing. So there was hidden subsidy from the beginning.

MOVING ON

Things could not go on the way they were going. Expenses were increasing. The revenue from 247 seats would soon not be enough to keep the theater open, no matter what economies were made. Ms. Fichandler decided to close the theater until she would find new and larger quarters for it. Arena Stage shut up shop at the Hippodrome in July 1955, after fifty-five productions in five frenzied years.

OTHER THEATERS

While Zelda Fichandler was sleeping on the floor of the Hippodrome, Nina Vance at the Alley Theatre in Houston and Herbert Blau and Jules Irving at the Actor's Workshop (now defunct) in San Francisco were undergoing similar tribulations. That is how resident theaters were begun, by local zealots who made them happen. "I clawed this theater out of the ground," said Nina Vance of the theater that had begun in Houston in 1947.

Later, things became easier. The success of the Arena and others provided models to follow; it became clear that professional theater was possible outside New York. In 1963 Sir Tyrone Guthrie opened the theater that bears his name in Minneapolis, not in tiny makeshift premises but in a brand-new, custom designed $2 million, 1,437-seat auditorium, with Hume Cronyn, Jessica Tandy, and the no-longer-unknown George Grizzard in the company. It is unlikely that anybody at the Guthrie had to sleep on the floor.

After the Guthrie, it was a new time for the resident theater. Solidly established amateur theaters in Buffalo and Richmond turned professional (as indeed the Cleveland Play House had done decades before, though few had noticed). Bright young men from drama school shopped around for a city, found one that seemed suitable, persuaded local businessmen to contribute money, and opened resident theaters. In some cities, businessmen and civic leaders got together, raised money on their own initiative, and went shopping for an artistic director to come out to Seattle or wherever and start a theater. A number of universities set up professional theaters on campus. The privations of the pioneers smoothed the way for those who came later: an old story. But that is what the privations of the pioneers are for.

All this, however, was still in the future when Zelda Fichandler decided that the Hippodrome was more trouble than it was worth.

Act Two: The Old Vat

In 1955–56 there were no Arena productions; the Fichandlers spent the year looking for a new site for their theater. For a while they were negotiating for the local Masonic auditorium, but the Masonic board of directors stipulated, "We don't want any actors hanging around here during the daytime," and negotiations collapsed. Arena came to rest instead in the former ice-storage room of the old Heurich Brewery in the Foggy Bottom section of Washington. Someone thought of the Old Vic and nicknamed the new brewery theater the Old Vat. As such it is still remembered affectionately in Washington for its warmth and intimacy, even though with 500 seats arranged arena fashion around the four sides of a rectangular central stage, it had twice the capacity of the Hippodrome (which nobody has ever called the Old Hip).

SUBSCRIPTION AUDIENCES

The Old Vat opened on November 7, 1956 with *A View from the Bridge*, directed by Alan Schneider. It was a popular success, but the plays that followed it were not. Ms. Fichandler responded to this situation with Arena's first all-out subscription campaign, and signed up 2,300 subscribers for the following season. (In 1976–77 Arena had 16,750 subscribers.) A solid group of subscribers guarantees an audience even for unpopular plays, frees the theater from excessive dependence on the verdicts of the critics, and diminishes the temptation to wreck the rhythm of production by closing the flops right away and running the hits halfway to forever. It has been argued by radical critics that a theater dependent upon its subscribers (as practically all resident theaters now are) is enslaved to those subscribers, forced to meet their tastes, forced to deliver them X productions a year, ready or not. Perhaps, suggest these critics, a theater ought rather to choose poverty and freedom, or perhaps foundation or government grants and freedom, on the model of off-off-Broadway. But to Zelda Fichandler "a subscription plan is not just a mechanism. I mean, it's not just a way to purchase tickets. It's a way to sign your recognition of what the institution is about." When the question of subscription comes up, she likes to quote Jean-Louis Barrault: "There is only one way to create a real theater: to strive unbendingly to attract the devoted adherent as opposed to the transient public interested only in the hits."

THE FORD FOUNDATION

It was in 1957, during the Old Vat years, that Arena—and the resident theaters generally—attracted another "devoted adherent": The Ford Foundation. As late as 1961, Howard Taubman could write in The *New York Times*, "We have only a scattering of professional companies outside New York." In the middle fifties these theaters were scattered indeed: few, small, obscure, struggling, and only dimly aware of each other. W. McNeil Lowry, then the Foundation's man in the arts (and now the editor of this volume), introduced the theaters to one another, and made them for the first time conscious of themselves as a movement. More fundamentally, The Ford Foundation enabled the key ones among them to grow—sometimes, perhaps, enticed them into growing. The Foundation's strategy was to provide a theater with money to expand, develop, raise artistic standards, but with a challenge to the community to help maintain the theater at its new level. It is hard to go back. Most communities, prompted by vigorous fund drives conducted by the theaters, got used to meeting the challenge.

Other foundations, most notably the Rockefeller Foundation, have given money to the resident theaters, but the Ford contribution was the largest—some $19.5 million as of 1976—and it was crucial. It stimulated the theaters not just to get bigger, but to stabilize, to institutionalize themselves. Augustus, it is said, found Rome built of brick and left it built of marble; The Ford Foundation did something analogous for the resident theaters, and not just in terms of architecture. There were those who said that Rome had been better off in brick—that the resident theaters had lost something in independence, flexibility, spontaneity, had lost their chance of becoming theatrical pioneers and radical critics of society, because The Ford Foundation had got them hooked on big audiences and big budgets. But this is a minority view. You cannot tempt a person, or an organization, with something that he, or it, does not find tempting. "Thou marshall'st me the way that I was going," as Macbeth said to the dagger. It seems clear that The Ford Foundation helped the resident theaters to become what most of them wished to become all along.

THE RESIDENT COMPANY

Zelda Fichandler, at least, knew what she wanted. In 1955, when the Hippodrome had closed and for the moment there *was* no Arena Stage, she had said:

> It is my belief that the time is now ripe for the creation in the United States—in Washington, D.C., in particular—of an American acting troupe which would gather, preserve, and develop a theatrical tradition, represent the theatrical culture of America abroad and which could stimulate by its example the creation of several similar companies in other leading cities. An acting company is a group of actors who work together over a long period of time, who share a central unifying objective beyond the presentation of a given single play, who have a common set of artistic principles—a common style—and who share either materially or psychologically or both in the welfare, prestige, and development of the group as a whole.

Three years later, invited to apply for a grant, she wrote a long letter to Mac Lowry of The Ford Foundation: "At the center of Arena Stage," she wrote, "is the idea of a permanent acting company." Yet she was making

> monthly trips to New York to round out my casts. . . . The problem . . . is to get the actors I want to come and to *stay*. And an acting company is built, first of all, on permanence and, at the very least, on some sort of continuity.
>
> While I have no difficulty in "jobbing in" an excellent actor even at our modest fee to play a particular role of his choice in a particular play that interests him, and while he may come back again during the season for another such role in another such play, Arena Stage simply does not pay enough to keep in residence for a season, or desirably longer, a sufficient number of the kind of actor it wants and needs to move further towards the formation of an acting company of first-rate quality.

She wanted a grant to enable her to raise actors' salaries to $125 a week; in 1959 she got a Ford grant to pay ten actors $200 a week each. (The Alley and the Actor's Workshop got similar grants.) As of 1977, The Ford Foundation had given Arena some $3.4 million. But Ms. Fichandler is still wrestling with the question of how to attract and maintain a permanent company.

MOVING ON AGAIN

The Old Vat was only a transitional phase for the Arena; the Fichandlers knew when they moved in that the site of the brewery would eventually be needed for the approaches to a new bridge across the Potomac. So the last years at the Old Vat were occupied with planning for a new theater.

The 1960s were a boom period in America both for "urban renewal" and for the building of theaters, and the two booms had a lot in common. Plans for the bulldozing and rebuilding of "blighted arreas" in the cities often called for the building of theaters, either singly or as part of "performing arts centers," and these theaters were often designated either for the resident companies that had grown up in makeshift premises, or for new resident companies founded to occupy the buildings. (The details of who paid for what, and how, were of course different in every case.) Arena, as usual, did it a little before it became fashionable. On October 18, 1960 ground was broken for a new Arena Stage down by the Potomac in the Southwest Redevelopment Area.

NONPROFIT STATUS

The need for a new theater precipitated other developments. In 1959, at Tom Fichandler's initiative, Arena finally became officially what it had always been in spirit: a not-for-profit organization. To receive foundation grants to pay for the new building and to treat with the redevelopment authorities, Arena had to be officially noncommercial; like subscription audiences, nonprofit status was part of the resident theater's way of life. (Arena's stockholders were duly paid off, and asked to return the value of their stock in loans and gifts; most of them did.) And in January 1961, after serving since the beginning as Arena's part-time business manager, Tom Fichandler finally left his job at the Twentieth Century Fund to become Executive Director of Arena, a job he still holds.

The Old Vat closed on June 7, 1961 with a performance of *Man and Superman* by George Bernard Shaw, after forty productions in five years. Zelda Fichandler made a triumphant speech:

> The concept of the independent repertory theater with a continuing policy and a definite point of view operating outside New York is a sound concept. And the idea that audiences outside New York are ready and eager to catch on to this kind of theater and the sort of repertoire it chooses to present is a sound idea. We have come to take these twin principles for granted, but five years ago they were still in the early testing stage.

Act Three: The Arena

THE NEW THEATER

This time there was no hiatus between theaters, only the now-usual summer breathing space between seasons. The new Arena Stage opened on October 30, 1961 with a production of *The Caucasian Chalk Circle* by Bertolt Brecht, directed by Alan Schneider. Harry Weese, the architect of the new Arena, had never built a theater before. But this was before the theater building boom of the sixties was well underway, and when Weese was hired, hardly any American architect had built a theater, unless you count high school and college auditoria.

The new theater cost upwards of $850,000. It is a brown brick structure, sober but not sombre, neutral but not unfriendly. As Ms. Fichandler said, "It is all bone and sinew, no paint and powder." It had 750 seats (later increased to 811) arranged on all four sides of the stage. She said at its dedication:

> We have not built quote—a flexible—unquote theater, representing every form of theater and ultimately no form of theater. We have built an arena and have stated our belief in the validity of this form of theater in brick and concrete.

Later she elaborated:

> It is a high, vaulted room with a ribbed ceiling pierced by infinite sources of lighting. The stage cube is not small: thirty feet by thirty-six and twenty-four feet [up] to the bottom of a large catwalk—a brooding, dark grey metal machine larger than the stage rectangle, bisected several times in both directions. Hundreds of lighting instruments hang on the catwalk rails. All the machinery of lighting and sound is exposed. . . .
>
> The stage can be small or large. With light it can alternately expand and contract within one production. It can be sunken or raised. Platforms can be built into one or all four of the tunnels or into none of them. The space may be used as *one* place. Or, because of the capacity of light to define numberless areas WITHIN A TOTALLY NEUTRAL CUBE, it may be used as an *infinite number* of places.

The new theater has no nickname. It is called simply "the Arena." ("Arena," without the definite article, is the institution; "the Arena" is the auditorium.)

THE SIXTIES

It was a good moment for opening a theater, and not only for opening a theater. In 1962 Ms. Fichandler wrote in a program note,

> When the power of men and the power of the moment came together, anything and everything can happen. It is possible that the American theatre is on the edge of such a time or even already within it, and that this is the time when our theatre is to come of age.

In 1962 a lot of people were talking like that, including John F. Kennedy. The resident-theater boom of the 1960s was part of a larger boom; it seemed for a while as if everything in America was expanding and would keep on expanding—as if there was no problem we could not solve, no need we could not supply, no good thing

we could not have. Uncle Sam might have said with King Lear,
"They told me I was everything."

Later, after John F. Kennedy was assassinated, after Vietnam was
revealed as a quagmire, Uncle Sam might have said, again with King
Lear, " 'tis a lie, I am not ague-proof." "The important thing," says
Marat in *Marat/Sade* by Peter Weiss, "is to pull yourself up by your
own hair/ to turn yourself inside out/ and see the whole world with
fresh eyes." Not easy, but Arena was trying to help. During that
decade, from the new stage, not only Peter Weiss but also Bertolt
Brecht, Bernard Shaw, Eugene O'Neill, John Arden, Howard
Sackler, Arthur Kopit, and others warned those who would listen;
there was even a production of *King Lear*. But Arena, too, went on
expanding. What else should it have done? It too was part of America, and its job was to use such American resources as it could get
its hands on, to do what American good it could.

In any event, the euphoria did not last. In 1965 Ms. Fichandler
wrote:

> We have conquered the black beast of housing and the black beast of
> public apathy, and now we have to deal with the black beast of the art
> itself. The regional theater movement has got some kind of recognition
> today. Now it has to reach its promise.

That was the challenge. Toward the end of the new decade, looking
around her, she saw the challenge, in the main, not being met. The
resident theaters were a success, all right: ". . . such a big thing
they ought to make a musical out of it." But they had become bland
and routinized; they had lost their sense of purpose.

> . . . we [in the resident theaters] need—individually—to find, heighten,
> and explore the informing idea of our theaters. We need to find our
> own faces. And not by looking at each other but by looking within
> ourselves. We already look too much alike. It has become a bore.

In the early fifties, a lot of people had complained that the plays
of Shakespeare, Molière, Ibsen, Chekhov, Shaw, and so forth were
not being professionally produced in America. Now these plays were
being produced all over the place, yet somehow the millennium had
not arrived. It was very disheartening. Newly established, newly institutionalized, the virtuous liberals of the resident theaters were
reacting with pangs of self-doubt to the moral challenge issued by
the radical left against all established American institutions. "I don't
want to be doing *Mary, Mary* when the bomb drops," said Jules

Irving of the Actor's Workshop in San Francisco (and later the Repertory Theatre of Lincoln Center), expressing the credo of all serious theater people. But in the face of the bomb, and the other disasters and shames it symbolizes, is it really that much better to be doing Shakespeare instead?

LIVING STAGE

At Arena, one product of this period of challenge is Living Stage, a small improvisational company that works with children. Children in Washington are mostly black; Living Stage is an integrated company (though its director, Robert Alexander, is white), and it represents a way in which Arena can connect with the black community and others not attracted by the regular Arena programming. Living Stage is sponsored by Arena, and has its headquarters there, but it functions independently; Alexander's orientation is very different from Ms. Fichandler's. He is concerned with helping children to release "their own natural creativity" by getting them to improvise with the actors; for this purpose, already written plays are of little use, and the company creates its own material in rehearsal or improvises it on the spot. In 1977 Living Stage appeared at The New Theatre Festival in Baltimore, the annual gathering of experimental companies, where no one would expect to see the regular Arena company.

THE TRAINING PROGRAM

With her own company, Zelda Fichandler fought the dangers of success, of institutionalization, and of despair by keeping things in a state of ferment. In 1965, with money from the Rockefeller Foundation, she started a three-year "experiment in the training and development" of the company, involving

> summer training workshops, when we were free of the rehearsal-production cycle, and . . . during the active season, a teacher of acting technique . . . a teacher of movement, and . . . lecturers, experts in dance, mime, fencing, make-up and the like, consultants and specialists.

At Arena it did not work, as she acknowledges. There just wasn't time.

> A repertory actor performs seven or eight times a week and rehearses every day but one, at the same time that he is learning a role, probing

a role, shopping for make-up, going to costume fittings, posing for publicity shots, appearing on TV guest spots, and hopefully sandwiching in some kind of personal life which now and then includes a nap. Fatigue eventually took over.

And there were further problems with the natural insecurities of the actors, some of whom were reluctant to submit their own ways of doing things to scrutiny and possible revision. Robert Prosky, the company's senior actor, recalls it as "a time of great strife." When the grant money ran out, the training program was dropped, and the great goal of the Ideal Company, a common goal of nearly all the resident theaters, was thereafter pursued by other means. The American Conservatory Theatre in San Francisco has had more success in maintaining an ensemble constantly in training; so have several off-off-Broadway companies that are experimenting with new performance techniques.

REPERTORY

Concurrent with the training program came another experiment in company building: real, regular, rolling, rotating repertory. "Repertory" means, first of all, the aggregate of plays that a theater does. Loosely speaking, any resident theater can call itself a repertory theater, and many do. But most of them produce a series of plays, one after the other, for uninterrupted "straight runs"; this is rather dismissively called the "stock" system. Strictly speaking, "repertory" (also called "true repertory," "alternating repertory," "rotating repertory") is a system whereby two or more productions, given by the same company, alternate on the same stage: *Hamlet* on Monday, *Twelfth Night* on Tuesday, *Hamlet* again on Wednesday, with maybe *Getting Gertie's Garter* at the matinée.

Repertory in this sense is an old dream of many in the resident theater movement. It is the system of the great theaters of Europe —the Comédie Française, the Moscow Art Theatre, the Old Vic—to which our American theaters have looked for inspiration. It was Zelda Fichandler's dream as long ago as her letter to Mac Lowry in 1958, though even then she was well aware of its difficulties:

> Rotating repertory is the method of production that is organic to theater. . . . Its advantages to the actor and the acting company—in terms of developing a role over a long period of time with alternating intervals of playing and gestation; of enriching the performance of

Lear with material derived from playing Algernon [in *The Importance of Being Earnest*] the night previously; of finding the common ground of all "styles" and where they differ, through alternating experience in various periods and with various plays; of knitting performances jointly with one's fellows over long periods of time; and, from the producing director's point of view, in terms of attracting actors to come and to stay because the "nothing-butler role" falls on Tuesday between, perhaps, Macbeth on Monday and Tony Lumpkin [in *She Stoops to Conquer*] on Wednesday instead of for thirty performances in a row—all these advantages are absolutely and without a doubt, entirely persuasive and convincing if what one is after is the very best that Theater can give. . . .

It is less expensive to run a stock theater and it is easier to be successful with it. Stock theater doesn't require the maintenance of as large or as versatile an acting company. It can get away with jobbing-in directors, whereas repertory theater should desirably maintain two directors in residence. Stock theater needs fewer technical people since shows are changed less frequently. It doesn't require extensive storage space to keep simultaneously accessible the sets and costumes for four or more shows. It is easier and cheaper to promote and sell a stock theater since favorable reviews and word-of-mouth can spiral a show into a hit over the scheduled period of its playing and since the theater-going public is conditioned by Broadway to this kind of attendance. And it is easier to maneuver a subscription series and the selling of blocks of tickets to organizations when productions are produced and scheduled in a series. However, it has become quite clear to me . . . that without rotating repertory there can be no first-class and permanent acting company. . . .

And so, nine years later, Arena's 1967–68 season began with a repertory of Shaw's *Major Barbara* and Anouilh's *Poor Bitos*—two tough political plays—and ended with three plays in repertory: *The Tenth Man* by Paddy Chayefsky, *Room Service* by Murray and Boretz (which had saved Arena from bankruptcy in the Hippodrome days), and *The Iceman Cometh* by Eugene O'Neill.

But repertory did not work at the Arena the way it works at the American Conservatory Theatre or the Tyrone Guthrie. "The space didn't lend itself to a constantly changing set," Ms. Fichandler explained later.

It was too expensive to maintain such a large company. We had thirty-five actors on the payroll and some were just acting once a week. The actors enjoyed it, but to the audience it seemed to make very little difference. And it cost us $100,000. Around the theater it's called Fichandler's Folly.

Now and again, Ms. Fichandler still manages to put two or even three plays into repertory for a limited time, but she sadly recognizes that Arena Stage will never be a true full-time repertory theater. She regrets losing the chance that repertory would have provided to keep alive certain "important productions that represent our style and our theater's sense of society"—productions "whose arbitrary abandonment on a particular date smacks always of crime and death." But you have to give up a few dreams over the years.

THE GREAT WHITE HOPE

Even in the repertory season of 1967–68, repertory was suspended for several weeks in the middle of the season to allow for a huge special project: the world premiere of a play by Howard Sackler with nineteen scenes and an integrated cast of sixty-two. *The Great White Hope,* based on the life of the black boxing champion Jack Johnson, was a spectacle, a melodrama, an all-out attempt at a modern classical tragedy, and a serious problem play about racial oppression in this country. It had a magnificent leading role, magnificently played by James Earl Jones. And its black hero had a white mistress, at a time when miscegenation was a subject of even more forbidden fascination than it was ten years ago. The Arena production, directed by Edwin Sherin, was a tremendous success in Washington, moved almost intact to Broadway, won the Pulitzer Prize in 1969, ran two years, and was sold to the movies. Arena had no share in the tremendous profits made by *The Great White Hope* after it left Washington, a source of some bitterness to the Fichandlers, who had put a great deal of work and faith and money into it. But its success was an important moment in the history of modern American theater.

Until the sixties, resident theater, particularly those outside New York, had generally tended to produce new plays reluctantly, out of a sense of duty. Audiences did not want them. And to the agents a regional theater production was often the kiss of death for a new script; after four weeks in Podunk, it was never seen again. *The Great White Hope* proved that a new play could be a hit with a regional theater audience and then go on to be a hit on Broadway. It made resident theaters eager to do new plays, and it made authors and agents more eager to have new plays done outside New York.

Traditionally, theaters outside New York have been dependent on Broadway for many of the new plays they do; from the time of *The Great White Hope*, the traffic has been two-way. *Indians* by Arthur Kopit, *Moonchildren* by Michael Weller (two important American plays), and *Raisin* (the musical version of *A Raisin in the Sun*) have all gone on to Broadway in their Arena productions. *Sticks and Bones* by David Rabe, *That Championship Season* by Jason Miller, the musical *A Chorus Line*, and *For Colored Girls who have Considered Suicide/When The Rainbow is Enuf*, a "choreopoem" by Ntozake Shange, all came to Broadway from the New York Shakespeare Festival, New York's own very distinctive resident theater. *The Shadow Box* by Michael Cristofer, which won the Pulitzer Prize and the Tony Award for Best Play in 1977, had been seen at the Mark Taper Forum in Los Angeles and then at the Long Wharf Theater in New Haven before coming to Broadway. And there are other examples.

No longer can Broadway ignore the resident theaters, or dismiss them as a bunch of arty amateurs. If Broadway once had a virtual monopoly on new plays in the American theater, it is now deeply dependent on work from noncommercial theaters, American and British, to keep its own theaters lit. This is some kind of revolution. And yet the resident theaters seem uncorrupted by it. As yet anyway they have not turned into farm teams or mere places for tryouts. Their work is still done first of all for their own communities.

THE INTEGRATED. COMPANY

In addition to Broadway scouts, *The Great White Hope* attracted another, rather larger, unfamiliar group of spectators to Arena. The District of Columbia has a mainly black population, but before *The Great White Hope*—and after it, when the regular repertory was resumed—Arena played to an almost entirely white audience—not surprisingly, perhaps, since the acting company also was almost entirely white. This was disturbing to Ms. Fichandler, who is more conscious than most of a need to connect the theater to what is going on outside it. And so, with the help of a Ford grant, Zelda Fichandler hired an interracial company for the 1968–69 season—not to do "black plays" or "racial plays" but to perform "a repertory that makes organic sense—that is to say aesthetic sense—to be presented by an interracial company." The season began with *The Threepenny Opera, Six Characters in Search of an Author,* and *King Lear,* in repertory. Ms. Fichandler had high hopes: "The creative casting of Negro and white actors in a repertory selected with that end in mind should make it possible for us to explode the theater event to a dimension that we have rarely experienced. . . ."

But many black actors were not trained to play this kind of repertory; many others preferred to work in all-black companies. The experiment was abandoned, though Ms. Fichandler is still glad to produce a black play (*No Place to be Somebody, Raisin*) when she finds one she likes. When she does, black audiences come; when she doesn't, they don't. The problem of reaching "minority" audiences —of reaching anyone except the white middle class—is one that the resident theaters have never satisfactorily solved.

Act Four: The Kreeger and After

The seventies have been for America at large a decade of retrenchment, or retreat from the inflated assumptions of the sixties. The resident theaters have had to retrench too, here and there, but on the whole it is amazing how little they have suffered: how few theaters have disappeared, how few have drastically curtailed their activities. A few theaters have even been founded in this decade— the Alaska Repertory Theatre in Anchorage, for instance, opened in 1977—and some older theaters have continued to expand.

Ms. Fichandler appears to mark the beginning of every decade with a new auditorium; Arena opened its new Kreeger Theater in January 1971. But this time the new theater adjoins the old, and was built to supplement, not to replace it. As early as 1962, Ms. Fichandler had been talking about a small studio theater for new plays. This eventually grew into the Kreeger (named for David Lloyd Kreeger, who pledged a quarter of a million dollars to aid in its construction), a $1.5 million, 500-seat fan-shaped house, much like a conventional proscenium theater, for plays that would be happier in such a house than in the Arena. In an ordinary year, four plays will be produced in each theater, or perhaps five in the Arena and three in the Kreeger. The Kreeger is also handy for booking in occasional special attractions (Hume Cronyn and Jessica Tandy in short plays by Samuel Beckett, Emlyn Williams as Charles Dickens or Dylan Thomas).

THE TOUR TO THE SOVIET UNION

On September 29, 1973 Arena's forces, sixty-eight strong, set off to play *Our Town* and *Inherit the Wind* in Moscow and Leningrad, under the auspices of the Department of State. American touring companies of *Porgy and Bess* and *My Fair Lady* had preceded them, but Arena was the first American resident company ever to appear in the Soviet Union. The tour was a huge success: sold-out houses, extra performances, flowers thrown on the stage every night. When she came back, Ms. Fichandler told the Women's National Democratic Club that "Arena Stage has just returned from a love affair with the Soviet Union."

The tour seems to have been a moment of special significance in the development of the company's sense of itself. One actor called it "a great unifying experience." Ms. Fichandler said, ". . . it was in the Soviet Union, not in America, that we were recognized, evaluated, and defined on the basis of our real goals and achievements."

Yet in between the performances and the parties with Russian theater people where "the wine flowed like tears, and the tears flowed like wine," several members of the company found time to meet with Soviet Jews, and when these actors got home they publicly urged America to increase its efforts on behalf of Soviet Jewry. One actress brought out with her six short stories by a Soviet dissident writer. A few months later, Arena produced *The Madness of God* by Elie Wiesel, an excoriating account of the plight of Soviet Jews. A year later, Arena presented the American premiere of *The Ascent of Mount Fuji* by Chingiz Aitmatov and Kaltai Mukhamedzhanov, a Soviet play that Ms. Fichandler had seen in Moscow, but a play that raised serious questions about contemporary Soviet society.

Resident theaters, as civic institutions, inevitably come into contact with governments—and that kind of contact can be dangerous. "When you sup with the devil, bring a long spoon." The Russian tour involved Arena Stage with both the United States Department of State and the Soviet Ministry of Culture; yet Arena seems to have avoided being co-opted by either.

The Soviets were evidently encouraged by Arena's success. Arena's tour was the forerunner of a tour to the Soviet Union by the American Conservatory Theater in 1976: this in turn led to a visit to the Soviet Union by representatives of seven American theaters in May

1977, out of which came plans for productions of Soviet plays, staged by Soviet directors, at the Alley Theatre in Houston, the American Conservatory Theatre in San Francisco, and the Tyrone Guthrie Theatre in Minneapolis. It is hard to imagine the Broadway theater participating in this sort of cultural exchange.

"IN THE PROCESS"

The resident theaters are increasingly aware of a responsibility not only to perform new plays but to develop new plays not yet ready for regular public performance. In 1976, with money from the Mellon Foundation, Arena Stage began the "In the Process" series, to stage new plays for small audiences under workshop conditions. After every performance the playwright and the director meet with the audience to discuss what they have seen, and the playwright rewrites on the basis of what he learns about his play. In Ms. Fichandler's words:

> . . . we are giving to a group of plays an environment where every criticism is a loving one, and nothing hangs on the outcome (not reviews, not box office, not monetary rewards, not any leftovers from the success-failure syndrome) except what can be found out in the doing.

The purpose: to "serve 'in the process' of the playwright's finding his or her own voice more surely and deeply."

The "In the Process" performances take place in the Old Vat Room, a cabaret theater space installed in 1975 in the basement alongside the Kreeger, and named in honor of the old, happily remembered theater in the brewery. This room can also be used for full productions of plays that are comfortable on a small stage before a small audience.

THE TONY

The Antoinette Perry Award to Arena in May 1976 was an event of less personal significance to the people who work at Arena than was the tour to the Soviet Union. But it was a landmark in its way: not because the Tony authorities are infallible arbiters of taste, but because the Tonys come from Broadway, from that great though compromised institution that Arena Stage and every other noncommercial theater was founded in reaction against. The nonprofit theaters have not sold out to Broadway; Broadway has sought a truce with them. Broadway needs their help: needs to borrow their plays, their actors, their ideas. Alan Schneider once complained, "Nobody on Broadway seems to know any other theaters exist in the United States." Now they know.

Epilogue: Present and Future

In the mid 1970s resident theaters no longer look so boringly alike as they used to. In San Francisco, the American Conservatory Theatre (ACT) under William Ball's direction goes in for extroverted, swashbuckling versions of popular classics (*Cyrano de Bergerac, The Taming of the Shrew*), acted with plenty of light-footed movement and flash-and-dazzle theatricality by a tightly-knit resident company constantly training toward greater virtuosity. Gordon Davidson of the Mark Taper Forum in Los Angeles is particularly interested in sober, dialectical, documentary political plays (*In the Matter of J. Robert Oppenheimer, The Trial of the Catonsville Nine*), cast from the talent pool attracted to Los Angeles by the movie and television industries. At the Long Wharf Theatre in New Haven, Arvin Brown produces a large number of new British plays (*The Changing Room* by David Storey, *The National Health* by Peter Nichols, both of which went to New York in their Long Wharf productions), and specializes in warm, mellow, finely detailed naturalistic acting. At the Trinity Square Repertory Company in Providence, Adrian Hall stages phantasmagoric extravaganzas for which the text is only a jumping-off point. Yet none of these characterizations is iron-clad; at any given moment you may find a modern realistic play at ACT, a comedy at the Taper, an American play at Long Wharf, a highly verbal British play at Trinity Square. All these theaters—and most of the others—do works from the standard resident theater repertoire: Shakespeare, Molière, Wilde, Shaw, Pirandello, Brecht, Beckett, Pinter, and the best that has come from Broadway and off-Broadway. They also—thanks in good part to the success of *The Great White Hope*—produce new American plays.

ARENA STAGE TODAY

And Arena? Arena Stage lives in a $3.1 million complex of three theater-spaces on the shores of the Potomac River. In 1976–77 it offered a total of thirteen productions between October and June in the Arena, the Kreeger, and the Old Vat Room, at a top price for a single ticket of $7.50. Arena's individuality is hard to define, though not hard to sense. There is something open-ended about it. Partly this is because in most theaters, the producing director or artistic director stages two or three plays a year himself, and sets the company's style by doing so. Zelda Fichandler directs only about one play a season, so her influence can be seen less explicitly. Perhaps, however, it is felt more pervasively, since she has time to be deeply involved with every production, working closely with the director, the designers, and the playwright. She herself says that the theater is all the people who have worked in it, but it was she who hired them all, she who put them together.

Arena's personality has everything to do with the personality of Zelda Fichandler: high-minded, yet very shrewd, but with the shrewdness at the service of the high-mindedness, not the other way around. When you meet her, she may very well be singing to herself, "I'm a ta-may-*ta*," from a number in a show she produced in the Kreeger. She has plenty of charm, and warmth, and even mischief; she is deeply divided about a number of issues, and not afraid to share both sides of her ambivalence. But you would have to be very insensitive not to realize immediately that this woman has a purpose, and even though she subjects that purpose to a constant process of reinvestigation and reformulation, she is not to be turned from it. All these qualities are reflected in her theater.

FOUR CONTINUING THEMES

In the years of Arena Stage since 1950, a number of unresolved themes keep reemerging: the company, the audience, the plays, the money.

The Company—What *is* an acting company; or what, in America, should it/can it be? In 1957 Ms. Fichandler wrote:

> To make the artist shift his foundations, to make his work discontinuous, as is practically the rule of the Broadway commercial theater, is to make him begin his work anew with each effort. The result is not only wearing and discouraging, it is profoundly uncreative; the individual artist needs a permanent base that allows for a continuity of acting and experience to reach the peak of his powers. The permanent acting company is the actor's best friend.

But the actors have not always seen it that way. According to Howard Witt, an actor who left Arena in 1977 after nine years (nine productive years, of which he speaks very warmly):

> There are certain things you have to give up when you come into a regional theater. You have to give up the idea that you're going to become famous, that you're going to become rich, that you're going to be recognized, even in the profession. . . . I have an old saying that my mother had two sons, one joined the Foreign Legion and one went to Arena Stage, and neither was ever heard from again.

Robert Prosky, the company's senior member, is staying with Arena (he has bought a house on Capitol Hill), but he makes ends meet by going to New York every summer to do television commercials.

The temptations of fame and fortune, of Broadway, television, and the movies, are very strong for American actors—even Arena actors. Ms. Fichandler notes that the company of the Sovremmenik Theatre in Moscow has been together since its members came out of drama school in 1957. Arena Stage, on the other hand,

> has already had three acting companies in its history: one that dispersed in the dark year between the Hippodrome and the Old Vat phase; one that split up with the movement of *The Great White Hope* to Broadway (some of those people have since returned); and one that now exists.

In common with most American theaters, Arena has had to redefine the idea of a company to suit the realities of American life and the "nomadic" temperament of the American actor. A company is now often conceived to include not only permanently resident actors, but also those who come and go and return again often enough to feel some identification with the theater. In addition to these two kinds of company actors, of course, there are often actors who are signed for this play or that, and then disappear back to New York, which is still the central casting market. A few theaters have no actors at all on season contracts and cast every production from scratch.

The Arena company is more of a resident company than most. As of May 1977, one actor had been there for nineteen seasons, one for eleven, one for nine, three for six, and three for five. Ms. Fichandler says, not unhappily:

> The company we have now [1976] consists of a solid nucleus of fifteen actors surrounded by the equivalent number who come and go; surrounded by a dozen or so young actors culled from our relationships

with various training institutions, especially Boston University. It is a company with a unified approach to work (achieved through the selection of actors, the rehearsal process itself, and the careful choosing of directors), common standards of what is good acting and what is not, and a generally accepted belief that the art of the theater is intimately linked to society at large.

Artistic standards at the resident theaters generally are much higher than they used to be. Older actors have learned by experience how to play the resident-theater repertory, or perhaps directors are learning by experience how to cast it. Young actors are emerging from the drama schools with a much broader training than they used to get. Budgets have gone up; not so often do you now see an apple-cheeked boy play an old man because no mature actor would work for the salary attached to the part. The loosening of the company ideal has brought some good effects: fewer actors, needed in Play A and Play C, are miscast in Play B because they are around and have to be used. Robert Prosky, after nineteen years at Arena, says that it is good to have new faces passing through; it keeps the resident actors on their toes, prevents things from getting too ingrown and incestuous.

The Audience—Some theater people are contemptuous of their audiences; some are condescending; some are content to give them what they want. Ms. Fichandler is none of those things; her attitude is a complicated, ambivalent one. She likes to tell a story about the great English actor, Sir Henry Irving, who is told during an intermission that "They don't like it." "Well, isn't that a pity," says Sir Henry, "because it's what they're going to get." She wants to serve her audience, but on her own terms:

> For while a theater is a public art and belongs to its public, it is an art before it is public, and so it belongs first to itself, and its first service must be self-service. A theater is part of its society. But it is a part which must remain apart since it is also chastiser, rebel, lightning rod, redeemer, irritant, codifer, and horse-laughter.

And yet, "The only real criterion for judging a production is the power of the impression it makes on the audience."

And who is this audience? Arena has kept expanding, doing more plays for longer runs, but attendance has held steady at about 88-90 percent of capacity, which in 1976–77 amounted to a total attendance of more than 200,000 people a year. But at the same time there were 16,750 subscribers and seven plays on the subscription series, which means that out of that 200,000-plus attendance, 117,250 —or about half—was presumably accounted for by only 16,750 separate people, unless subscribers are in the habit of giving away or selling their tickets. Arena has a prosperous audience of government workers, lawyers, doctors, academics, and so on; but this is neither a sizable fraction nor a general cross-section of the population of greater Washington. In common with nearly all resident theaters, Arena has not discovered how to attract a steady audience beyond the well-educated middle class.

The Plays—And what kind of plays does Arena present to its audience? It is an eclectic repertory, but Ms. Fichandler does not simply make balanced seasons, pacifying the audience with Noel Coward this month in the hope that it will sit still for Brecht or Beckett next month. She has never been afraid to do plays that all the other resident theaters were doing or had done, but does not do plays merely *because* other theaters are doing them.

She said to her stockholders back in 1955:

> Probably we will continue to do our best work within the general style of modern realism, since that is the dominant style of today and the majority of our actors are most at home in it. But we must continue and by all means enlarge upon our efforts to discover the correct stylistic idioms for doing before a modern audience the plays of Shakespeare, the Greeks, Shaw, the Restoration playwrights, Molière.

There is an ambivalence here: "We feel most at home with modern realism; but we feel an obligation to Shakespeare, the Greeks, and so on." Nowadays Ms. Fichandler is more comfortable with her own preferences than she used to be. She admits (so does everyone else around the theater) that Arena is not at its best in Shakespeare. She has never produced a Greek play; she has not figured out how a Greek play should be done at Arena. She does not do Restoration comedy; it does not interest her. So modern realism it is, not entirely, but mostly. Modern realism, of course, is the basic style of Broadway, but the Broadway realists have traditionally confined themselves to new plays of contemporary American life. Arena's repertory includes these, but also ventures beyond them in a number of directions. Ms. Fichandler is particularly interested in plays from Central and Eastern Europe, not only Chekhov but Gorki and others. So she has partly, though not entirely, fulfilled her 1955 aspiration "to break away from the currently rather limited stylistic range of the American theater." It is the nonprofit theater as a whole—the resident theaters *and* off-off-Broadway—that has accomplished that task.

Arena's ideological position is, generally speaking, one of worried liberalism (if that is not a redundancy nowadays), but it is open to various points of view. Ms. Fichandler produced *The Great White Hope* and *Indians*, two strong attacks against American complacency. She took *Our Town* and *Inherit the Wind* to the Soviet Union: two reaffirmations of American tradition. After she got back, as has been noted, she produced *The Madness of God* by Elie Wiesel, about the plight of Soviet Jewry, and *The Ascent of Mount Fuji* by Chingiz Aitmatov and Kaltai Mukhamedzhanov, a modern Soviet play critical of the scars left from the Stalin era. She has also presented *What the Butler Saw* by Joe Orton and *A History of the American Film* by Christopher Durang, two comedies of camp nihilism. The criterion seems to be not *what* is said, but *whether* something is said.

Arena has a reputation as a serious theater, but Zelda Fichandler has no compunctions about comedy, even farce:

> . . . I think there is a place for *Three Men on a Horse* alongside *Oedipus Rex* in the repertory of an American theater for reasons of its theatrical exuberance, the deliciousness of its design and its sly, askew glance at the American way of killing the goose that lays the golden egg by not knowing when enough's enough. . . .
>
> I think one must guard against uppishness. Plays like *Room Service* and *You Can't Take It with You* and *Three Men on a Horse* are not "trashy comedies."
>
> At any rate, I produced *Three Men on a Horse* and *You Can't Take It with You* (and over a hundred other plays from the past including Molière, Giraudoux, Shaw, Shakespeare, Pirandello, Brecht and O'Neill to an average of 90 percent capacity over the years) for the life that is in them, and, particularly, for the life that, like a tuning fork, sets off and responds to vibrations that are in the air today.

The Money—And how is all this to be paid for, since it cannot pay for itself? Says Ms. Fichandler:

> People have such faith that Arena Stage will continue. . . . But there is really no guarantee. Where is it written that American society is capable of identifying Arena's function on its own terms or, even if it should identify it, of giving the theater tangible support so that it can enlarge upon its achievements. Our situation is not unique.

In 1976–77 Arena's budget was just under $2 million. Its earned income was a little over $1.1 million, leaving an earnings gap—the highest in its history, thanks to inflation—of about $800,000 to be made up by gifts and grants. Arena is generally conceded to be a well-run theater; there is not much fat on that budget. The Ford Foundation, Arena's ace in the hole for decades, is withdrawing from operating support of the resident theaters; its last grant to Arena terminated in 1977. Fund raising from the business community is difficult in Washington, where the only sizable industry is the federal government, and national corporations appear to limit their support of theater in Washington to the Kennedy Center. State governments are increasingly active in funding the arts, but Washington, D.C., has no state government, and its local government is impoverished.

Since 1966 the National Endowment for the Arts, an arm of the federal government, has steadily increased its contributions to the resident theaters. As Ford Foundation support diminishes, the government becomes, like it or not, more and more the necessary, primary patron of the performing arts in America. For 1977–78 the Endowment allocated to Arena $200,000 or 10 percent of the budget. Tom Fichandler thinks this is much too low a percentage; at least one-third of Arena's budget will have to come from the government, he insists. And Zelda Fichandler says: ". . . the first question remains the last: exactly how important are our artistic institutions, in a real way, to those who formulate political policy and determine appropriations?" That is the question, all right—the question of survival. And not only for Arena.

THE LAST QUESTION

Beyond that, however, is yet one more question: does Arena—do the resident theaters—*deserve* to survive? The "subtext," as actors say, of this chapter is meant to be an emphatic "Yes!" to that question, but the question needs to be asked.

Arena represents the best in American resident theater. Its productions have been admired in Moscow, New York, Washington. Ms. Fichandler said in 1955, talking big, "It is not out of the question that if the potential promised by the record is realized, Arena Stage could become a theatrical landmark of not only national but international significance as well." And it has come to pass. Yet for all its excellence, Arena is still bound by certain limitations of the resident theater movement as a whole.

In her moods of skepticism and discouragement, Zelda Fichandler is a brilliant devil's advocate:

> Among us [in the American resident theaters] there has been no Antoine rushing into his makeshift theater with his mother's dining room furniture and real meat from the butcher down the street, discovering the breathtaking reality of an actor daring to turn his back on the audience. No Stanislavski and Danchenko putting together—out of an amateur theater and some acting classes, and out of the work of a genius playwright whose plays demanded a different vision—an entirely new system of behavioral acting based on the physiology of the human body and connected to allied biological and physical research of the day. And where is our Molière? Inventing plays to act in for himself and his troupe, elevating and freezing into art his own interior experiences, building a dramatic tradition on the shoulders of the improvisational *commedia* form, mocking himself, mocking his age, mocking his fellow man and still catering to and pleasing both? Yeats and Lady Gregory and O'Casey and the Abbey, making a theater of protest after their own style, making a literature to help make a nation: we have not made one of these. . . . Who is our Bertolt Brecht, theoretician, transformer of form, social architect, director-dramaturge-dramatist-institutional head in one mind and body?

What this means is that the resident theaters have not yet produced any geniuses. True. But when the geniuses appear, there will at least be theaters for them to work in and audiences for them to work for. And in the meantime there is plenty of work worth doing that can be done without them. And when you think about it, Ms. Fichandler's litany of pioneers, of movers and shakers, is an evocation of the possibilities of theater, and therefore an argument *for* its survival in whatever form.

Resident theater is not radical theater, either aesthetically or politically. It feels guilty for not being more radical than it is, but it has taken as its task to address the educated middle classes in terms that the educated middle classes understand, though it tries to broaden those terms as best it can. Zelda Fichandler says, "I've nothing against the middle classes. I'm a member of them. This is a middle-class country."

There is one way of phrasing the last question that makes it especially disquieting: in these times, is it justified to spend government money—your money, my money—on a form of art that reaches such a tiny percentage of the population? (This is, of course, a question that extends beyond Arena, beyond the resident theaters, to the subsidized performing arts in general.) Well, the percentage cannot be increased if the art does not exist. What it comes down to is whether the theater is important. The resident theaters are trying to realize the theater's potential for being important to the people it serves. Zelda Fichandler has this to say about the *nature* of this importance:

> Theater is educational in that it teaches man to recognize, by means of the events acted out before him, his own human condition, to understand that condition and to have compassion for it. Theater is educational in that it causes a change to be brought about within the nature of man, so that he becomes more knowledgeable, more sensitive, more responsive, more enlightened, more aware. . . .
>
> I think it [theater] has an opportunity to reach deep places, and its journey to that inner place is very inexpensive compared to that journey to the moon, and while no one can measure it, it has the opportunity to be equally rich in implications. . . .
>
> To think isn't enough. You have to think feelingly. To know what those thoughts mean feelingly. You can't change the way people think by talking to them. So you put them through an experience and hope they come out a little different from the way they were before. It's not to make them feel good about themselves, but to make them *ask* about themselves.
>
> Money is well-spent to create sensitive people capable of transforming their world a little bit by knowing about themselves.

7

The Individual Artist

Training and Career Development

Introduction

This chapter was edited by W. McNeil Lowry from the transcript of a symposium held in New York on May 3, 1977. The participants:

Robert Bloom, oboist, is Professor Emeritus of the Yale School of Music. Currently a member of the Major Faculty at Juilliard, he performs with the Bach Aria Group.

Paul Freeman is Conductor-in-Residence of the Detroit Symphony and Artistic Director of Columbia Records' *Black Composers Series*, a national program of recordings of Afro-American composers. Before going to Detroit he was Associate Conductor of the Dallas Symphony.

Earle Gister, Director of the Davis Center for the Performing Arts at City College, New York, was for many years head of the Department of Drama at Carnegie-Mellon University.

Stuart Hodes, after a career as a dancer and choreographer in modern dance, is now Professor of Dance at New York University.

Robert Joffrey is founder and Artistic Director of the Joffrey Ballet, director of the American Ballet Center and Co-President (with Yuri Grigorovich) of the International Dance Committee of the International Theatre Institute.

Robert Lindgren, after careers as a dancer with the Ballet Russe de Monte Carlo and the American Ballet Theatre, is currently Dean of the School of Dance at the North Carolina School of the Arts and Director of the North Carolina Dance Theater.

John Ludwig, who helped to found the Minnesota Opera Company and was manager of the Spring Opera in San Francisco, is now Director of the National Opera Institute in Washington.

Alan Schneider, an active theater director in the United States and abroad over the last generation, is now Director of the Juilliard Theater Center, an advanced conservatory training program for theater artists.

Douglas Turner Ward, playwright, actor, and director, is founder and still Artistic Director of the Negro Ensemble Company.

The members of the symposium were given five principal questions:.

1. What has been the institutional pattern for training and apprenticeship for each category of the performing artist? Has the pattern shifted significantly in some of these categories? How have training and apprenticeship programs outside educational institutions been planned and supported?
2. What is the point on the career ladder for an artist in your field that presents the greatest obstacles to be overcome? What changes could be made or programs planned which could help alleviate these obstacles?
3. Do young performing artists with professional potential have it better or worse than did young artists twenty years ago?
4. What mechanisms exist for identification (or audition) of young performers in your field who might not otherwise be visible? Has the existence of these mechanisms had any effect on the standards of university or conservatory programs?
5. What has been the influence of artist unions on professional training, apprenticeship, and career development in your field?

Mr. Lowry, who chaired the discussion, asked the members of the symposium to begin with individual statements from their own experience. He then invited comments on these statements from the other participants before proceeding more systematically with the agenda.

Three General Principles

Mr. Ludwig: Three relationships seem to me to create the fundamental situations which will govern the answers to your questions as they relate to opera.

First is the relationship of supply and demand. As one considers whether or not artists have all the opportunities one would want for training and career development, it seems to me at any rate that the answer relates directly to the extent to which the public wants the thing that the artist does. If the public wants a lot of opera, one is more likely to have a greater wealth of programs for training people to do the desired thing and a larger number of opportunities. This seems simplistic, but it also seems to me to be a fundamental relationship.

There's another relationship which is perhaps more peculiar to opera than to other art forms. Opera is a multiple art form combining several other art forms. Specifically, it is a combination of music and theater in proportions and under conditions which have been a subject of debate amongst opera people from the word go.

I think the fact that opera is this kind of amalgam has very serious implications when one talks about training of artists, and later I want to relate that to supply and demand.

The third relationship that came into my head was the relationship between the capacity to perform and the physical maturity of the individual. I believe that it is fair to say that individuals develop the capacity to perform in different art forms at different levels of physical maturity. I would say that there is no question that one can mature physically as a dancer before one can mature physically as a singer. Many singers don't mature physically until they are well into their late twenties or thirties.

This relationship also affects the length of time it takes to train, the time in which training can profitably take place. It governs a pattern of training and employment vis-à-vis the life span of the individual which not only affects the extent to which the individual can train, but also affects the career opportunities available.

So to me, these three ratios, relationships, whatever they may be, have seemed to be key points in considering the kind of training available to young artists in opera and the employment opportunities available to them.

Mr. Freeman: I was just recalling this morning an experience of ten years ago when Mr. Lowry and I had a meeting on minorities in classical music. And I think this is an area certainly that we would want to touch upon in our discussions, because the training of the minority musicians has certain psychological implications and demands which, so frequently, may be overlooked. I shall deal with that later in a specific way.

I think I should like to make just a few broad comments, as I am most anxious to see the direction in which we are going. But to speak about the symphony orchestra musician, per se, I would simply like to touch upon two points.

The Soloist versus the Ensemble Player

One has to do with the training of the soloist versus that of the ensemble player. I think if one considers that the musician almost becomes a musician not by choice, and that he must start at a very early age, it is impossible to become a professional symphony orchestra musician without having started before choosing one's profession. In surveying the development of the orchestra musician, one has to bear in mind that the child becomes special in his family and becomes more or less a prima donna. Then the child becomes special in the educational institution, be it private or public school. Then arises the problem of competition as he or she moves into the more specialized institution of the conservatory.

Unless the child is also special in the conservatory, it is not likely that he will succeed to a great degree in the profession. So there is a great deal of pressure over the years placed upon the emerging orchestral musician, not unlike that in some other disciplines. Ironically, however, through all of these years of being special, one is usually special as a *soloist*, as opposed to being special as an *ensemble player*, which he must become.

I think there is not enough attention given throughout the years of training to the psychological preparation for this participation as an ensemble player. For so much of his life, regardless of the instrument, even be it tuba, the student has been featured as a soloist.

The Avocational Musician

It is also interesting that we have so many nonprofessional orchestras which contain musicians who have music as an *avocation*, which are in fact better than some of the professional orchestras abroad. Now this brings about a special climate as it relates to the preparation of the artist, if he can be called "artist" in a situation in which he functions without receiving his livelihood therefrom. (In so many communities this is a necessity in order to make a symphony orchestra work.) And, I am wondering in my own mind how to segregate the two, the "professional" artist as opposed to the "avocational" artist, many of whom are as good as some people who are earning their keep as full-time professionals.

I think this is a very interesting relationship considering what is happening throughout the country in the public schools, and I think this is something we might want to touch upon. In so many centers throughout the nation, the first thing that is cut from the budget is the arts, even before sports, and in some instances *because* of sports. The result is that a great deal of attention is given to high level training, the conservatory, and professional jobs. But what about 1985? What about 1990? We are already beginning to feel the effects in many large urban areas in this country. Many young people do not have the advantages of musical training. Will this ultimately affect the supply of potential professionals? I think this is a very serious and challenging question which the nation must face up to rather soon.

The Special Problem of Dance

Mr. Joffrey: Dance, I feel, is perhaps the least understood of the performing arts. Parents have very little knowledge of what is required in the training of the dancer. The public schools give very little attention to dance. There is art appreciation and music appreciation. But when one brings up dance, it remains a big question mark. Parents most often do not have the background to decide upon a good teacher, how long the training should be, or at what age the training should begin. So there is a very large problem of educating the public if the parents are to have the knowledge to help their children.

We have music in church, we have music in so many other ways, but there is so little dance in which the family can participate. Furthermore, classical dancing is very new to our country. Our oldest school, perhaps our most distinguished school, the School of American Ballet, started in the 1930s. A great deal has had to be accomplished in a very short period of time.

The High School of Performing Arts began in the late 1940s.

Many of the training schools in America are still commercial studios and that is an enormous problem. The dancer is faced with deciding to stay in his own community or travel to a larger city where he can receive adequate training. Who is going to pay for that? At what age does he make the jump? How will he obtain his general education along with his dance training? It is an extremely difficult problem.

I think when we look at the fact that the Bolshoi School has celebrated its two hundredth year, and our best and most famous school started in 1933, we see the enormous amount of work that must be accomplished for us to have the standard of dancing that we need.

Mr. Gister: I am already stimulated by what has been said by the three who have preceded me. I have a page of notes already that I would like to get at.

Confusion about the Actor's Craft

My principal concern is theater. Although I agree with Mr. Joffrey that when we consider an art as perceived by the audience, dance probably is the least understood of all the arts, I think that by the same token people who perceive and look at theater are equally ill-equipped to ascertain the skills and the techniques required of the performer. The enactment of dramatic actions is viewed in terms of its being realistic or naturalistic. The more real or natural it appears, the better it is perceived to be, and therefore we get a confusion in the public as to what constitutes good acting.

This complicates the question of training, particularly at the very young age levels, where I don't think we know what to do at all, in terms of how to prepare young people for lives as performers in the theater. Certainly, nothing exists in the grade schools. Very little that is decent exists in the secondary levels of training, where the major way in which training is handled is to put on plays. This simply reinforces some very bad notions about what it is to act, or what is required to realize that thing called a dramatic event or a play.

At least in dance, if you can't move and use space properly and have a whole sense of tension, form, shape, you don't even try it. You don't even get up and put your foot on the stage before a public. But in theater, there are all kinds of people who are willing to put their feet and their emotions and everything else on the stage before they are ready.

Audiences in this country have no sound criteria for evaluating performances in the theater. It is left to "I liked it," or "I didn't like it." Personal preference substitutes for well-informed reasons for appreciating or making distinctions between what two individual performers may bring to an enactment.

The Recent Improvement

I think that at the postsecondary level we are moving out of this stage of confusion into a little enlightenment, at least over the last ten or fifteen years. Does the young performing artist with potential have it better or worse than young artists had it twenty years ago? I think they indeed have it better, insofar as they have available to them many more opportunities at the college or post-secondary level to seek training as part of normal educational process.

There are now, offhand, twenty schools that I would not hesitate recommending to students. Twenty years ago I don't think I could have named four. So that there has been a good development in that respect. Some of those schools have now formed themselves into the League of Professional Theater Training Programs (I was, incidentally, instrumental in getting the League started) to bring trainers together and to formulate some principles of training that would serve as guidelines. The League has increased, for instance, the possibility of identification of talent, because these schools have gone out into much more of the country to try to identify talent through immediate contact.

The Obstacle of the First Job

However, I would like to go to the question of the places in the career ladder where artists find their greatest obstacles. The greatest obstacle is still the first job, how to get the first job, no matter how well prepared you may be for it. I don't think that has changed drastically in the last twenty years, even though we have gone through a fantastic change relative to the number of acting jobs available in the country. We now have resident theaters across the nation. We had only a very few twenty years ago. But in their early years some of the resident theaters provided a kind of continuing education for young performers. They developed acting companies rather than jobbing in actors on a show-by-show basis, which is what is happening now. And the sheer fact of a group of actors staying together for a year or two provided a system of development that was essential to the young person coming out of training. The only company I know of now where this goes on systematically is the American Conservatory Theatre, where actual classwork was built into this producing theater from inception. The concept created all kinds of problems in the beginning, but now that they have years of experience under their belts it works out beautifully for some actors.

The Drain at Mid-Career

The other place on the ladder where there seems to be a great obstacle is mid-career, for a number of reasons. After actors get their first few years in the theater, there are obviously the dry times, and during those times they seek other ways of employment—making commercials, for instance. That may become so lucrative that many of them don't go back, or they try to expand their experiences through film. They get trapped out in Los Angeles in the sun, and it starts to lull them into a kind of complacency. They find it difficult to get back to the rigors of New York or of the professional theaters across the country.

I think we lose a huge amount of talent for live theater in this country through the related media of television and film. I think it is a problem that has to be confronted, because the drain is going to continue to the point where the theater could be seriously damaged. Our best young writers, for instance, will write for television and film because of the greater financial remuneration.

The Influence of the Entertainment Media

Mr. Ward: I'd just like to ramble a little, addressing my remarks primarily to the actor. I think, in our field, the question of training is vague and diffuse in that we live in a society which really places a premium upon entertainment, and there are so many commercial outlets where the question of training is not significant. The whole field is affected by these amorphous standards or lack of standards. In the most lucrative performing outlets there is really no particular demand or need for the trained artist. A recognizable figure, a football player in many instances, can very often become a star. What is most visible to youth around the country is the presence of the "star"; and in many instances the aspirations of these young people may have nothing to do with understanding that there is any acquired craft or skill involved in acting. And why should there be? When over a week's period of time you look at television, it seems that most of the performers involved do not necessarily have to know anything about the craft of acting.

This situation is the source of many of our problems—the society we live in and the values we have to contend with. In my experiences I know that in dealing particularly with young actors I have almost wanted to quit, because more than half of these people have merely declared themselves to be part of a profession or a vocation. In some instances they don't even have the minimum background that would lead them realistically to consider themselves actors.

When we first started the Negro Ensemble Company I used to wonder whether it was just us blacks, because of our "deprived background," but as I went along I found the situation applied to white actors as well as black actors. Sometimes actors picking up a script lacked the simple ability to read the text, and the script would emerge as a foreign language.

As far as acting goes, there is no clear standard, there is no understanding of craft and skill and their relationship to the discipline. Consequently, we have a professional acting community which runs the gamut from A to Z. You will find the accomplished actor, the craftsman, the skilled performer many times existing on a lesser economic scale than the untalented, the personality or star performer who functions in the field with just enough amount of skill to make a commercial or appear on television.

Lack of Education

In training actors, the first requirement relates to general education. Many lack a solid general education starting from grade school. We do not have a general educational system which puts very much value upon some of the rudiments that actors need. I have often thought that in comparison to, let's say Britain, even their bad actors have something on us when it comes to understanding words, how you can use words, how you can make words "act" for you. To spit is to spit, and they will make the spit spit. An American actor will often act in between the lines. He wants to do that which is do-able, but to ignore the word itself—its sense, its sound, its texture. From an early age, the question of general education is one of the basic sources of our problem.

The Varying Standards of Actor Training

Mr. Gister referred to the quality of specialized education. But even by the time you get to college or drama school, I'm not so sure that there are quality standards of measurement. One can put up a shingle in New York City and start an acting school. I have seen people who claim to be actors start a school. And I'm very cynical about assessing this acting instruction because, in the first place, if I know they could not themselves act, there is no evidence that would lead me to think that they could "teach" acting. I know about the universities, but in traveling around I've seen university departments which didn't seem to be any great shakes either.

I think we come down to the final question: once you've had the training, then what do you do with it? How do you consistently grow and develop? Are there avenues and outlets to continue to grow and develop? There comes a time in an actor's life when he might stay in school for the rest of his life and do five-minute scenes, which will be of no value to him, because suddenly to confront a three-hour play and sustain a characterization has nothing to do with five-minute scenes in a class.

The Radical Changes in Dance

Mr. Lindgren: I think, perhaps, of all the performing arts, the dance has had the most tremendous growth. Those of you who are familiar, perhaps, with The Ford Foundation's concentration on dance know what that did. It really changed the whole look at the dancer. It changed the whole look at dance training in America. It is not so many years ago that there were in the United States really only two dance companies, one a domestic company that was foreign dominated, and one completely a foreign company. Today in New York we have three major dance companies, the New York City Ballet, American Ballet Theater, and the Joffrey, and the lesser ones, the Eliot Feld, plus the best modern dance companies in the world, Martha Graham and others.

What we have done in dance is unique, in that we have started from almost nowhere. We have had to create a whole sense of dance. I think by nature we're dancing people. We always have liked to dance, we feel dancing. How you get young people interested in dance, really, doesn't seem to have been a problem. It seems there have always been young people who want to dance, whether it be a sugarplum fairy or swan queen or something else. The idea that they wanted to dance was always there. But then a sophistication came in when some of the early dancers left the centers, left New York, left the major companies and went out to the regions and decided to start something.

These people were the ones who really first organized training into the first decent system, instead of having the tap, baton, elocution kind of dancing school. The training was now centered on dancing, and people began to want and expect good training. Companies were traveling around the country, and young people felt this was what they wanted to make their careers in. These young trainees have had much more selection in good training, perhaps, than in some of the other arts, in music or drama. I think that what they have produced has shown the quality of dance training in America. We do still have a problem in how to reach their parents. Why should children want to be dancers? Where is the career offering for them? What is the potential? What happens? Because unlike some other arts, dance is still a youth-oriented art form. Perhaps that's one of the reasons we have been able to attract so many young people. It is something people can do when very young and be involved in and organized, whereas in the other art fields perhaps it comes in later development. By the time the dancer is in his late thirties or forties, his career is over. So we have a different problem. What happens to all those people? Where do they go in our society? They cannot all become teachers.

The Spread of Opportunities

I think we have created tremendous job opportunities. We have regional ballet companies besides the major ones that provide lots of opportunities. We have smaller dance ensembles. We have, I think, developed regional dance to the nth degree; it almost covers this country like a blanket. Everywhere you go, there is dance. The cream rises to the top.

The best talents will always be attracted to the major companies and obviously to New York. That's a problem, because many of the young people don't want to spend their lives in New York. But still this is where not only the major companies are but really the major audiences. I guess I mean the difference between a sophisticated and an unsophisticated audience, the amount of dance you can see in the New York area. Do other audiences really understand the significance of choreography in dance? The meaning of some of the works the choreographer is doing?

The Perception of Audiences

It is very difficult, because they have nothing to relate to. There is not much literature that you can read. You really have to go and see ballet to understand it, or you don't. I think that in order for people to understand more what dance is, more must be done in the education of the audience. Somebody may come and see a ballet like "Les Sylphides"; it may mean nothing to them except people jumping around, in pretty white dresses, but it means something. But if a ballet has something of a deeper meaning, psychologically or socially, people are not quite sure how they should take it. How to make people understand that dancing is just another way of communication through the arts?

I think this is an area of education that perhaps should happen in the schools, along with training in dance. You just can't give everybody steps and exercises to do and say, "Are you learning how to dance?" I think the appreciation of dance, either as art or as entertainment, is part of our social life. Not everybody likes a baseball game, either, the first time he or she sees one. It may be boring, but when someone explains it to you, you understand it more.

I think the schools might treat it as something not quite so sacrosanct, but something that is much more human. I think most people who practice the so-called "arts" never think of themselves as "artists." But on the outside it is sometimes the label placed on "the arts" that keeps people away. They are a little bit frightened of it. I certainly think that often the word "ballet" is a very unfortunate word. If we had some other word that would describe what we do, I think it might help people understand it.

Mr. Schneider: My first job was in a university, teaching acting and directing; and toward the end of my career I seem to have drifted back to the problem of how to train actors and, to some extent, directors. I have certain fundamental attitudes and prejudices, and I think at the beginning I should just share a few of them with you.

Training and the Theater Institution

I believe that training in the theater is specifically affected, usually adversely, by the nature of our values and the structure of our society. I want to be very specific about that. I feel that training too often becomes an end in itself, rather than a means. Training for the actor, of the actor, seems to me to be related directly to what happens in the theater, in the institution of theater.

When I was at Catholic University at the beginning of my career, I used to talk about the idea that a school should not so much have a theater as that a theater should have a school. It seems to me that the whole idea of training should always be related to a practicing institution, an institution with an artistic attitude, an artistic continuity, and some relationship to the community. I don't think it's an accident when we talk about Mr. Balanchine and Mr. Kirstein having changed the American dance. They changed it because they were training dancers for a specific institution, and that institution, following on their training, changed the dance. I have always been a believer in institutions in the theater, and I've always felt that training should be part of, connected to, related to, an institution. That is my first prejudice, and I don't think I've so much changed as simply been solidified in that view. And my work at Juilliard at this point is specifically connected to an institution, that is, a theater institution or the creation of a theater institution, and not simply training in a vacuum.

Defining the Art

My second prejudice, I guess, and it is connected, is that I'm not sure that we can just train people without constantly defining the nature of the art itself. Even in my relatively short time in the theater, the very nature of acting and directing has changed. It has changed fundamentally several times. It has changed peripherally a dozen times. What is "acting"?

Again, I have to go back to my own situation. Mr. Lowry has asked us to talk first from our own experience. The reason I am at Juilliard today is that for the first time in my experience I see an opportunity for training actors not just in some more organized way, but in a way which has to do with what I consider acting *to be*; the process not simply of being oneself on stage but becoming someone else, being expressive in a variety of styles, being able to play in a variety of theatrical periods. For the first time, in a sense, I feel that acting training is doing what musical training has always done. It is teaching people not only to doodle or to improvise or to play contemporary music, but to be able to play classical music, in this case classical theater, not only for the sake of being classical actors but for the sake of being better contemporary actors. For most of my life in the theater, I watched a kind of acting training that consisted of telling people, showing people, pushing people to be the best possible waitress or the best possible taxi driver. But I have always wanted actors actually capable of dealing not only with language but with *any* kind of behavior on stage, other than their own behavior or contemporary behavior or colloquial behavior.

The whole idea of training actors for classical roles seems to me to be a stage not only forward but different from what has been done before. I think that until American actors can play the classics, they will never be able to play the contemporary playwrights as well as they might. That's another prejudice on my part.

The Importance of Apprenticeship

I believe very strongly in the performing arts within an apprenticeship system. I do not think that training means just classroom. I do not think that training means just a school or something apart from the actual work itself. I think that actors must apprentice in theaters. I am sorry that Actors Equity abolished the journeyman category. I am all in favor of internship programs, or call it whatever you want, apprentice, intern journeyman, young company, anything at all. I think it is essential for people to have the opportunity to apprentice.

I don't know whether the director is considered a performing artist in this discussion, but I have made it a practice over the last thirty years of my life always to have a young director as my assistant, whether I've been able to pay him, or the institution I work for to pay him, or whether he just comes and works for me for nothing. I have given twenty or thirty directors an apprenticeship in directing, and a lot of them have gone on and taken jobs away from me later (which has occasionally made me wonder). Nevertheless, it seems to me that in the arts it is essential to make apprenticeship possible, rather than just to assume a kind of training period and then a professional period. I wish that the medieval craftsman apprentice system were more widespread in our field.

The Absence of Continuity

It is sad for me to end on a joke, which you may know, about the five stages of the creative artist in America, but it is true and I do want to end with it. These are the five. The first stage is very simply: Who is Alan Schneider? The second is: I want Alan Schneider (or Robert Joffrey or Marlon Brando or Al Pacino or Vanessa Redgrave). The third stage is: I want somebody like Alan Schneider (or Mr. X) but I don't want Schneider because I've already seen him enough. (That's that middle stage that Earle was talking about, when nobody wants Mr. X or Ms. X because they've already had too much exposure.) The fourth stage is: Whatever happened to Alan Schneider (or Mr. or Ms. X)? And the fifth stage is: Who is Mr. X or Ms. X? Who *was* Mr. X?

Unfortunately, all of that is too true, and it is my serious, sincere, passionate dedication to make it not so funny or not so apt any more. I'm really concerned about keeping Mr. X or Ms. X or even Alan Schneider employed as an artist in an institution with continuity and growth and appreciation at various stages of his development.

I think it is essential to the training process that we have more institutions, more opportunities, more theaters, more connection between theater and training, and better ways of breaking from the training period to the professional period.

Mr. Lowry: I would like now to start again to see if you have a comment, a disagreement, a modification you want to make of some point of view one of the others has advanced. If you do not have that to do now, you will pass, so that we shall get that much more quickly to a general discussion.

Mr. Ludwig: I think, in general, I would end up simply seconding a lot of statements that have been made, which is unnecessary and a waste of time. One general idea that has occurred to me throughout all this, one theme that comes back again and again, is not about training artists, it's about training the audiences. And while I wouldn't for a moment say we don't have problems that need to be solved in training artists, I note with interest the recurrence of the theme that an underlying problem is the need to train audiences.

Classical Music and Television

Mr. Freeman: I have to say that I have several pages of notes as well. But one area which I would like to have some expression about at a later stage, since we are speaking about audience development, is why we have not been able to utilize the most accessible form of exposure for classical music, namely television. In this regard, I address myself to the detachment of the professionals in music from the professionals in the public communications media. I think until that gap is bridged, we shall still suffer from much mediocre television. How can we capitalize on this in such a way as to make it a viable force for the arts?

Exposure to Dance

Mr. Joffrey: I think one of the major unsolved difficulties is how can we show the people around the country the best possible dance that exists? We played Detroit last year, and it was the first time in ten years that a major company had played that city. And I think that's a very serious problem. How many people have seen "Agon," outside a few critics in America? And that is a problem that I think the dance world must face, because one realizes that we are not educating enough of the people in the things that are happening in dance. When one plays Missoula, Montana, one sees how

little people know of what is happening in dance. And we have
so few publications, mainly only *Dance News* and *Dance Magazine.*
And there are very few magazines and books one will find in
libraries in universities that will help enlighten dancers and help
educate the audiences.

Mr. Lowry: I think we need to decide whether the last two topics
raised by Mr. Freeman and Mr. Joffrey are directly related to the
question of training and career development or whether they are
related to the broader question Mr. Ludwig wanted to throw in
about the development of audiences.

If we have mediocre television in the presentation of classical
music, is this going to affect the interest of young people in becoming trained in music? Is it going to miss opportunities with the
audience, and in the larger area of the whole society will make for
less understanding and therefore fewer resources, because there will
be no strong motivation to support the arts, including training in
the arts? Are we relating this question or leaving it separate?

Mr. Freeman: Actually, I suppose, in dealing with classical music
and television, this is almost exclusively restricted to public television with the exception of the recent New York Philharmonic
presentation à la Bernstein. What we have for the most part is the
live concert rather than the television presentation. We were mentioning job opportunities, we were mentioning the degree to which
a person who is trained can be considered an artist. Now, how we
cut across it and how we define it for the purposes of this presentation, is another thing. But I just wanted you to know my own
thinking. I think you will have to say to us where the lines of
restriction are.

Mr. Lowry: Well, one occurred to me in the fact that in Europe,
particularly in Central Europe but also through the BBC, one of
the largest social resources in the support of the arts comes through
the support of national or provincial television and radio, and there
are as many artists supported through those media as in the direct
government programs. Whereas in this country, except for public
television on very limited economic returns and new job opportunities, we have not yet found a great deal of support of the arts
and the training of more artists coming from this source. This is
one way I could see the topics related.

Otherwise the remarks seem to point more toward the development of audiences than toward the question of training and career

development. And that they don't see "Agon" in Detroit has an effect perhaps not just on the audience that Mr. Joffrey will find when he gets there but on the stimulus for a young person who might say, "I'm going to study dancing because I just saw 'Agon,' and I think it does this or that to me." Is this a part of it, or were you going to leave this subject related only to audience building and not to training?

Mr. Joffrey: I think, in dance, it is very important, because I think we still have so many areas to break down. And talking about training, one of the problems is to educate the family to allow the dancers to have the correct training. We get to those same old basic problems: "She must graduate from high school; I want her to go to college." And then the child is torn: "I want to become a professional dancer." I think that somehow the parent has to be enlightened in order to help the children.

Mr. Gister: Mr. Joffrey refers to touring. He is talking about the need to take the better companies out into areas of the country where they have not seen such companies perform, giving audiences a broader perspective on the art form itself.

Institutional Survival versus Touring

I think that the major responsibility facing this country today is stabilizing the arts institutions. Through stabilizing the institution comes the system of the continuing development of the artist, comes the way of bridging between training and the profession, comes a commitment to educating the audience. Therefore, from all perspectives, the institutions themselves are in the best interests of the public.

The Primacy of Training for the Stage

Mr. Ward: Just one thing I'd like to make clear in addressing the question of training as it relates to actors. I would not like for it to be thought that we are talking about an elitist sort of training which is only valid for the legitimate stage at its best. My experience and my contention is that an excellently trained actor, in particular, can make an adjustment to film and television. There are certain unique crafts and skills involved in these media. But in my experience I think with a good director it would take a trained stage actor only about six weeks to adjust totally to cinema or television. Training for the stage is the most complete training, the most intense and thorough. Adjustments to the other media can be made easily. The stage is where the best training will take place because the demands are more rigorous.

Mr. Schneider: I do want to add a couple of things. I think training changes the theater or dance, and also the institution of the theater (or the institution of dance) which as it changes also changes the nature of the training.

No One Method in Theater Training

The thing that I most disagree with is that there is one method of training or one philosophy of training or one way of dealing with actors that is the "best" way. I think I'm always nervous about homogenizing the training, institutionalizing the training, or making it uniform. I would like to think that there are many different ways. All the ballet companies that I know are quite different from each other. It seems to me that although there is a fundamental approach to dancing or a fundamental school that you go to if you want to be a dancer, ultimately the training must branch out. The training for Bob Joffrey must be different from the training for Alvin Ailey or someone.

I also feel that it is essential that we not think of training in the arts as being similar to that given by a vocational school. The training of values, the training of attitudes, the training of habits (human habits as well as artistic habits) is very essential to our work. When people ask me at Juilliard why I do not teach a course in acting, I say I have a very good acting faculty and I do not feel that I have anything more to contribute than they are contributing. But I very much want to teach a course in values at Juilliard, and in a sense I do, whether I have such a formal class or not.

I'll say something that you can disagree with right away. I think, for example, if actors would not do commercials, even if their kids were starving, we'd have the greatest theater in the world in about five years, because they would then have to work in the theater. You cannot prohibit them from doing commercials, and I certainly have great sympathy with their various desires and needs, but I believe the fact that the actor has that escape valve changes our theater, degrades our theater, degrades the profession of acting and the art of acting. And I would like at least to suggest this thought to our young actors.

Mr. Hodes: In view of the fact that I arrived late, I'd like to make some kind of statement on my concern in dance, and that I see it as an art form in a broader context than is generally discussed.

No Real Training for Choreographers

We are talking about professional training, but to many this means technical training of the dancer's instrument, and no more. In music, the instrumentalist is certainly basic, but composers, conductors, musicologists, and a whole range of artists and scholars are also trained. In dance these needs are hardly acknowledged and this works to the particular disadvantage of choreography.

You can say that American dance has produced more choreographers than the rest of the Western dance world. But still, good choreographers are much rarer than composers or playwrights, whose works also require performance. Is choreographic talent inherently rarer? I don't believe that. I do believe there are problems peculiar to choreography and problems in the conceptual limits of dance training. The first problem is simply setting choreography down. There is no choreographic tool comparable to written language or music notation.

The first problem this presents is that there is no written tradition by which a 20th century choreographer may know precisely how a ballet was danced in the 19th century or earlier. There is a kind of kinetic memory handed down by generations of dancers or ballet masters, each of these "setting" the ballet for younger dancers. But there seems to be little doubt that each time the ballet is handed down inevitable changes are made. Today there are several systems of dance notation, some of real power and utility, and there is the new tool provided by videotape and film. This permits the creation of an archive, and presumably the handing down of tradition to our own posterity which will provide an invaluable resource for future dance students and choreographers, as well as companies. As important as this is, the percentage of works secured in archives is still small.

But existence of an archive does not touch the problem of the contemporary choreographer, who, even with notation, must work in a studio with live trained bodies. And a dance can't be said to be finished without performance, which also requires live bodies. Live bodies equal dance companies. Dance companies commonly have apprentice dancers and often associate with schools which train dancers. The big companies even have entire second companies of apprentices. But there is nothing comparable for choreographers. As long as professional training is conceived as no more than instrumental training, it's not likely there will be.

Conditions in this country make it possible, not easy, but possible for choreographers to attract a few dancers and start companies of their own, and this certainly has a lot to do with American preeminence in the field. And I'd never want to see this stop. But must young choreographers take on the burdens of company director, business manager, booker, fundraiser, and all the rest when all they want to do is dance?

As to technical training itself, it certainly has improved, but I don't think there is a change in kind. There is more opportunity, a lot more people are entering the field, and standards are higher. But after all, there is a centuries old tradition here. I recall twenty-five years ago splendidly trained dancers were arriving in New York from Dallas, from St. Louis, from the West Coast. But choreography? When a choreographer appears, you can't give the credit to any training program I've been able to identify. There's nothing we know that is sure to produce brilliant choreographers, as our centuries old technical training produces brilliant virtuoso dancers. The process is mysterious. But that's no reason to give up on it. I think it's the most fascinating challenge facing dance training today.

Mr. Ludwig: I should say again that my background is as a person involved in production at the professional level, and not as an educator. My impression is that the institutions that are training people to perform opera—and I'm talking about performers now—respond slowly and considerably behind the time of the demands of the profession.

Limitations in Opera Training

In the past ten years, perhaps, one has seen more attention paid to the theatrical and dramatic aspects of opera than in the years prior to that; and yet even so, I think the main point is that the training institutions lag very far behind the profession. The evidence for this can be seen in the discussions of the professional trade organization of opera companies called Opera America, which at a recent meeting lamented considerably that the artists being turned out by the schools were of less use than they would like because they simply did not know how to behave on stage.

One understands that the European countries in the time between the end of World War II and up to about the last five years, had placed very high value on American singers as being the best trained in the world. But I think perhaps this reflected more the fact that European populations were destroyed by the war and the educational institutions were wiped out. For a time, in addition to their native ability, Americans had an unnatural advantage. That this advantage was unnatural, I believe, is to be seen in the lessening of interest in foreign companies in hiring such high percentages of American artists.

Mr. Lowry: But at a panel I heard you recently chair on training programs, you were featuring programs of apprenticeship in which opera companies themselves were training. Now, is this not a slight difference over the last twenty years?

Importance of Apprentice Programs

Mr. Ludwig: Yes, indeed. The apprentice training programs came about, according to the profession at least, because training in schools was not adequate. Young singers would be auditioned for companies to work in chorus or small roles and would be found inadequate, and therefore the companies undertook the burden of completing the training process. A cynical point of view might be that there were other more pragmatic reasons, but whether or not that was so, the producers are telling the whole truth in saying that the artists, as they came out of schools, were far from ready to hold their own on the operatic stage, even in a chorus, on which high theatrical and dramatic demands were made.

The idea of providing a training program for a young artist which will allow him to move from the point at which he finds himself upon the completion of formal education to the point at which he can hold his own in the profession, is still a valid one. This may be seen not only from the flourishing of these programs, and even the addition of programs operating at a slightly higher level, called journeyman programs. These journeyman programs are similar to the apprentice programs in that they combine the opportunity to perform professionally with a degree of pay higher than for the apprentices but with the opportunity to participate in certain kinds of formalized learning.

Apprentices in Symphonies

Mr. Freeman: Has the pattern shifted significantly in some of these categories of apprenticeship and training programs? I would like first to address myself to the minority training programs, because I think that this is a recent trend with symphony orchestras, and it is, I think, a very positive, affirmative action program. Recently, the National Endowment for the Arts and one of the Rockefeller philanthropies established an apprenticeship program for major orchestra minority players, and it works in this way: A grant to the orchestra of $10,000 per player permits the orchestra to have a base of payment; the orchestra supplies the difference between the $10,000 and its minimum scale, and the player is auditioned, not through usual channels; you place the musician in an environment where he can get more experience until he is ready to audition on a regular basis for full-time employment. In Detroit we start with those concerts which do not depend on just one rehearsal or perhaps even on sight-reading. This is a relatively recent program for minority musicians and it has been in effect only about a year. And the various persons who have participated are, without exception, now getting regular jobs with different orchestras. I would like to say that this is a pressing problem with the symphony musicians, as well as with the operatic musicians. There is the gap between what is taught at the conservatory and what one is expected to do in the professional environment, and I don't know that this has changed that drastically over the years. I think there is still a gap despite the fact that many of the institutions have more sight-reading orchestras, and the teachers try to place more emphasis upon orchestral material. I go back to my original statement that the greatest thrust is still placed upon that solo appearance.

Democratization of Leadership

And finally, I think there is a great need to face the matter of democratization in the arts. What we are facing within the symphony orchestras now is resistance to leadership. There was a time, you know, when if the conductor gave a musical or any kind of demand it was automatically followed. But now we have the orchestral committees and a feeling among the musicians that some works the conductor may choose do not merit performance. Someplace along the line in the training process, we have to tackle the matter of the participation of the artist in the ensemble. I think this is almost excluded from his preparation.

The Changes in Opportunities

Mr. Joffrey: I was going to answer Mr. Hodes' question. I think we have always had a certain number of good teachers, and they are in two categories. There were the teachers who never danced professionally but devoted their lives to teaching because there was no way they could dance professionally. There was the Anna Pavlova Company and the Diaghilev Company, and since, I believe, perhaps only Ruth Page ever made either of these companies, the general rule was that Americans had to go into vaudeville or they had to teach to make a living. And there were outstanding pioneers—Edna McRae in Chicago, Mary Ann Wells in Seattle—they were unique people. But the number of students that became professional is very small. If I go back to my own class and the class behind me and the class in front of me, only three to five of these students became professional, not because there was no talent but because there were no means.

Then where did you go? It was very expensive to come to New York and train. There were no in-between jobs. You either made the Ballet Russe de Monte Carlo or the Ballet Theatre, or you went into musical comedy. You had no way to make that jump from the school to a professional career. If there were apprentice groups, they were never paid, as you may remember.

Now we have all the large companies competing for the talent.

Every year each of the companies sends someone out to scout different areas. We have auditions; we go to regional ballet festivals; we have certain teachers who will tell us they have a talented student. And one company competes with the other by offering a scholarship or paid apprenticeship and perhaps even transportation to New York. Then when they arrive in New York, where do they stay? That's a major problem because they are generally minors. Also how do they get their general education? One talks people into giving money so they can go to a private school. Some dancers are immediately guided into a private school, such as the Professional Children's School, while continuing their study with the ballet school. That is the way the whole thing has evolved.

Broadening the Training

If you happen to remember the High School of Performing Arts in 1950, they had Arthur Mitchell, Eddie Villella, and Allegra Kent. Allegra and Eddie never graduated. The second year, Balanchine offered them scholarships and offered them funds to go to a private school. What is still needed is a general education with dance training at a high standard. But also a general education in the arts. As we know from the Russians, every single dancer must play a musical instrument. We have all seen Nureyev at the piano. We have seen Baryshnikov at the piano. The same was true many years earlier for Balanchine.

There is another thing: classes are too large. Usually the classes have thirty or forty students. Never, in a really fine school, should there be more than twelve in a class. The classes should of course be divided between the male and the female. They should be geared to include both the classical training and the modern. They should have some form of character dancing and also basic elements of acting, which certainly would make for a much finer performer.

In my work with the opera, one of the problems I always have with the singers is trying to make them move. I'm always saying, please go and take some ballroom dancing. If you can learn how to waltz and fox trot and polka, you can do almost any opera you are going to have to do. But you do have to have some sort of basic dance training.

Returning to ballet, we now have, in a way, the first generation of American teachers. The teachers that we had before were mainly Russians, who did not speak the language very well, and it was hard for them to communicate. Now we have not only Americans but Americans who have been in professional dance companies. This has all happened in a very short period of years, since our companies are so new. Now, a good school sends a dancer to a dance company because the teacher has worked with that company or is acquainted with the artistic standards.

Mr. Gister: I'm going to try to begin where Mr. Joffrey left off, in the world of dance and what happened in the last twenty years. Very similar things happened in theater. Twenty years ago there were certain schools, but they were not recognized training institutions and they existed in the wilderness. The rest of the 1,200 colleges and universities in the country were doing what I call educating, which is all well and good, but they were not engaged in training.

Expansion of Theater Training

Over the years there developed a core of trainers, for some reason. Perhaps because more schools came along wanting to train and not simply to educate, and the need arose. Perhaps, therefore, more people familiar with the profession left it and entered the world of academic training institutions. At any rate the arts curricula across the country were significantly changed, so that time, attention, and credit were given over to the development of techniques and crafts that before had been subsumed under the rehearsal and performance of plays.

We are still trying to learn how to systematically coordinate all those elements that go into the training of an actor, so that at the end of the period of training the actor comes out knowing how to put together all the elements that he or she has come into contact with.

Today we have excellent voice trainers, movement trainers, speech trainers, acting trainers, but all those things are not necessarily coming together at the end of the training process. Today, we have considerable diversity in training. Separate schools are, indeed, standing for a particular approach to theater and theater training. And as Mr. Schneider said, the influence of the institution is basic:

the training institutions affect producing companies and theaters affect the training institutions. I do not have time to describe all the university departments doing things in distinctive ways. It is not always known what they are doing because they do not necessarily advertise themselves as unique. More or less the word has to seep down and hopefully reach those people who are interested in getting that training. This may account for the development of groups of people finishing their training and saying: "We want to stay together; let's form a company in this location that has never had one." And I think that is healthy, a healthy reaction to training and to creating institutions.

The Identification of Talent

The Theatre Communications Group has existed now for eighteen years. It is the organization that brings together the not-for-profit theaters. I mentioned earlier that some of those theaters operated more or less on a company basis. They would hire actors who would stay together at least one season and frequently two seasons. That slipped away, but the Theatre Communications Group still has national auditions in Chicago, and the resident theater companies come to Chicago to try to hire the talent that is coming out of the university training programs each year. Since Actors Equity abolished the journeyman contracts, however, there has been less hiring going on. The journeyman formula used to be the apprenticeship system for the people coming out of theater training programs. Informal and ad hoc apprenticeship systems have been developing over the last four or five years between particular universities and particular companies. These ad hoc experiences, however, must somehow or another find their way back into a more systematic approach. It takes up so much time and energy, it is a kind of hit-or-miss thing, and it does not really connect the training programs with the actual performing institution.

One final word: writers for the theater today, I think, have more opportunities if they are willing to take advantage of them. The resident theaters are willing to do new plays. They will read new scripts. They will attempt to produce them. This also has been an uphill battle.

Training and the Black Minority

Mr. Ward: I would like now to address myself to my own area of involvement, and this is the question of training as it relates to the black performer. Prior to the mid-1960s, it was probably only the really tenacious, determined black who was able to get trained or pursued it relentlessly. The fact that there was not much of an environment for black talents to be utilized created a situation in which a career was not thought very feasible. Indeed it appeared hopeless. There were always exceptions. I think that I and a few others you may know of my generation who stuck with it did find some way, various ways, to get some formal training.

In the mid-1960s, as we all know, the climate changed and improved, socially, politically, and in many other ways. It is obvious that in the last twelve to fifteen years you will find a greater presence of black performers even throughout conventional white institutions. I think that has been a positive development and the black theater movement itself has benefited from it.

My only observation about how blacks have fared in the majority institutions, whether educational institutions or adjunct companies of resident theaters, is that very often they have had questions, wrongly or rightly, about whether those institutions met their needs. I am not here concluding that what they considered to be their needs were 100 percent valid or accurate.

My own company is located right next to New York University. New York University has had a large proportion of blacks in its theater program, and at some point, somewhere along the line, I would estimate that probably the majority have come to me to talk about doing something at the Negro Ensemble Company because they didn't think that NYU was exactly meeting their needs. And when I visit around talking with various black students from schools all over the country, this issue often arises. I have counseled them to be very pragmatic and to take advantage of whatever those schools provided that was of incontestable value. For instance, I advise, if there is a good speech department, take advantage of it; if a good dance department exists, take advantage of it. Then find, or create, other circumstances to fulfill other needs.

The Negro Ensemble Company

How have training and apprenticeship programs outside educational institutions been planned and supported? As many of you may know, the Negro Ensemble Company was always conceived from the beginning to feature training as an almost equal component of our professional theater. Over the years we have had programs which to one degree or another touched more than a thousand black performers. There have been problems. We have not had the developed cadre to do the training itself, I mean in the conventional instructional sense, particularly in teaching acting discipline. I would say we have had more instructional success in dance and some other aspects of training.

In relation to acting training, the basic benefit I feel that our company has provided has been that we have given people access to professional work experiences. The training that they have benefited from has derived more from this on-the-job experience than from a conventionally structured program.

On the second point, the irony is that in terms of support, at this point, when the company itself finds itself fighting for its existence economically, the first thing that must probably be cut out is the training program itself. Productions take priority because without a professional performing program, there is no future because you won't have a fighting chance.

Mr. Lindgren: To be positive about how the pattern of training has shifted significantly, I think it's certainly in the teaching. We all know now that there has been more communication, the teachers are more analytical, and the teachers have organized themselves so they can share teaching experiences and can share ideas. And students can also see each other. They are no longer isolated. They can see the difference between good training and bad training.

A National Network

Now the students have to expose themselves to recruitment, which was something brought about by The Ford Foundation originally, with scholarships in the East to the School of American Ballet and in the West to the San Francisco Ballet School. But the pattern was followed by many other companies—Mr. Joffrey's company, I think, and American Ballet Theatre and Harkness—whereby the best students in the country would be seen by the best dance minds in the country, the ones who could offer the opportunities. No longer was one teacher carrying a pupil from the beginning to the end, and then a dance company would come into your hometown and you'd go down and say, "May I audition for your company?" Which is how I got into the old Ballet Russe de Monte Carlo. I did not come to New York; I auditioned in Victoria, British Columbia, for Mr. Massine and he said, "Come with me." That's how it used to be done.

But no longer. The directors of the dance companies or their representatives can go to the regional companies or involve themselves with teachers in any small town in America. These teachers now feel a bridge between their school and New York or the many fine companies like San Francisco, Houston, Pennsylvania, et cetera, where students can be seen.

Now the prospective director of a company can see a young talent both in a classroom situation and in a performing situation, talk to that student's parents, find out the background, communicate any kind of problems that may exist. This creates a line of communication for the young dancers from the first day they walk into a dancing school almost to the professional job opportunity, which I think is incredible.

Mr. Schneider: I want to agree with what was said about our knowing how to train dancers but not having a clue about training choreographers. In theater, we feel the same way about directors versus actors. We don't know very much about how to train directors, except as actors who might become directors. We begin to think that we know something about training actors; and I am especially fortunate in being in a context where we are training actors but at the same time where we are also training musicians, opera singers, soloists, ensemble people, et cetera.

Externalizing the Art

I said earlier that the basic difference today in training had to do with the shift from dealing with the individual's internal life to dealing with his external life. That's slightly superficial. It is not 100 percent true, but it is somewhat true. The thing that most impresses me with current acting training is the degree of versatility expected of the actor. Our actors today take for granted that they are not only going to have to act, but they are going to have to sing, they are going to have to dance. Anna Sokolow, who is a choreographer, a dancer, teaches our actors, and we feel that we benefit a great deal from having a cross-fertilization from someone as dominant and creative as she happens to be.

Actors have to be acrobats, they have to be not only skilled in fencing but in unarmed combat, in armed combat. We also deal with masks. In other words, we are basically stimulating creativity, and the only place where I disagree a little bit with Mr. Joffrey is in his saying that he wants the dancer to communicate *himself* to an audience. I want an actor to communicate the playwright's theme, the playwright's material. We want him to be expressive; we want him not to exclude himself from the process, but fundamentally what I am interested in is having him express something outside of himself, other than himself, more than himself, to the audience. I remember an English director once saying to me that the difference between American actors and British actors (this was twenty or twenty-five years ago) could be expressed very simply, that the American actor was seeking to find himself on the stage and that the British actor was seeking to get away from himself on stage. And I am of the latter school, and I think that the emphasis has, indeed, shifted in that direction.

General Differences

Mr. Bloom: Let me go back to when I was a student. I was at Curtis Institute, and we had a very good music school there; we wanted to be good musicians. In other words, we wanted to express ourselves, and it didn't make much difference where we did it. I was going to school at Curtis, and we found there was a symphony orchestra in Frankford which was nearby, and we went there wanting to be in the orchestra. We worked at it for nothing. At Juilliard I find an entirely different attitude. This may have something to do with New York—the students have this feeling of having to make good, at least of having to make money while they are going to school. I have a concert tonight of my class at Juilliard. They are very good kids and some are very talented young people, but all through the year I have had the problem of students who did not show up for rehearsal. I would say, "Where is he?" Well, he got a small job some place. I could not say he could not have this job, because he needs the money. We did not have this problem when I was going to school, but we do have it now. How do you get these young people to realize that their real chance is right now while they are going to school? They can always work after they get out of school. I tell my students, "Borrow the money to go to school; do something to go to school. Get the money and spend time, because after you are out of here, nobody is going to bother you the way I keep after you to be good." It is a hard concept for them to grasp.

Curtis Institute was an all-scholarship school. When Mary Louise Curtis Bok found out that some of the more indispensable students in the orchestra were taking outside jobs, she said, "If we allowed you a certain amount of money for an allowance each week, could you devote your whole time to Curtis?" And, of course, we said yes, because, at that time, some students were supporting whole families. You could support the whole family if one of the members of the family was a very talented young musician. I got twenty-five dollars a week while I went to Curtis. This was a long time ago, and twenty-five dollars a week was enough to pay for my room and board and I even saved up enough money to buy an instrument.

Now young music students have to go out and earn money, and you can't say they can't miss a rehearsal. But we do say they still have to play the concert, and play well. Where is the balance? If you have enough authority and charisma to say this is what you have to do, well they'll do it, but it is a rough fight, it really is. Frankly, I don't know, I'm comparing it with my student days and I just don't really know what to do about it.

Mr. Joffrey: May I say one thing? Companies are now beginning to add apprentice companies; we didn't really bring that up before. Ballet Theatre has an apprentice company. We have an apprentice company in which we have twelve dancers who are paid fifty-two weeks a year, an American Guild of Musical Artists (AGMA) weekly rate during performance weeks, and an eighty-dollar stipend during nonperformance weeks. I think Ballet Theatre pays the same. And the School of American Ballet has an annual performance with advanced students who participate in a workshop.

I disagree with one point Mr. Lindgren made. We haven't had the golden age for dancers. It is coming. In my time it was very, very difficult to study. I have always looked with envy at the Curtis Institute of Music. In the field of dance there is no equivalent to

Curtis. Even the School of American Ballet has very young children whose parents pay tuition.

Mr. Lindgren: The North Carolina School of the Arts comes the closest, in the dance field. The problem is that then it becomes a competitive thing, where students are offered opportunities, and they become school hoppers and scholarship bargainers and all that.

Mr. Joffrey: The apprentice company is a major shift, and it is a big improvement because, as we said, the big jump is from the classroom to that in-between stage, before dancers actually have to take on complete professional responsibility. It happened, in another way, in the opera ballet. Our young dancers at the beginning went to the New York City Opera, which again did not have big demands; it is only seven or eight minutes that you really have to hold the stage in opera, usually. You are only a part of the opera, which is something I had to learn, and it took me twelve years. I thought people came to see the dancing, and one day a very famous director said, "You know, they really came to hear the singing." It took me a long time to realize that.

Mr. Ludwig: May I have a minute on the same subject? When I was talking before, I was talking, I realized later, about the profession's response to training in the school, and that response being largely in apprentice and journeyman programs. I want to give some thoughts about what is going on in the school that produces that response. In general, I think that training in the undergraduate and graduate schools must be several decades behind that offered to people in the legitimate theater. And to compare it to dance, if comparisons are of any use, opera training is probably more institutionalized and this, I think, also works against excellence in training.

Opera: A Multiple Form

One of the basic problems in school training for people who wish to perform is that opera esthetically is a combination of at least two basic elements, music and theater, and unfortunately it is taught either in one area or the other and almost always in the area of the music department, where I have yet to encounter anyone with any understanding of drama and very little of the theater. There are exceptions, beyond doubt, but they certainly must be few in number.

Comment was made earlier about a problem that exists even in theater training programs, which seem so much better than opera training programs, and one must say even in theater that the student is taught many specific disciplines but not enough time is given to putting them together. This is certainly the truth in opera, where to begin with the student is not taught all of the disciplines he needs, and is never taught how to put them together. One opera teacher—stage director—expressed it by likening training to a supermarket, in which the student is paraded before a huge selection of items but given no help in deciding which items he should take off the shelf, much less how to combine these items into some kind of coherent thing.

The latest development has been the inclusion of a formalized program in a producing opera company. I believe there are only two such instances at this moment of professional opera companies which combine rather complete and advanced training programs from which artists may go into the work of the parent company. I am excluding from this statement the ten or eleven apprentice programs which do, in fact, do something of this nature, but I exclude them because they are limited to a duration of ten weeks out of the year. The companies I refer to have programs that run virtually for the whole year.

A comment was made earlier that a good development recently in theater training is that some schools are pointing their students away from Broadway toward the nonprofit company, away from the star concept toward the ideas of ensemble. This has yet to dawn in the training given to opera singers as far as one can determine by auditioning them. On the basis of auditions we must assume that each one is encouraged to believe in his own capacity to be not only a star performer but a performer suited only to leading roles at the highest possible salaries.

And finally, I think there is almost nothing to be said for the training of the opera composer, for the opera librettist, for the opera stage director, and for the opera conductor and his vital ally, the opera coach. There is some training for the conductors and coaches, especially in some of the very large and highly specialized institutions such as Indiana University, but for the composers and librettists, who must have a forum in which to work, and a very expensive forum, there is very little, and for the stage director there is also very little.

Obstacles at Different Stages

Mr. Hodes: The biggest problem in dance is the very first step. If one is born near a good teacher, one has a chance. How many students have I seen with a God-given instrument, high energy, real desire to dance, who grew up in a town without a decent dance teacher? They get out as soon as they can, but it is mostly too late. There's not much to be done except hope for a general enrichment as the arts grow. Perhaps the in-school programs will help, but they can't be the whole answer.

The next big problem is getting into the profession itself. Some of the things already mentioned might apply differently in dance. Mr. Bloom spoke of a young musician torn between further training and taking a job for temporary gains. When this happens to a dancer in training, I am often afraid to advise against the job because it could be an important transition. Not merely the big break sort of thing, but a turning point in a career. Unless a dancer is clearly headed into a specific form, say classical ballet, in which case the transition point can be better identified, there are many ways to go, and any opportunity can point out one of these ways. I believe that part of the job of professional training is to keep close to the real world of dance. We will advise a student against a job if we feel the opportunity is not worth taking, but it is always specific, never a matter of a policy of waiting until training is complete. Actually training is never complete, even though dancers become employable earlier than is usual in music. Of course they stop earlier too.

Training must lead into a career if it possibly can. If I hold a dancer out of the profession until graduation, then thrust him or her into a strange world, that is a failure of the training.

The matter of survival is particularly a problem to those who don't go into mainstream, major company, institutional dance. The importance of these dancers can hardly be overstated since most of our seminal artists worked a long time, surviving somehow as individual teachers, choreographers, concert dancers, before they became institutionalized. This is a subject unto itself and extends out of dance, since how artists survive before their work has some economic value is important to all of society.

In a recent talk with a group of young and old dancers, a young dancer asked how to get to know important people in dance as the old people do. The answer was, "Survive. If you're still a dancer twenty-five years from now, you'll know everybody."

Mr. Ludwig: One very difficult point of passage on the career ladder is getting a chance to perform, because opera is enormously expensive, and for that and other reasons probably there are relatively few performances as compared to certain other media.

The other is unlearning what seems to be the prevalent bad training, which makes most products of the schools unready to go onto the stage. I think this is really the more interesting difficulty that the performer has to overcome, but it is certainly a difficulty and is evidenced by the amount of training and the kind of training that the professional companies themselves have to take on.

Getting that first job is quite difficult in every profession, not only in the performing arts. I do not think, however, it is the greatest problem in our book, because I think there are a number of ways to bring to the attention of the producers a very broad cross-section of the young talent coming out of the schools.

Oversupply of Virtuosity

Mr. Bloom: I represent the foot soldiers of music here, the orchestral musicians, the chamber musicians. For every job that comes up, there are sixty and seventy applicants now. They are all quite good but the real top ones are not any better than they were twenty or twenty-five years ago. So how do we distinguish between all these applicants? The conductors really do not know what they're looking for. There is a famous overture by Rossini, the *La Scala di Seta*, which has a very fast oboe solo, and one of my friends said, "You know, the person who plays the fastest gets the job." And in a way it is quite true. The conductors do not understand what they are supposed to hear. Sometimes they hire people and then after about six or seven months they call me and say, "You know, I'm not quite satisfied with so and so, and so and so. Do you have somebody you can recommend?" What they're looking for is people who are musicians, who can express themselves. And to me, that's the most important thing. Are you expressing yourself and the music?

In my early years there were not that many people involved so that if there was a job that became available there would be five or six people trying out for it, and it was pretty easy to find out who was the one suited for it. Out of fifty or sixty people how do you make up your mind?

So you have to call the teachers, and if one teacher is a little more persuasive than another, his student gets the job, and if one teacher gets a reputation for having his students get the jobs then students go to that teacher. It is a very, very uncomfortable and commercial situation. I wash my hands of the whole thing, you know. If you call me and you want somebody for the position of first oboe, I say, "This is the person and take my word for it or do not take my word for it, but if you are going to call me and then try forty or fifty other people, just don't bother me about it."

It is very difficult now, Mr. Lowry. In the old days, when we met for the first time, somehow things were not that difficult. It was a question of so many oboists available for so many jobs, and the good ones got them and the other ones got lesser jobs, too. Now, we keep turning them out, and one has a feeling of guilt. You keep teaching them and then what happens to them? I am sorry to be so pragmatic about it, but we teach people and then what do they do? I recommend to my students that "if you can't get into a symphony orchestra, get a teaching job some place. Get a job in a small college."

And they say, "Yes, but there's no music there."

I say, "You make the music, you do it, you organize the music." And a lot of them do just that. They go somewhere and they get a job as an oboe teacher and they get their fellow faculty members and they say, "Let's make some music here." It takes a lot of effort and they have to keep at it. But there is no real chance for them to make music in these jobs unless they do it themselves.

Mr. Freeman: I have already said this: so many people who have had excellent training through the conservatory have to settle for a combination of jobs, but one of them may be outside an orchestra.

The Influence of Chance

The unfortunate thing is perhaps a person who could have got into the New York Philharmonic or into the Pittsburgh Orchestra, and because of the auditioning process was not discovered or fairly treated, therefore ended up in the Evansville Symphony and teaching at one of the nearby universities. By and large, while there is an oversupply (I think of orchestral musicians), there are now many job combinations, and this is what I meant about levels of professionalism.

The Detroit Symphony Orchestra is now the seventh highest paying in the country of the thirty major orchestras. The starting salary is $20,800. It does not matter if you are just out of the conservatory or if you have no degree, the starting salary is still $20,800. And the Chicago Orchestra, which is the highest as of the recent contract, starts at $26,000. Well, we had recently eighty-some applicants for the English horn position in our orchestra in Detroit, and we listened to only thirty-two. But even to listen to thirty-two English horn players is unsatisfactory. By the time you get to number eighteen you don't know what to listen for, as Mr. Bloom has said. A musician is selected on the basis of what he plays on one day, during a fifteen to twenty-minute period, and many musicians become nervous. So the auditioning process certainly should not be the final selection process, although it usually is.

At least in most major orchestras today the audition is held behind screens. You no longer take into account what the musician looks like, how he responds, whether or not he has found himself or has not found himself. You just hear the notes coming from behind the screen, and it is no longer just the conductor who is listening. Elaborate systems have come into play whereby the music director is given only a certain number of points on the audition committee.

Two other points, and I am finished on this question. Let's deal with the matter of pianists and conductors very quickly.

The Conductor Needs an Orchestra

What does one do in a country where out of the thirty major orchestras there are fewer than seven native-born and trained music directors, and of the top ten orchestras, only one? And in all deference to Maestro Rostropovich, it is highly unusual for a world power to appoint a music director who is not a national as Music Director of its national orchestra. On the other hand, it sometimes works the other way around because some other countries have the same attitudes. They like foreigners too. Except that our point here is— how does the American conductor reach the pinnacle of his career after all of his training and experience? And on the training level, how does a conductor really learn to conduct without an orchestra? That is the big obstacle for the student despite all the training at Indiana and Eastman and Juilliard—and of course, Juilliard is perhaps an exception in that there are so many opportunities in New York for experience in smaller ensembles. But even at various stages of one's development as an interpreter, one needs to get through three centuries of orchestral repertoire. And few conductors can conduct a major work for the first time with the greatest interpretation on any level. They must go through this work several times to live with it and know it.

Pros and Cons of Competitions

Next, about the pianist. What does one do about the wealth of pianists and the large number of extremely talented artists that we have created, not just in this country but in the world? And is there a better way than the competition to ascertain this talent? Now, while the competition has identified the outstanding talents for the stage, at the same time unfortunately the competition has killed so much talent that would have forged ahead, had they been students of a certain person, and entered a certain competition, and made a certain grade. This is a very serious problem, and it is one we might at least acknowledge.

The Difficult Stages

Mr. Joffrey: I think in dance there are two difficult ages. The most serious of course, is thirty-five, about which we have already spoken. And I find the teens is also a very difficult time, especially for young boys. At about sixteen they begin to question if they should continue to dance, especially in large cities such as New York City where there are so many things happening and so many things they want to participate in. You know we all have classes for seven or eight little boys who are wonderful, but when they get about thirteen and fourteen they begin to lose interest. Somehow we have to maintain that interest.

"Nutcracker" has of course been wonderful in helping to do that. They can get on the stage and be a part of a theatrical production and that seems to help them over that barrier.

Other Uses and Careers

At thirty-five, I think we have to utilize dancers more effectively in other posts. And there are many opportunities. We need teachers. There is still a shortage of good teachers in America. We cannot fill the number of applications that come in for teachers. We need stage managers who know something about dance and know something about music. It is very difficult to call light cues for dancers unless one has a basic background in movement and in music. Also we need dance notators. And we certainly need people who are educated in dance in order to raise the standards of dance on television. When you go into a television performance there is no one there that has any understanding of movement. The best cameramen are the ones who have worked in sports. At least they can follow you because they are used to moving quickly. We always ask for the ones who are experienced in football or basketball. I think we are just now hitting that period where we do have a lot of people who have been trained professionally and need to go into other things. And the art, the field, needs them.

Training the Theater Director

Mr. Gister: I want to say just one thing about the position of the director in a theater. There is no continuity in the training process for the director. What is his career? He comes out of training, and there is nothing waiting for him to do. He is lucky if someone like Mr. Schneider will allow him to be an assistant, but that is rare. I have been trying to deal with it by asking the nonprofit theaters to take on assistant directors and to hire them in some capacity where they can be around the theater, observe the theater, try to give them a chance in the second company, if they have a second company, or a touring group. Many artistic directors did not want them around. They did not want us to deal with that problem.

Mr. Lowry: There are people here from other fields who may know a good deal less than you and Mr. Ward and Mr. Schneider. I want to be sure you want to leave the subject of the director at that point.

Many of the directors you say do not want another director

around have a minimum of two or more assistant directors or have visiting directors brought in for one play. Many of them themselves came out of theater companies evolving from other theater companies and from directing around a circuit of professional resident theaters. There are a number of people in the theater whom we think of as directors. And I have met them and dealt with them and talked to them around tables like this for twenty years. There is a career for a director in the American theater, is there not?

Mr. Gister: Yes, there is, but I'm not sure I can describe it for you.

Mr. Lowry: Are you saying there are no recognized successive stages of development in that career?

Mr. Gister: That is right. I mean, I know what his job is, but not how he goes from one stage to the next.

Mr. Lowry: I just want it to be clear for the record.

Mr. Gister: Without doubt, there are many artistic directors across the country who do employ people who come in and do a show and others who develop directors out of their own company. Some companies, for instance, were created by two or three people who would share the directorial burden of that particular theater. There are other companies where someone was brought onto the staff and stayed for years and has indeed been, in a sense, associate director or co-director of the theater. That, it seems to me, is not the norm, however. It is contrary to the norm. Generally, an artistic director hires a visiting director for a show or two, because he or she cannot handle the whole season. But sharing the season and providing the artistic vision for a company are two very, very different things. To create a process whereby someone can have the experience of shaping a vision, of seeing directing as not just the responsibility of one show at a time, is a very different process. I don't think, at this point, that experience is provided very frequently in our country for the developing director.

The Problem for Blacks

Mr. Ward: It is all dependent upon the stability and even the breadth of a company's activity. I'll just give a personal experience. I have over the years created the Negro Ensemble Company and have helped to develop many black directors who have since become known. However, there may be about at least eight young black directors whom I have some faith in, but there is no place to see their work. The only way you can gauge a director's ability is to see him function in a working situation. If I do not have a sufficient amount of subsidiary activity, a workshop or what have you, then in my company the situation is that very often my only choice is to entrust the young director with one of the major productions. You have only four weeks to mount that production. It would be unfair to that young director to entrust this responsibility upon him. So even when you want to, there are so many circumstances which impede your ability to give him his chance.

The Strength of Motive

Mr. Bloom: Many years ago when Toscanini was conducting the NBC Symphony there were some little internal problems, and he asked me to come to see him. Of course I went immediately up to Riverdale. He had a little study upstairs. He was childlike; I mean, he had Puccini's snuffbox and Verdi's eyeglasses, et cetera. On this day he looked very tired, and I was supposed to be there for lunch but I said, "Maestro, you look very tired. Why don't I go home. I don't have to stay for lunch and you can nap." He said, "Oh no, *caro*, it is just that this morning I got up at five-thirty, and I was studying the symphony." (The symphony that week was the Beethoven Fifth.) And I said, "Maestro, how many times have you conducted this?" He said, "Oh many times—fifty times—many times." And I said, "And you're still studying the score?" He said, "I'm always afraid I missed something."

Mr. Schneider: But how do you train people to have that attitude toward whatever it is they are working on or in?

Drive and Necessity

Well, I'm glad we got on to directors a little bit because I know something about directors from direct experience. I did not get started until I was thirty-five. Dancers may be finished when they are thirty-five. Directors sometimes don't get started at thirty-five. One thing that struck me, as my colleagues were talking, is that so many of those directors who now have the top jobs in these

various theaters could not originally get jobs as directors at all and
therefore started theaters in order to give themselves opportunities.
This includes Zelda Fichandler or Nina Vance or Bob Kalfin. I do
not mean that that was bad. They made themselves into directors
out of necessity. Yet I do not believe for a minute that there is not
a way to train directors. I just don't think we are willing to lend
ourselves to it. Roman Polanski went to the Polish Film Institute
and took a twelve-day entrance examination to get in. André Serban
studied in Romania and took a three-year course in directing, including dialectical materialism, and so on. I think there are ways
of training directors, but we have a different rhythm in our society;
we have a different attitude. We are more mercurial in our tastes
and attitudes.

The interesting thing to me about the fact that Zelda Fichandler
could not get a job as a director and so started her own theater,
is that without her theater I would not have survived as a director.
I was trained as a director insofar as one can be in undergraduate
and graduate schools, but I could not get a job in the commercial
or even the noncommercial theater on a regular basis without the
Arena Stage. Had that theater not happened at that point in history
I think I would have lived out the rest of my days somewhere in a
university, maybe quite happily or unhappily, that is not the point.
The point is that there was no specific pattern established either
for her to get a job, or for me to get a job.

On another subject: Mr. Bloom was talking about the seventy
oboe players. Every time we try to find actors for a play, I would
be happy if there were only seventy for each role. There may be
seven hundred. Unfortunately for them and fortunately for me, I
am under no obligation to see them. I could see seven hundred for
each job, and I am not so sure that there would be fifty or sixty
that I could use. Nor am I sure after seeing fifty or sixty that I am
any more capable of evaluating them than a conductor is able to
choose the oboe player.

I am not sure that in the arts there are mathematical formulations
of anything. But there is something on the other side. Robert Anderson, a playwright friend of mine, has a sign over his desk that
has given me some encouragement over the years. The sign says
"Nobody asked you to be a playwright." Now all I am saying is
that nobody asked me to be a director, and when things get really

tough I somehow know these conditions exist, and I somehow have to go on pursuing my career in spite of that; otherwise I feel even more guilty. I do not feel guilty about Juilliard because I know that by the level of their talent and the level of their craft, and even more through the level of their dedication, the Juilliard students may eventually create those opportunities without which that talent and that craft and that dedication could not exist. The proportion of graduates of the Juilliard Theater Center that are working at any given time is very high. It is 75 or 80 percent. Despite what Mr. Hodes said, we have very strict rules about our students not going out to work in the New York theater while they are in our school. We tell them that. Sometimes they don't like it, and they quit. We do not blame them. We say, "Okay, the spectrum of your opportunities will narrow. You are not going to be one kind of an actor. You are going to be this other kind of an actor and your range of employment opportunities is ultimately going to be narrower; and that's okay, if you want that."

Discipline and Use

It seems to me that the point on the career ladder of greatest obstacles for an actor is almost every moment. One of the finest actors I know of in the American theater is Henderson Forsythe. (Not everyone agrees with me; you may never have heard of him.) I had him in twenty-one shows. He is totally unrecognized. He has to struggle for a theater job, although he makes a very good living in soap opera. His career opportunities are severely limited. Yet he is as talented as anyone I know.

Our real problem is that people tend to jump rungs on the career ladder. That is almost the main problem. They do not want to work through an apprenticeship process. They do not want to suffer through the small roles. Their expectations of salaries are greater than the theater can afford. A lot of actors with whom I have had contact just in the last few years who come from a conservatory or a university theater situation simply do not want to work for a hundred and fifty dollars a week. When I tell them the opportunity they are getting at the Arena or some other theater is worth much more than that, they don't want to believe me. They want to be something else, right away.

What can be done to deal with such obstacles? Anything that creates more companies, apprentice companies, touring companies, internships and so on. The growth of the Acting Company, which came out of Juilliard, has been tremendously helpful not just to those graduates but to every single graduating class since, because almost all our students look forward to joining it, to feeding it, to being part of it. Everything that happens at any point in the arts changes the field, including what happens in the training.

Mr. Hodes: The mere presence of trained artists seems to stimulate the market for the art. Fifteen years ago the existence of far fewer professional training programs than we have today was seriously questioned. Where would all the dancers find jobs? Today there are ten times that number of companies, an audience tenfold larger, and the question is still being asked. Sometimes I ask it myself.

Training and Artist Unions

Mr. Lowry: What has been the influence of artist unions on professional training, apprenticeship, and career development in your field?

Mr. Hodes: I've been in unions since 1948, a union deputy, on a governing board, and member of seven unions as a dancer. Today there are still five unions a dancer must join depending on where he or she dances. Each is concerned with dance only on its own turf. A musician can work Broadway, ballet, television, nightclubs, films, and be in one union, the musicians' union. There is no dancers' union. Dance is fragmented, and to no union is it a primary commitment. Each accepts a piece of the action, and the sum of all the pieces amounts to no more than an economically visible fraction of dance performance.

On top of that, or beneath it really, lies the basic union perception of its role as a power center. We know unions fought bloody battles for the right to exist. Now that dancers are forced into the adversary relationship with employers, that is the only union reality. Dancers certainly need to make a living, and when one becomes employable by major institutional companies, or in commercial work, the union is encountered and the dancer accepts this union reality. The reverse is not true. The dancers' reality is an artists' reality, the need to do dance, which is shared with choreographers and company directors. This doesn't mean dancers don't need union protection. But they need it in a context that accepts the conditions under which they live and includes understanding of what is real to them. The unions deny them this, and deny the whole existence of much of dance because it has no economic visibility. In dance, as in any art, activities taking place that are economically invisible can have great importance for the art. Concert dancers, loft dancers, small companies, apprentice companies, and all who dance in ways that don't earn a livelihood can be said to benefit from union blindness to their activities, since it frees them from interference and gives them time to develop their ideas. But this is a very negative kind of benefit, and results in a pervasive fear of the union among those who ought to be seeking to become its constituents. Much that is vital to dance is underground as far as the union is concerned, and as small companies approach the economic threshold they literally go into hiding as long as possible. This is obviously antithetical to a performing art, diminishes it, and is bad for the dancers involved who are often at that stage of their lives when training and early professional work are not easily distinguished.

In the 1950s, when talk of merger was heard, it seemed that perhaps the tradition of artist guilds, on which the AFL was built, might be achieved for performers, and within it dancers could have a coherent, unified place where their realities would be understood and included. But merger is long dead and the idea of a dancers' union was never born. I believe a deep conceptual change will have to precede any change in this discouraging and sterile situation. It will probably have to originate with the arts and the artists, since what I've seen of the young staffers gives me little cause for hope.

Instead of seeking understanding of the dancers' need to 'dance regardless of economics, they are impatient and contemptuous, seeing it as a weakness and a flaw. Instead of trying to expand their view to perceive dance in its wholeness, they focus ever more narrowly upon economics, missing most of what we know as the dance explosion as they zero in on funding programs.

The origin of the union movement is identified with a courageous, idealistic, unswerving humanism. Dance emerges from these same spiritual sources. How ironic, and tragic, if the dancers' union is unable to reach into them now to achieve understanding of its own membership.

The Rigidity of Union Rules

Mr. Schneider: I'm sorry to say, I share Mr. Hodes' feelings, particularly on the question of the journeyman contract in the resident theater, which was a way in which young actors could bridge the gap more easily. Actors Equity eliminated it. As a result young actors were not hired so readily and so simply.

The rigidity of the union in terms of our working conditions or the number of hours actors are allowed to rehearse is ridiculous. I am on my union's board too, and I fight all the time as much as I can. I do not know of any positive influence of the artistic unions on professional training. They are not interested in making distinctions. As far as career development is concerned, the union keeps changing the minimum wage, but that is about all. I don't know how to deal with the unions.

But Variations Exist

Mr. Ludwig: I have had different experiences with various unions but I shall comment only on AGMA only as it deals with singers. It may deal with the dancers in different ways. I had contrary experience to both Mr. Hodes' and Mr. Schneider's. It may have to do with the fact that the experience I have had has not been in New York City but in Minneapolis, Washington, D.C., and San Francisco. These experiences have varied considerably. San Francisco was a very highly structured union situation. In Minneapolis there was no union, and the producer was in the perhaps enviable position of being able to write the contract and send it in to the union for ratification, which we eventually got. But in general, outside of New York one finds that while AGMA has problems dealing with its own rigidity, in my experience its executives have tried very hard to overcome it.

With reference to training programs, AGMA has allowed a very special contract to be drawn up for the apprentice artist. That contract has limitations. For instance, it allows the apprentice status to endure for only approximately twenty weeks spread over two years, which is not a long time to be an apprentice. But AGMA nevertheless accepts the concept of an apprentice system. It has allowed the creation of a higher level but still subprofessional category of contract to exist, which we call the journeyman contract. And in general, it has not been unhelpful in dealing with work situations that call for different rules. I have never had to suffer through a contract which was written for some other purpose. There are certainly some instances in which this particular union has been to some extent positive in the area of training programs and perhaps, therefore, career development.

Mr. Bloom: Well, as for the musicians' union, whether local or national, I do not think it has contributed anything to the growth of musical excellence. But they have set certain time limitations so that a man who is in charge of a production has to know his business, and he cannot spend all day doing something that could be done in one hour. That much has been a good influence. It saves a lot of time.

Artist Members' Responsibilities

Mr. Freeman: I think one of the problems has been that in the early stage of the development of the musicians' union there was too little participation on the part of the artist himself. The unions were allowed to be controlled by nonpracticing musicians. And now, because the machinery has become so complex and many of the situations have developed into job problems, there is a gap between the participating artist and the employer. For sure, we can advise the more militant young performers that they should participate in the union. In other words, they should be more involved in participation, in becoming officers, in the voting process, and so forth. And I think this might eventually improve the situation somewhat. For example, there is no question that over twenty major orchestras were driven out of the recording industry as a direct result of national unionization. The negotiation process is geared more or less in favor of the top six orchestras. The other twenty-four major orchestras have refused to band together and say to the union, we really should have governing conditions relative to pay for recordings, which will make it possible for us to benefit from recordings. And this is why so many recordings are made in Europe for American companies. And I do not know how we explain that to the young people, except to tell them to become involved in union affairs.

Finally, for the most part the union has created the atmosphere which contributes to lack of communication between management and player.

Mr. Joffrey: I think we are lucky in that we do have good leadership in AGMA. What I think is very difficult is that there are so many different types of companies that one contract is not suitable for the San Francisco Ballet as compared to our company in New York or for the Pennsylvania Ballet. The contracts have to be adapted to the company, to the size of it, its location, and so on.

The other thing I feel is that there are not enough dancers who are in control of the union. I feel that somehow the dancers are just a little part of that very big union. And I do not see how AGMA can really solve the problems of the dancers because its interest is in the majority, which are the singers. I wonder if it may not be advisable at some time for the dancers to get together and hopefully form their own. My company was the first to do the "Dance in America" series on television. Our greatest problems were with unions, because in television you work five hours straight. We almost did not do the show, because we had to come to a compromise. Naturally we compromised with television because it was so expensive to give all the crew an hour off. We made other concessions. But all that, I feel, should be involved in a union that really is devoted to dance, because there are so many problems that need to be taken care of, especially as dance goes into other things like television and film. For years we danced on cement, even Nureyev, on every television show that was done, but we had no power. They finally have built a wooden floor which is used for the "Dance in America" series, but before that there was no suitable floor. And you could understand why. How could those big cameras roll across a wooden floor? It requires a whole other way of photographing.

Mr. Gister: I do not really think that the unions representing theater performers have had much to do with training. They do not represent a standard of achievement, a performance capability, a competence, so they have no influence on training. The scenic artists, on the other hand, have had an influence on training, because their exam is a rigorous exam. It is much more objective. It does indeed deal with competencies. And, therefore, anyone who is training potential scenic or costume designers knows that the students eventually have to qualify for that examination and they must be taught certain things.

The Need for More Diversity

Mr. Ward: I consider myself as a member of the profession, a union man. However, I think the question now is that the actors' union does not confront the diversity developed in theater in the last ten years. I think that as long as its rules are being used to protect the union member in a highly commercialized situation, they are probably beneficial, and I would want these protections to safeguard actors in those highly commercialized situations. But when you are dealing with the type of theaters that some of us have been involved in, you will find that rigidities do not help, particularly in the area of training. Sometimes I have hired a young actor for a particular play because his talent was right and almost urged him not to join the union. For his continued development and growth he needs to do a wide multitude of things. Yet if he gets that union card and pays the money, as he has the right to, he may restrict his access to further growth outlets and never change. He may not value the need for further training, not leave himself open to work in a variety of situations.

The Union at the Base

Mr. Lindgren: I came into AGMA when dance first came into the union, which was after a strike in Cuba by the original Ballet Russe. And at that beginning it was obvious what the union did for us. It gave us basic working conditions, it gave us a basic salary, and it gave us some sort of identity. Before this, the practice of hiring young people with a kickback was one of the things that was happening. And the salary was $41.50, so there was nowhere it could go but up. And we got such things as toe shoes when they were needed. And during the war when we traveled two in an upper berth we got paid the difference between an upper and a lower. All those working conditions were greatly changed. But once you got past what I call a corps de ballet stage, I don't know what the union ever did for you. It certainly was not interested in a dancer as far as training was concerned. They did not offer job opportunity; it was a closed shop.

Present Auguries for the Future

Mr. Schneider: In spite of my generally skeptical attitude towards the profession and its relationship to training, I feel much more optimistic about the theater today; and I do not quite understand the logic or the rationale of that. I feel much more optimistic about the opportunities for young people in the theater. It has partly to do with jobs, in the sense that there are growing numbers of nonprofit theaters, ensembles, experimental groups, individual companies, whether they are resident or touring or repertory or pretending to be repertory. And there are not only more jobs, but the quality of the work is better. There is the idea of a company, the idea of doing classical plays, the idea of being skilled in a variety of different styles, the idea of the theater as an institution that has continuity and permanence and direction and a point of view, rather than simply getting a bunch of second basemen and shortstops together to play every ball game. All of that is changing. I wrote an article thirty years ago, almost thirty-five years ago, titled "One Theater," in which I talked about the possibility of a national theater, and I think that we are on the verge of having a national theater, consisting of a nationwide theater and a nationwide attitude toward the theater. I think more people go to the theater today on any one night than ever. Whether the quality is always good, or it happens to be spread out in such a way that we are not even aware of where it is, I am not sure. But in any case, I feel more optimistic and more hopeful of the opportunities and, therefore, of the need for bettering our training and making more possible that first step: some way of helping young people into a profession which they respect. The only time I've ever seen American actors respect themselves as artists was on a trip to the Soviet Union, which the Arena Stage company and I embarked on three years ago. Suddenly, they felt that they were not just actors, not just workers, not just rogues and vagabonds. They were artists and they were important to a society. We talked about that a great deal, because their whole idea of themselves changed. And I think that we are at least one step closer to having that sense of ourselves as being part of something essential to a society, rather than peripheral to a society. And I find that very hopeful, and I am delighted to be part of the process that is feeding that potentiality.

Lincoln Kirstein

8

The Performing Arts
and Our Egregious Elite

The Hazard of Imagination

The metaphysic of intellectual and moral energy is no simple matter. The human imagination, poetic or scientific, has few limits. It is impossible, and once one might have thought it undesirable, to try to control either. Imagination—lyrical, artistic, or mechanical—is the mortal enemy of habit and routine. Sir James Fraser, the great master of "The Golden Bough," wrote: "Imagination works upon a man as really as does gravitation and may kill him as certainly as a dose of prussic acid." Habit and routine are the safe or accountable practice of all quadrupeds and most bipeds. Anything threatening habit or routine, those relatively safe paths by which we endure to survive our hazards of accident or circumstance, causes suspicion and fear in various kinds and degrees.

The scientist, since he or she is associated with metrics which impinge upon the necessity of maintaining breath and blood, is always protected and supported more than poets or artists whose imaginativeness, invention, or fantasy are both unmeasured and immediately unmeasureable. The measure used by lyric makers and their colleagues and partners, performing artists, is neither so obviously secure, safe, nor tidy. Their very ensign flags refusal to con-

LINCOLN KIRSTEIN *is founder and director of the School of American Ballet and the New York City Ballet Company. In addition to editing* Hound and Horn *(1927–1934) he has written six books on ballet, two books of poetry, and books on Tchelitchew (1947) and Nadelman (1949).*

done or accept habit or routine. Indeed, their egotistical, selfish, or reckless renunciation of safety, the proud or vain embrace of hazard or chance, is the first gauge of creative energy or artistic quality. Naturally this has always inspired suspicion, which can grow easily to something approaching fright. This fear, inchoate or focused by prejudice, is always to be triggered at some level, whether it is manifest by distrust of disorder, a rational protection from the impractical, spendthrift, or capricious, or merely a dislike of the unlikely or unfamiliar. It is only assuaged by flagrant signs of economic neatness, interpreted as the stability of institutions or artifacts which somehow have managed to survive previous shock, terror, blame, or failure. It was Saint Augustine among the early Christian fathers who laid down the fundamental ethic of distrust of the sensory imagination: "The devil insinuates himself in sensuous forms; he adapts himself to colors, attaches himself to sounds, abides in perfumes and flowers, lurks in conversation and clogs the channels of understanding." This was an echo of Plato's exile of artists from the ideal republic because of their danger to the stability of the state.

Artistic Quality and Demography

If some political recklessness may be tolerated, together with a bit of sanguine pessimism, one might start by attempting to define what the performing arts signify on the level of absolute quality, rather than auditing their dilution by demographic assignment or median societal acceptance.

The performing arts at a high qualitative level have been and always will be majestically urban phenomena, simply because the economic base of a repertory audience lies only in cities with centers which can attract and pay for them. The bigger cities have the better audiences, indeed the single big-scale publics which can afford prime producing institutions. By and large television so far has absolutely nothing to do with quality culture, except as it squirms uneasily to pay miserable dues to a substitute for live performance, whatever the size of the screen or the integrity of the choice of images. Our big performing companies can no longer travel widely as once they could since the costs of labor and transport are highly inflated, and local subsidy, even with some cautious aid from federal pittances, seldom sanctions the necessary guarantees. But television, once and for all, is not a substitute for live virtuoso performance.

"New York is not America!" This is demonstrable fact on any map. However, if the megalopolis is not capital and criterion of our culture good or bad, where else are they located? Ask any performing artist whether, if given the choice, he or she would prefer to remain loyal to the native hearth or risk an appearance on Broadway. Without the criterion of the highest professional levels, sustained by metropolitan audiences alone, there are few standards of quality left by which the face of a nation's culture can be estimated or, indeed, displayed.

THE CONTRAST WITH LIBRARIES AND MUSEUMS

Regions avid for capital evidence of the performing arts find it hard to match the hugely greater prevalence of absolute quality in the service of great libraries and museums of the visual arts. Objects of art, apart from historic or aesthetic value, have an immediately visible, riskless, negotiable, and marketable appreciation. Museums and libraries are warehouses of success. Whatever the mortal failure of a Blake, Van Gogh, Seurat, or Cézanne in their lifetimes, they have become saints of success, canonized in their expensive endowed sanctuaries which now replace more orthodox sites of worship. There is neither danger nor hazard in an enshrined masterpiece whatever the initial cost in neglect or suicide. But the arts of performance always involve hazards, both moral and physical. Performers are also acrobats whose tendons may snap, or voices fail, or whose ill-assorted careers may founder on commercial mischance. Failure is unfriendly, but worse, magically unlucky, and while we as democrats prize our right to fail, even in building repertories and audiences, failure is finally judged as an unpaid debt, damning testimony to sloppy judgment or bankrupt operation. And should a performing arts institution by some miracle end a year in balanced fiscal condition, the state councils funding it may easily decide that it therefore needs no support. In fact, it may be penalized for a proper operation, since there are a majority of others in more desperate need whose very deficits inspire superior pity and terror.

The National Fear of Failure

Repertory institutions have a rule of thumb that one in three to five novelties may not add to the repertory past the season of their debuts. This third or fifth can be translated into waste, which rarely includes the excitement stimulated by risk, free press coverage which anticipates it, or the moral stimulation of the artists responsible. But its evidence is forgiven far less than failed litigation, bankruptcies of shops or banks, or surgical operations with drastic consequences. The allocation of artistic responsibility lies with individual, nameable imaginations or talents, artist managers or producers. This failure is focused in the field of operative fantasy. Their daring is unforgiven and the threat of it guarded against by those whose fantasies are satisfied by formulae. Courage and imagination in the act of invention are impalpables, two costly and feckless luxuries in the minds of those who recognize neither, but who by endemic apathy or ignorance are self-appointed guardians of the public purse. However, the chance of failure, the risk of unpopularity is treated as a moral naughtiness. The fright of failure is an active illness of our national health. A century ago in his essay on "Culture and Anarchy," Matthew Arnold wrote: "Our society distributes itself into Barbarians, Philistines and Populace; and America is just ourselves [the English], with the Barbarians quite left out, and the Populace nearly."

ARTISTS NOT TO BE FORGIVEN

This fear of lyric or artistic imaginative risk is not to be mitigated by comparison with other common or popular services, for the performing arts are scarcely acknowledged as service, to say nothing of necessity. It has not proven useful to reiterate that museums, libraries, hospitals, and schools fail to run themselves as profit-making successes. These are bound to the self-evident necessities of life-maintenance; any granted expenditure is forgiven as prime need. These do not "lose" money; they are able to raise money and spend it. Rarely has so evanescent a property as artistic culture been recognized as anything approaching first importance since the decline of the age of faith, except by artists, poets, makers, or inventors who are possessors of gifts, talents, vision, and energy different in kind from purveyors, maintainers, or manipulators. With their lurid "problems" or presumed "temperament" artists are deemed unstable (unlike psychotic statesmen or demented tycoons); hence a condign threat to the body-politic. When Plato in his wisdom exiled artists from the ideal republic, this was not an ironic attitude. We remember that Phidias was indicted for embezzling gold and ivory from work on his colossal statue of Pallas Athena intended for the Parthenon, and that the trials and tribulations of Richard Wagner, despite personal support from the greatest music lover of the nineteenth century, were colossal, persistent, and, befitting his talent, Napoleonic.

Ignorance and Apathy

There are two threadbare statements which serve as keys to self-protective ignorance or apathy, and which are wielded powerfully by those whose self-centered criteria arrange the subsidies from which we starve. "I don't know much about art, but I know what I like." Boasting a seemly ignorance, both modest and honest, has its own mindless artlessness which, while not exactly endearing, is a locution which makes a whole world kin. Parallel to this is the declaration, when wandering through a museum gallery or marooned in a concert hall: "This [painting or tone-poem] doesn't do a thing to [or for] me." "Fortune," said Louis Pasteur, "favors the prepared mind." Clinically, the inability to attach meaning to sensory perception is called *agnosia*. In such a state the act of perception cannot be completed, so that a person while capable of scanning or viewing an object is unable, owing to lack of focused energy or illness, to recognize its essential nature. There is a common supposition that art has some heavy and overwhelming obligation to affect a blank or resistant field, unprepared by curiosity to enliven itself. The very instinct to disdain, whatever the vapid emptiness in the observer or listener, vaunts its own beefy innocence. Condemnation of the complex, multilayered, or unfamiliar is a proud assertion of the ordinary citizen's right to be simplistic and ordinary. It follows that everyone else should be equally and democratically passive and mindless. After all, as we say, who needs it? Art, the broad and deep practiced play of imagination, therefore requires no prior preparation, attention, or sympathy. We cannot trust our artists as we trust any banker or surgeon. And, as for the problem of elitism, the

elite as possessing a discrete place or attitude (unlike blind prejudice or apathy), is clearly supercilious, superior, undemocratic. The
terrified doubt of superiority, of failed claims, or unproven prestige
lies, mental or moral, at the heart of opposition to the poetic
process.

VOLITION AND WISH

Metaphysically the problem of resistance to an imaginative elect
is a question of will. In man, will is maintained as an agent of
necessity, of survival. Each act commences with the energy or heat
of volition, of willing. On higher levels, will is something more than
choice between opposites or alternatives. It can be directed by energetic focus toward a particular creative or inventive target, even
serving as a mighty tool toward personal ambition. But, alas, the
average biped is a miserably weak and pitifully deenergized unit.
This disturbing and distressing truth is one of the many obscene
facts of existence, and one which an affluent, democratic society
both ignores and battens on, while the imaginative elite manfully
labors against persisting conditions of apathy and ignorance. The
gross consumer body forming our potential audience is indolent in
thought, lukewarm in desire, and only exceptionally generates
enough energy for a will strong enough to gain its desires, to say
little of first being able to formulate what such desires might intend.
It rarely wills but only vaguely wishes. It is restricted by habit, by
the dross of received ideas, by setbacks, perplexities, and annoyance
on daily levels. With the first hitch, inconvenience or discomfort,
it abdicates and abandons the struggle toward the ideal or the more
difficultly superior, the elitism of perfection which is the artist's main
existence. Energy has not chosen it as a repository for magic. It
behaves like a sleeper awake, and we must ever contrive to engage
it at least in its minimum of wakefulness to support our fortunate
or unlucky energetic chances.

Signs of Impending Change

Optimistically we can show that since the last three major wars
there has been considerable public interest in the promulgation and
hope for a more ideal situation to be enjoyed by the performing arts

in the not-too-distant future. If not in this administration, then possibly by the next, or at least sometime in the new century. Almost every city in the nation with a population of half a million seems to be planning or has already built some sort of civic center which hopefully can house music, drama, or dance. Certainly facilities have not exactly improved parallel to the resources of the average provincial hospital; but we should be grateful for what we are given. But lest we congratulate ourselves unduly on such very often ill-planned accommodations in which local pride does nicely without expert opinion as to the needs of dancers' feet or players' dressing rooms, we may forget that until the close of World War I, artists like Duse, Bernhardt, Sir Henry Irving, Caruso, Pavlova, and the Diaghilev ballet toured even the tank-towns of the far and middle west, while today the most that widespread touring offers middle America is music-tents and the traveling circus.

THE CARDINAL IMPORTANCE OF TRAINING

While music training in the United States has enjoyed a comparatively long history in capital schools for virtuoso performance; although today there are few enough academies in the traditional sense which teach the elemental crafts of draftsmanship, painting, and stone-cutting; and apprenticeship in the drama still suffers perhaps from a lack of regional companies, there has been a wide quantitative and qualitative improvement in the instruction of the classic dance. A national school of music, parallel to the French or Soviet conservatories, is hardly our present need for the larger urban centers, and a dozen universities and conservatories have fairly stable, if perennially needy, continuity. At the moment, whatever the idealistic expectations of a few artists and educators, a national theater in terms maintained by British, French, or Russian governments, all of which include music, drama, dance, and film, is scarcely thinkable. And while we must all be grateful for Washington's Kennedy Center, both as it functions as a national ensign of cultural interest and as a magnetic center where our legislators can actually view live performances, it is more a very welcome booking house than a fountain of noncommercial productions on the highest creative and artistic level.

NATIONAL ACADEMIES OF THE FUTURE

Certainly our Congress will not soon be ready to match West
Point, Annapolis, or the Air Corps Academy with top educational
facilities for training in drama, dance, music, or film. From the
geopolitical aspect, the nation is too expansive for any single isolated
central school, either in the Washington area or on neutral ground.
But if, as one hears, the Kennedy Center is ambitious to maintain
under its own roof a National Opera, Drama, and Ballet, these
should require supporting academies as well as a coordinating
bureaucracy for recruitment and massive budget to insure subsidies
for production and touring. The cost of such a centralized effort
on any absolute scale might well exclude any such support, at least
for this century. It took the British, with their world repertoire,
from the Elizabethans to today to achieve a national edifice, even
though their new dramatic theater exists on the fringes of state
bankruptcy.

Lacking a criterion of academic excellence, it will be difficult to
canalize opinion in the direction which may even in the twenty-first
century support the kind of selective and qualitative standards ensur-
ing virtuoso efficiency, a pool of superior performers comparable to
the training of the great technical and medical schools with their
mandatory collegiate affiliations. Such a productive educational ab-
solutism is unquestioned for the national defense and security but
hardly as an appanage of culture. The majority of taxpayers are not
disturbed that cash annually appropriated for arms (to say nothing
of health, education, and social welfare) is seldom questioned either
as to essential need or allocation on any qualitative basis. But what
can justify any considerable fraction of even a billion dollars toward an indeterminate, unmeasured and perhaps unmeasurable
across-the-board cost of national culture? The very act of proclaim-
ing or subsidizing superior talent, on the grounds of quality rather
than popular appeal, will be left to specialists who do their minimal
best via the foundations or private donors.

THE GREATER DIFFICULTY OF DEFINITION

Sooner or later the quality of education for the performing artist
must come into question. The medical profession in the United
States grew from the tradition of medieval barber-surgeons guilds.

Licensing was almost a question of self-election for generations. Abraham Lincoln's law office was not graced by a diploma from the Harvard Law School nor J. P. Morgan's from any business school. However, if the state started to qualify dance studios today to the same degree that dentists, chiropractors, or even lay healers are licensed and held accountable, possibly a large portion of the industry would be out of business. This is not to claim that present danger threatens unsuspecting children who are put on *pointe* at the age of four, although this is certainly more dubious as to future careers than premature baton twirling. But there are only relatively few first-rate teachers who have themselves never performed in public, who have gained their science mainly from observation, books, or peripheral instruction. It is only a gauge of the superficial interest of the gross public in virtuoso performance which permits anyone who wishes to set up a dance studio to start to teach young children in a corpus of information which has accumulated by trial and error over three centuries and which compares in complexity, subtlety, and practice with English common-law, *materia medica* or musical composition. The recent proliferation of regional dance companies, the broad and loose instruction of "modern dance" on whatever permissive, self-indulgent, or amateur basis, particularly in the colleges, calls for some critical standards and qualifications. Separations are not easily made between what is art appreciation, life enhancement, audience building, the amateur, dilettante, and modestly professional. It would be decent enough to equate the schooling of a professional dancer with that of an aspirant pianist, violinist, or singer, candidates for instrumental mastery, and these cannot start instruction in their hardy disciplines in late adolescence nor are they taught by those who have not themselves been professionally experienced. There exists in the minds of many Americans a notion of latent amateurism, the pride of the autodidact, the jack-of-all-trades, the pioneer improvisor, which invests the optimistic philosophy of can-do. The universal mechanic was a cheerful ideal when the country was still to be conquered in its physical boundlessness. But now a residual amateurism degrades a recognition of standards, and yet at the same time secretes a distrust and a resentment of the strict limitations of a professional elite. It is as if the performing arts, an area inhabited by entertainers, have a less serious right to elevate their skills into a necessary service.

CURRENT ADVANTAGES OF ANARCHY

Part of this problem is of course taken care of by the process of natural selection, by personal suitability, obvious talent or the glaring lack of it. The survival of the fittest and loose, happily upward mobility magnetizes or canalizes superior energy past puberty. This is perhaps one of the chief advantages of an anarchic popular democracy. Our loose, uncoordinated, even unlicensed system may be ultimately wasteful in its disregard of an ultimate potential, but its awkward mechanism has proven more productive than the tidy regimentation of the British system which inhibits recruitment of dance students on the basis of a preposterous outworn nineteenth century syllabus, a chauvinist restriction on international instruction, and the severe societal limitation of an entrenched teachers' association. The needs of our regions and centers have to be balanced and reconciled, yet one may hope that the pressures of a national movement can be firmly directed toward the truths of virtuoso quality in teaching and performance, which has little to do with the blind will or wish to perform or with the support of a passive liberal-minded community to award "A for Effort."

Obstacles to the Present

The social sciences over the last half-century have not convinced us that they provide a metric which is much more than a choice of statistics. Investigations and reports concerning costs or conditions of the performing arts rarely penetrate into the radical humane reasons for their stimulation or resistance, except for the presumption that culture is somehow therapeutic.

THE TWO SIDES OF THE COIN

Apathy and ignorance, energy and inertia, are not quantitative abstractions, and although they may be read as blanket numerical simplifications of persistent states of mind involving suspicion and resentment, they remain constants in any developed society. Weber, the famous sociologist, has imagined "we are moving from the simple legitimacies and irrationalities of traditional society to the desolation of instrumental rationality in a megalopolitan context." But however our present situation is offered or analysed, any grand revelation pointing toward a solution of a permanent dilemma seems far away. Costs (labor, managerial, entrepreneurial, artistic) have to rise, along with the rest of the economy. Inflation is only more death and taxes. The sole consolation history has to offer is that there has never been an epoch which has not had its well-informed prophets of imminent doomsday. We are not now in a situation for despair, and it is a selfish betrayal for anyone to try to gain an individual point by pretending that the demise of a single performing arts institution means the end of civilization. This has been a happy cry of "Wolf, wolf!" by those who can best afford to hire Madison Avenue to save their skins.

Rather than the terror of costs, it is the fear of the free-wheeling, far-ranging imagination whose products cannot be anticipated or measured by negotiable values which is not to be legislated away either by votes or cash. Indeed, we have much for which we may be thankful. In some ways we are quite in luck. Western civilization has managed to take for its models birds and beasts rather than ants or bees. Our mechanical and industrial energy or ingenuity, our brute physical force derived from the centuries of marvelous amalgam of the cream of European immigration have given us an affluence, however feverish, which is fat enough to permit a fraction of its waste to support the fruitful chaos of unprogrammed discovery, invention, and, yes, creation. When we look at the state of our performance efficiency today, no matter what its ragged activity, compared with the deliberate retardation (or death) of the ancient patrimony of Russia or China, we can soberly congratulate ourselves on our freedom from the kind of bland maintenance which only promotes a tyrannical, organized, and exhausted stasis.

THE PROTECTION OF "DE MINIMIS"

Nevertheless, we can never underestimate the millions of our own people who are taxed, and who must always resent any portion of their dollars being assigned to matters in which they find small delight. Yet even here art seems to protect itself, finding its own scale of survival on an interstitial level. The portion of the tax dollar likely to be spent on so impractical an action as the art of performance in theaters can hardly serve as a red rag to whatever bulls would smash our precious china shop. We are free to be poor, to conduct our poverty in private, free to fail, free to manage our improvisation, permitted to fool around with projections as long as they appear to satisfy the worst fears of our few but patient patrons. We live in a land fat enough to support our home-grown anarchy to which we are quite accustomed, and our abject respect for the name and category of "education" has its lucky as well as its specious aspect. All money raisers know that "education" is spelled "open-sesame," and that if art, or culture, can be identified with some general massive hope, it is that much less frightful. Many of our causes essential to the survival of the arts survive by some hygienic or ancillary attachment to a remote and often irrational "educational" process or service to the very young or the very old, where compassion forgives disquiet.

THE RECASTING OF PRIORITIES

Finally, what the performing arts need is not "audience-education," but the continued, adequate subvention of professionally educated performers, producers, and their products which their long and arduous education displays and requires. Money for preparatory levels is well spent, but not unless it is balanced by the maintenance of those self-elected and self-surviving institutions whose unique responsibility is the growth and tender care of repertories which sooner or later become the prime resource and residue of education itself. "Audience-education" has unduly legitimized nonprofessional attitudes in both acting and dancing. This hardly affects a far more sophisticated public for both sport and music; there is no dilettantism in the professional ball player, pianist, or violinist. The levels of improvisatory or dilettante performance in the ancient crafts of dance and drama only leave students with false notions of the time, task, and talent which alone produce peak performance. The overall lack of primary physical qualification for a dancer can at once be recognized as ridiculous compared to conditions controlling candidates for highly professional "amateur" players of ball games. But ball games are serious business, with vast alumnae and popular support. Also, they can be televised to sell cosmetics. It is accepted that ballet is an ephemeral and special diversion, while the *pas de deux* is about its only formal fragment (apart from the portraiture of individual star personalities) which can be currently photographed with a quality which remotely approaches live impact.

If anything positive can come out of societal analysis in the next years relative to a reduction of resistance to the aid of our performing arts, it might be well to spend effort on particularization, on trying to pinpoint those areas most sensitive to possible improvement, namely what works toward a more just and conscious appreciation of the nature of peak performance and its preparation, its difference from mere diversion or entertainment, its otherness from self-indulgence and amateurism, its capacity to prove and improve the limits of physical and imaginative possibility. Continued confusion and, with it, impotence is caused by peripheral considerations, rhetorical and political, and while one has to continue to talk to the apathetic and ignorant, there are limitations which must be accepted both as permanent and even endurable.

THE FINAL AUTHORITY OF ART

The main problem is indeed one of "education," but an education in strategic or tactical policies rather than secondary or propitiatory ones. If live performances were more widely dispersed on a proper broad scale, if vivid virtuosic action was in some more continuous position to be made immediate, there would be small need to educate a public as to prime quality. The mass public may "know nothing about art," but they are, or can be, electrified past ignorance by authority in skill. They cannot be fooled or confused by the essence of peak performance whatever their ignorance of refinements of grace or technique. Ballet or opera may not "do much for or to" overwhelming numbers of watchers or hearers, but those who are a bit more than idly attached recognize the veracity of the virtuoso, and even their numerical orders are not contemptible. Audiences need to be "educated" not only by participation and attendance, but also by the need to recognize the exact processes by which performances come into being and are maintained, with money or without it, when indeed there are no audiences present to watch such preparation.

THE COMPARISON WITH EUROPE

The performing arts may "entertain," although they have suffered grievously from hasty identification with entertainment. The dictionary includes among its definitions, indeed as its first one, but alas, italicized as *now rare*: "a. To maintain; keep up. b. To retain,

as in service. c. To give reception to; to receive." The meanings
of amusement or diversion, once subordinate, have become capital.
Today, if people cannot pay for being entertained, the rational
answer is that either they cannot afford it, do not want it, or do
not deserve it. How much and/or how many really want or need it?
If we want it enough, we could or should pay for it. Since per-
suasion on the scale of indeterminate necessity has so slight a clout,
since other pressures are so much more urgent, is there much hope
that we can do more than already has been done? We can console
ourselves perhaps even in the relative unimportance of cultural
prestige. In the United States, our prime complaint is not what we
do, or how it is done, but how little we have for what we might do.
Great Britain, despite or indeed because of its dependence on an
Arts Council as a centralized authority, has to face the rage of
Scotland and Wales and the provinces of Britain (which have not
been propitiated by nominal promotion to "regions") for an over-
emphasis on Greater London as the capital of culture and the seat
of national and royal ballet, opera, and theater. The regions have
little chance to witness shows they pay for presented in the home
counties with anything approaching the panache of Covent Garden
or the South Bank. Canada, despite its generous arts budget, has to
pacify legislative rancor in hiring expensive alien performers to
insure those foreign appearances in New York and elsewhere which
make a national prestige, something upon which the young native
institutions can one day be built. Russian support of the performing
arts surpasses all others in fiscal terms, but their development has
been catastrophic in the debasement of their own performance
morale, restricted on every imaginative level, surviving only in a
muscular limbo of mechanical activity. Certainly, admitting our
dollar starvation, the United States lacks nothing in talent, executive, inventive, or technical. In potential, we are incomparably the
envy of the world, and it is by no chance that Europe is increasingly
staffed by American directors, choreographers, dancers, and repertoire just as New York has replaced the hegemony of Paris in the
realm of the visual arts and architecture.

If one is impatient or greedy or just a worker in the field, progress in appreciation or development may seem in sad arrears; yet
perhaps without diluting our energy we should be grateful for
what we have and are. Our busy interstitial activity is more healthy
and active and free of imposed conditions than many more ancient

households. Consider the restrictions under which the Paris Grand Opera operates, with its unchanging nightmare of labor relation confusion, its haphazard dependence on a presiding minister or intendant who falls with each change of government, its entrenched chauvinism, all of which derives from the imperial patronage of Louis XIV but which still maintains a popular prestige as criterion of the world's lyric theater and ballet. Our pendulum seems to be swinging, however slowly, toward sympathy for the arts of performance. As appropriations increase at whatever snail's pace, and against whatever sluggish governmental encouragement, political and geographic distribution will be proportional, and with this inevitably comes spread and dilution. But in their supreme acrobacy or virtuosity, the performing arts cannot be diluted any more than professional sports will employ fewer prime ball players. And lonely, egotistical, hardy, willful, courageous, and talented individuals will continue to exercise their own priceless and indefensible gifts, no matter what support, or lack of it, allows.

POPULISM AND ELITISM

Programs for development, platforms for policy and diplomacy, aid for formal lobbying in the Congress will unquestionably pursue their useful paths. One can only hope that an immediate virtual desperation may make common cause on attractive populist grounds yet not vitiate principles or standards. The performing arts with their essential specialization cannot be popularized out of intrinsic quality. This quality, muscular, mental, and moral, aiming toward perfection in practice, will never be reduced, whatever compulsive political demands may come for adopting one stance or another as the chronological moment requires. Some epochs are chronologically unlucky. Franklin Roosevelt's enlightened and productive public works project was the greatest arts patronage this country ever enjoyed. The Congress killed it, mindlessly, as boondoggling. The time was wrong, but the precedent remains. We are indeed luckier due to the examples and sacrifices of our predecessors, artists, and lawmakers.

However, if there is one single primacy which can be presently considered, accepted, and then fought for, it is the assertion or admission that there is in fact and deed an *elite*, that this elite, not only on account of its peculiarity but despite it, deserves to be legitimized, fostered, preserved, encouraged. The word *elite*, like so many others which were once unprintable or almost unthinkable, must emerge into the vulgate and colloquial, in the frank and full illumination of its veritable intention. For *elitism* does mean something definite, discrete, apart. It is not a dirty word, a loose epithet, a convenient demogogic handle left to the barbaric defacement of professional philistines. Elite is a word to be fought for. Around it has accumulated a dusty web of vague negatives which have come to affirm a positive pejorative, a fair justification for mindless unpopularity and tacit antipopularism. Similarly, the term "esoteric" once meant what was known only to a select and worthy few, unavailable to the commonality. Most specialists deal in esoterics— neurologists, astronauts, mining engineers, astronomers. Their specialties deal in fact rather than fancy or fantasy, and constitute them as an elite. But the esoterics of the artist are no less special, apart, difficult, and demanding of legitimacy.

THE TRUE ELITE AND THE FALSE

The root meaning of the word *elite* is election, which implies also, selection. The big Oxford dictionary first defines it as "a person chosen," citing an early example: "a bishop *elect*." This involves further "the choice or flower of society, or of any body or class of persons." Election, selection, choice. Aristotle said man was a choosing rather than a rational agent. Who elects, selects, chooses? Who has the energy or capacity of rational choice? First of all comes a candidature. History or circumstance, at once or in eventual perspective, recognizes clear claims of peak accomplishments, personal or collective. But we must also admit that an elite is self-responsible, self-chosen, and in a rather lonely sense, self-serving. Who has the wit to choose? Only those who have been exposed to the vast possibilities in a range of choice. The commonality hardly appoints an elite; it merely confirms it, either by awe or acclaim. The very quality of difference, excellence, or superiority is so self-evident and proven by inherent capacity that finally, despite initial resistance which is almost a sign of its status, it elects itself. The elite is, perforce, an aristocracy; however impotent politically, culturally it is imperial. We know that to the Greeks *ariston* meant the best. It has become one of the ironies or paradoxes of our democratic dictionary that *intelligence* has, by recent historical accidental attachment, a meaning associated with sinister. *Shrewd, clever, ambitious* have all been reduced to negative epithets. These all connote or denote a presence of energy, rational or at least intellectual, and all act as offenses against apathy or inertia rooted in ignorance. The word *elite* is possible to use in a positive popular frame only if it is disqualified as applying to a suspect, localized, and hedged minority, with condign supercilious attributes. If the defenders, patrons, and promoters of the performing arts over the term of the Carter administration have one salient, modest, persistent duty or objective responsibility, it is to reason and clarify their claims to be associated with a legitimate elite alongside ball players, brain surgeons, or brokers. It is time for the inventive, lyric, poetic, creative elite to come out of their closets and declare themselves—their worth, their difference in kind, their capacity, their energy, and their strength. Most of all—their necessity.

Of course this last must sound more like a rhetorical boast or fantasy than a plank in a political platform which may soon be acted upon. Elitism should be a rallying cry for that band of brothers and sisters who bear the culture of their country, for it is this cultivation of the only memorable residue that marks and outlives their epoch which justifies their permission to perform and produce as free agents, whatever the risk or cost to their countrymen.

W. McNeil Lowry

9

Conclusion

The arts of performance in the United States, unlike what happened in Europe, reached their most extensive development outside either commercial or governmental initiative. The nationalization of culture in Great Britain, for example, proceeded from royal, parliamentary, or municipal charters to preserve for the British public treasures in the visual arts and later the artistic display of creations in music, theater, and dance. In the United States, federal initiatives were lacking until most recent times, except for the brief experiment of a WPA program motivated by a political concern with unemployment in all fields. Municipal governments sometimes made small contributions to the maintenance costs of artistic institutions, but these were institutions that had been established by private patronage and continued to depend on it for any real financial stability. Commercial impresarios penetrated even very small communities until the first decade of this century, but thereafter played a very small role except in the theater and in the management of concert artists.

Voluntary associations were the vehicle for the formation of orchestras and opera companies even before the second decade of this century when income and inheritance tax legislation permitted a broadening of the base of private patronage. Until 1945 symphony and opera continued to be the chief beneficiaries; dance and theater then slowly began to enforce their own claims. By the time public agencies began to accept limited responsibility for cultural resources in the nation, private and foundation patronage had legitimized all the performing arts.

This is far more than a matter of the economics of the performing arts. Orchestras, operas, theaters, and dance companies have developed in the United States through social, ethical, and political influences peculiar to this country and often contrasted with Europe's even before DeTocqueville devoted so much attention to them. Pluralism and diversity was one aspect. The reliance on voluntary rather than on public or commercial initiative was another and more basic aspect, however, and it conditions both the structure of performing arts institutions and the issues of policy concerning them. At this level, and only at this level, the issues about performing arts institutions are fundamentally the same. Six of the preceding chapters, including the symposium on training and career development, have characterized the differences. In this conclusion these differences will be largely, though not totally, ignored.

THE ARTISTIC PROCESS

Some of the most noted professionals in theater or dance often perform upon commercial stages in our largest cities, and many talented singers concertize under commercial management and record for commercial distributors. The claim persists, however, that the nonprofit voluntary association is in the United States the instrument best suited to the nature of the artistic process and allows for greater concentration on qualitative and aesthetic standards. An actor who is already highly trained may survive a very long run in a Broadway hit, not only to his financial but also to his professional credit, if the role is sufficiently rich. But to obtain the most varied and continuous training in serious dramatic roles and techniques he may require a producer who can, in part, subordinate profits to other goals. By extending the time spent on rehearsal and shortening the length of the run, the nonprofit producer offers the performer a variety of craft experiences and the public a serious repertoire both classical and contemporary. Even if the commercial producer were also subsidized for 30 or 40 percent of his costs, he would have difficulty limiting a run to four weeks. The concentration on the artistic process is taken by nonprofit producers as the best justification for the 30 to 40 percent subsidies to their operations. Here they believe they merge aesthetic and professional with social goals and the enrichment of experience for their audiences. Whether they are right or wrong, it is a question of public policy to consider what the quality of American dance, theater, opera, and symphony would be today had only the commercial mechanism been employed in their development. The same question arises when we consider what might be the career opportunities of dancers, musicians, singers, actors, directors, playwrights, composers, and choreographers.

GOVERNANCE AND ADMINISTRATION

The social, ethical, and political influences upon the development of artistic institutions in America also condition the way in which they are governed. The reliance upon the nonprofit corporation as the instrument is, of course, the most pervasive. Artistic producers or an association of patrons took the initiative for forming the organization and therefore had the responsibility for preserving it. If the initiative came solely from patrons, the trustees normally maintained the balance of power through the institution's history, though the emergence of a strong artistic or musical director could now and then change this pattern. If an artistic director were really the founder, even though without his or her own financial resources, the trustees gave up major control except over the outside limits of budgetary planning. This latter phenomenon largely showed itself after 1945 and affected theater and dance much more than opera or symphony, the models for which were set in the nineteenth century. The chapters on theater and ballet in this volume are useful case histories of the continuing administrative roles of two founding directors. The chapter on symphony details the continuing shifts in tension between a board and a conductor characteristic of that field but, by centering upon the Atlanta Symphony Orchestra, has no occasion to treat a new and sweeping trend among American orchestras—the administrative autonomy of the general manager now that all major orchestras rely on musical directors who conduct for only a part of the season or even share that title between two orchestras. The chapter on opera treats an institution that is atypical though not unique in its field, one founded after World War II by a strong general director.

The roles of the trustee in performing arts groups have been to elucidate and support the director's goals, to assist in (or at least to examine) its fiscal and management practices, and to contribute or obtain money needed above earned income. Since there is more than one role, there has been the need for more than one kind of trustee. The initial association of patrons may have done without an executive committee by a de facto assumption of that role while adding to the board any patron willing to contribute regularly to financial needs. Sometimes the proliferation came through recognition that particular groups or interests within the community were not represented on the board and were useful in enlarging audiences, selling memberships, or increasing annual gifts. Until recently this widening of the base of board membership still left most of them constituencies of the middle and upper class in economic terms. But since the sixties, two trends have emerged. One is the effort to break unwieldy boards between either voting trustees and patrons or an executive committee and a board meeting only annually. The other is the trend toward a board representing not only the broad community but actual delegates from labor, industry, government, and existing ethnic or racial minorities. The latter trend is fraught with controversy because it is often pushed on the institution by municipal, state, or federal funding agencies.

A more concrete description of the role of trustees can be made only in terms of its relationship to those of the artistic director and of the general manager. We have noted that these vary somewhat between performing arts fields and also through varying historical antecedents in the same field. Even the most experienced practitioners might agree that there is (to them) a *desirable* norm but would be hard pressed to find a charter for it, even one comparable to the *Professional Practices in Art Museums* promulgated by the Association of Art Museum Directors in 1971:

> Trustees, administrators, curators, staff, visitors, members, and public officials all have an interest in the institution. . . . Good governance depends on a reasonable allocation of responsibilities among all those groups. . . . It is impossible that all should decide everything or be consulted on every issue. . . . The administration of an art museum demands not only the acumen and procedural awareness needed in the administration of any corporation, but also taste, knowledge, and experience of a highly specialized nature. . . .

As in art museums, legal responsibility is invested in the trustees. The director or manager may or may not have a contract but has no tenure, and, until quite recently, no arrangement, however inadequate, to be pensioned off. Even today there are performing arts groups in which a committee of the board approves repertoire in each season, but what is significant about this is that within their own fraternities the existence of such an arrangement is now considered not only rare but notorious.

Bereft of a chartered authority outside any individual corporate bylaws, the artistic producer or director has sincere or tacit acceptance by the trustees as the final professional voice over the selection of performer, the works to be performed, and the creative goals of the institution. In many, many companies, until quite recently, this was thought to be enough when added (hopefully) to the strength of his or her talent, character, and personality. More recently, even the strongest director has come to realize that the group's objectives are more likely to be achieved where there is also a division of responsibility, a sharing of information, and a readiness to subject authority to the requirements of a well-defined system of accountability. The classic board and staff conflicts on the intervention of one or more wealthy trustees in artistic policies—and they have been legendary in each field of the performing arts—sometimes made communication and reporting seem like infringements upon the prerogatives of either the director or the board, but both the new scale and the new numbers of institutions have altered these attitudes (even while new conflicts arise and run their course). The greater presence of organized national sources of financial support and technical assistance has also worked to produce this result. Artistic producers now discuss long-range plans and goals more freely with their own trustees before annual budgets are formally submitted.

These developments have enlarged the whole question of management at both the board and staff levels. Traditionally the treasurer of a performing arts institution has been an officer from the board rather than from the staff. Now most boards have a finance committee to assist the treasurer, separate from the normal executive committee. And the manager, who a generation ago might have been the only full-time staff person not engaged in artistic and production activities, has a staff divided among three or more departments. The general manager has always engaged in more detailed reporting to the board than was required of the artistic director; and as accountability has taken on a more important role, relations between managers and artistic directors have been affected, often with by-products of tension or even conflict. Except in the symphony field, the director's leadership role has not been downgraded, though both in a few opera companies and in a few theaters, it has recently been challenged. (There are indeed a handful of resident theater companies in which the manager has continuity and directors are brought in for one or more productions.) The answer to the division of authority lies ultimately, of course, with the board.

In the main, even allowing for personality influences, boards of trustees recognize the artistic director as the apex. Ideally the manager informs the director of the agenda of his imminent discussions with a board or board committee even if the director is too concentrated on artistic matters to immerse himself in details. If board and manager perpetuate the layman's myth that an artistic director is impractical, improvident, or even fey, a manager may not only go around the director but attempt to wrest control of the institution from him. These attempts have proved to be either short-lived or disastrous in most instances, even when the director has been complaisant. Nonprofit corporations appear to have intrinsic laws, and when a university, conservatory, museum, foundation, hospital, or performing institution either dilutes or overinflates the authority of the chief executive director, important changes impend. Dilution is the more usual pathogenic agent for change. Overinflation allows a slower incubation of the crisis because the director has normally to be hanged in public before being interred by his board. (Sometimes public erection of the gallows draws a board together to protect the institution and with it the director.)

In the norm, the artistic director also is the institution's public voice. By the seventies most nonprofit companies had both a special board or allied committee and one or more full-time staff persons under the manager working on fund raising. But many donors, not only organized foundations but even private patrons, expect to deal with the producing director particularly to hear his or her own exposition of the institution's artistic goals. To ease the burden on the director's time, original contacts and presentations may be made by others. This will not always work, however. Foundations with a specific program interest in the arts continue to be reluctant to deal with development officers or individual trustees as substitutes for the professional director, who often may have served the foundation as an informal or formal consultant. In dealings with the National Endowment for the Arts, the director may be not only a consultant but a member of one of the panels of selection in his own field.

In the growing concern with public advocacy of the arts, artistic directors, managers, and influential trustees all appear to have a role. Artistic directors until the mid-seventies generally shunned the advocate's function except when working with a specific institution supporting the arts. The result was that most advocacy and all lobbying was dominated by laymen or by artist unions and the officers of institutional associations like the American Symphony Orchestra League. When the expenditures of the NEA were divided between the support of artistic institutions and a variety of social and educational objectives, many professionals in the field concluded that they must speak more clearly for their own objectives. To lobby simply for greater appropriations to the NEA did not automatically translate itself into greater stabilization of existing institutional resources. If the question were not *how much money for the arts* but *why money for the arts in the first place*, then the artistic directors and performers might have to take the lead.

Individual artistic directors may choose to delegate to their managers the largest role in representing the institution. The job of the manager in the performing arts generally has been converted into a professional only in the past twenty years, though even at the start of that period it was better defined and more organized in the orchestra field. Theater and dance companies may have had only one full-time person in an administrative capacity. Until the early seventies managers generally developed through internship on the job, often supported through specific grants from a national foundation. The interns may have originally been performers or stage managers; sometimes they were recent college graduates with a general interest in the arts. Since the sixties, university departments in one of the performing arts or special university programs in arts administration have supplied others. Now the managers of even a middle-sized company may supervise three or more departments with three or more employees in each. By 1971 administrative personnel accounted for about 17 percent of operating budgets, and, given the number of institutions in each field, young people could with some confidence plan a career in the administration of a performing arts group. Now they can even seek specialization—fund development, accounting and fiscal control, promotion and subscription, press and public relations. Twenty years ago, this would have been an impossibility outside the largest symphony and opera organizations.

THE FUTURE OF THE PERFORMING ARTS

As defined in Chapter 1, this volume has concentrated on music, opera, theater, and dance in their professional aspects and upon performing artists and artistic directors and producers who strive for or have attained professional standards. The level of discussion has ranged from the historical to the quite personal and from concrete to the broadly philosophical and aesthetic, but always in one way or another returning to the final objective—the moment of ultimate performance before the public. Though beginning and ending with individual vantage points, taken together the separate papers say that the future of the arts depends upon the answer to one question: What is the importance of the arts to the American society?

This is not merely a truism or an evasion, given the fact that even three-quarters of the way through the twentieth century there is no public policy about the arts. At first glance this would not appear to be unique. Despite a mass of legislation, there is no single policy about pollution, energy, conservation, surface transportation, or public housing. But there are policies that are understood and regularly advanced in each of these fields. They permit both choice and change, and they occupy federal, state, and municipal legislatures; the executive; the press and other media; and a whole variety of public and voluntary forums in the process. To have a public policy in any field, Woodrow Wilson said in 1910, "The man who has the time, the discrimination and the sagacity to collect and comprehend the principal facts and the man who must act upon them must draw near to one another and feel that they are engaged in a common enterprise." A defined public policy exists when it is generally *understood*; it need not be generally *agreed* upon. The contest between the federal executive and the Congress over energy questions, for example, would not exist if there were one agreed national policy. Its understanding of the executive's policy is what provokes the conflict in Congress, and far beyond Congress, to industry, labor, press, and the public.

But more than a decade after federal legislation in the field, there is no generally understood and defined public policy about the arts, and only recently have professionals in the arts, interested laymen, and the press even begun to point to this fact. To determine the policy of the most conspicuous national agency in the field, the National Endowment for the Arts, one must begin by looking at the beneficiaries of its expenditures rather than at its legislative authorization or the three general objectives which introduce its reports to the President (noted in Chapter 1). But this exercise is clarifying only to a point, and it leaves in suspension the question whether the national government's objective is the stabilization and expansion of artistic enterprises, the education of young children, the provision of community and welfare services, or the general education of adults.

If the future of the arts is dependent upon public recognition of their importance to the society, then a host of other questions is subsumed. Does their importance have to do with the question of values at the philosophical and ethical level? Are they important also because they are the professions (or would-be professions) of many persons who believe they have a social function equivalent to that of other skilled and unskilled workers?

At this philosophical and moral level, we must deal with what remains of the Puritan dilemma in American history—the ideal versus the useful, the sacral versus the materialistic. Though we are more than three centuries beyond Plymouth and the Massachusetts Bay Colony, how strongly does this influence persist? Or is it largely our historical consciousness of a stereotype that makes us wonder whether the public accepts artists or their creations only as instruments to educational and social ends? Who needs them? Mr. Kirstein asks in his chapter. Are they really icing on the cake compared to our "real" needs? Performing arts companies have higher proportions of earned income than either colleges or hospitals, but both colleges and hospitals have nevertheless done a much better job in explaining their need for subsidies.

But if art and the artist are important intrinsically and inherently, do they then represent elitism in a democratic society? No issue threatening their future has been more perverted and confused than this one, by the proponents of public support of the arts as well as by the opponents. The proponents, including most especially the National Endowment for the Arts, have engaged in elaborate numbers games about the economic side effects of theaters and centers for the performing arts in a city or region and the ever increasing audiences and have used commercial polling services to suggest wider and wider public interest. (Note that the writers on theater, ballet, opera, and symphony in this volume wrestle with themselves in answering their own questions about the size of audiences versus the cost of survival.) The opponents decry the use of either taxpayers' or stockholders' moneys for the support of elitist institutions.

None of this is more acute than before the federal government intervened in the economics of the arts in 1965; in fact it is much less acute. But the distorting effect of the argument is nevertheless real because it has been translated into the terms and objectives of the government's aid. It is argued that populism and democratization are ensured if the aid is pushed only partially to existing groups and institutions in the arts and more heavily to educational, community, and avocational activities in every corner of the country. But those who actually have built the bridge to the public in every region of the United States know that there is more than one approach to decentralization. If agencies, public or private, in the support of the arts seek to build on talented and forceful leadership wherever found, this is decentralization that has a chance to become permanent. It is more important, for example, for cities outside New York to have their own performing institution than to be left only as a spot on a tour or with only amateur groups that lack the means to do better. As Mr. Novick's chapter indicates, this was how the resident theater movement in the United States was brought about, and it stretches from lower California to Massachusetts and from Florida to the state of Washington.

If the National Endowment for the Arts were to regard everything that now exists as ipso facto part of the "establishment" and steadily proliferate in avocational or community service activities, its program would conflict with, rather than provide momentum for, the growth and expansion in the performing arts that began twenty years ago. "I clawed this theater out of the ground," Nina Vance is quoted by Mr. Novick about the Alley Theatre in Houston. The federal government can support educational and community services in their own right and be clear about what it is doing.

Without a more clearly understood public policy about the arts, the public and its legislative representatives are treated to many false antitheses between "elitism" and "populism." Whether working in New York or in Houston, Milwaukee, or Atlanta we can seek talent or potentiality wherever found and attempt to cultivate it. It cannot be found in geographical or dollar quotas. As Mr. Roddy notes in his chapter on symphony, one can set standards for the art or the craft in the nineteenth largest orchestra in the country as well as in the first. Robert Shaw of Atlanta is quoted by Roddy: "The vitality of the arts depends upon their reaching the people without losing their own integrity."

In its strict sense, before it became a pejorative, elitism meant the single exercise of choice—between two talents, two artistic performances, two companies of performers. Mr. Kirstein's extensive and eloquent analysis of the argument includes the caveat that the artist, at least, cannot avoid choice and must proclaim that position. If there is to be an effective public debate, one of the issues that has to be dealt with is that a democracy can have a national policy for the arts that does not abandon standards and disciplines by treating every manifestation alike.

To this, of course, the professionals above all must contribute. If the end sought were scientific policy or the importance of science to the society, could we find a realistic and practical balance of priorities by leaving advocacy to dedicated laymen and community leaders? Nor will the question of priorities be answered by a huge increase in public funds for the arts. Much time and effort has been expended upon this argument, and yet the priorities in the NEA's program have remained basically constant since the first of successive increases in its budget beginning in 1971 (see Chapter 1).

A more analytical policy about the arts, furthermore, cannot be confined to the question of public support, and the arts constituency continues to founder in a strategy that ignores this principle. The historical introduction in Chapter 1 presents some of the elements underlying it. Can the United States maintain a balance between private and public support of the arts (which is of course now unbalanced in favor of the private)? If not, public support itself will be affected. The growing acceptance by Congress of cultural activities as meriting federal encouragement could be one casualty. Bureaucratic control of the arts, even without the specter of censorship, is also at stake. If there are desirable limits to public support, they may have to do less with the risk of political control than with the steady public dilution of private and voluntary societies in the American tradition and the creation of a civil service concerned more about popularity than about discrimination and choice. Are there dangers in the yardstick of quality that in any way match those in the yardstick of popularization?

Private patrons, national foundations, and corporations are all necessary points of reference in any public policy about the arts. Though constituting the largest proportion of unearned income in every field of the arts, the private patron almost exclusively confines his support to one or more favorite institutions and leaves it to government and to national foundations to do more. In 1974 the largest of the national foundations used the greater appropriations to the NEA as an excuse to do less, though the level latterly reached in the Andrew W. Mellon Foundation was maintained. The loss of dollar support was important. What was more important, however, was a change in the terms of national foundation support. New groups responding to new artistic leadership were formerly given leverage to help stimulate private patrons. They were, in effect, established in partnership with an organized foundation. In the late seventies this became more difficult, and the annual grants in operating support by the NEA could not be used to launch a new company. Beginning in 1977, private patronage of new enterprises was again threatened by the pressures of existing institutions for moneys to legitimize "challenge" grants offered by the NEA. National corporations, like private patrons but on a much smaller scale, have made their direct grants largely to cultural organizations in the city in which their headquarters were located. When they used their own operational budgets in advertising and public relations, as noted in Chapter 1, the bulk of the funds went to the mass media. One of the questions in a public policy about the arts is to fix reasonable expectations about the growth of corporate support of the arts from outright grants. There plainly are ways in which a national corporation can make a national impact on a performing arts field, but an understanding of real or imagined obstacles to such a policy depends upon at least one national corporation's debating it with its stockholders.

The objects of philanthropy in American history begin with the individual donor and move clear across a spectrum of greater and greater organization until they have reached the opposite pole on the public tax roll, where they cease to be only objects of philanthropy and become objects of public policy. (Religious benefactions have been the exception.) The alleviation of suffering, health, social welfare, science, medicine, and education have gone this route.

How to support institutions and activities in each area continues to provoke controversy and frequently changes, but support for them in some fashion is accepted. And every one of these fields is still a complex of private and public support in vastly different proportions from one to another.

The humanities and the arts completed this route only a little more than a decade ago, and it is not surprising that as objects of public policy they are as yet somewhat tentative. They are not only volatile intrinsically, the arts most obviously so, but also have to do with the question of values in any society. And even from a miniscule historical perspective of a decade, the need for a public policy appears urgent. That it should comprehend the artists' own terms appears as reasonable as when almost thirty years ago the White House and Congress wrestled with the scientists' terms in the establishment of a National Science Foundation.

William Blake wrote: "He who would do good to another must do it in minute particulars: General good is the plea of the scoundrel, hypocrite, and flatterer."

Index

The American Assembly

Columbia University

About The American Assembly

The American Assembly was established by Dwight D. Eisenhower at Columbia University in 1950. It holds nonpartisan meetings and publishes authoritative books to illuminate issues of United States policy.

An affiliate of Columbia, with offices in the Graduate School of Business, the Assembly is a national educational institution incorporated in the State of New York.

The Assembly seeks to provide information, stimulate discussion, and evoke independent conclusions in matters of vital public interest.

AMERICAN ASSEMBLY SESSIONS

At least two national programs are initiated each year. Authorities are retained to write background papers presenting essential data and defining the main issues in each subject.

A group of men and women representing a broad range of experience, competence, and American leadership meet for several days to discuss the Assembly topic and consider alternatives for national policy.

All Assemblies follow the same procedure. The background papers are sent to participants in advance of the Assembly. The Assembly meets in small groups for four or five lengthy periods. All groups use the same agenda. At the close of these informal sessions, participants adopt in plenary session a final report of findings and recommendations.

Regional, state, and local Assemblies are held following the national session at Arden House. Assemblies have also been held in England, Switzerland, Malaysia, Canada, the Caribbean, South America, Central America, the Philippines, and Japan. Over one hundred thirty institutions have co-sponsored one or more Assemblies.

ARDEN HOUSE

Home of the American Assembly and scene of the national sessions is Arden House, which was given to Columbia University in 1950 by W. Averell Harriman. E. Roland Harriman joined his brother in contributing toward adaptation of the property for conference purposes. The buildings and surrounding land, known as the Harriman Campus of Columbia University, are 50 miles north of New York City.

Arden House is a distinguished conference center. It is self-supporting and operates throughout the year for use by organizations with educational objectives.

AMERICAN ASSEMBLY BOOKS

The background papers for each Assembly are published in cloth and paperbound editions for use by individuals, libraries, businesses, public agencies, nongovernmental organizations, educational institutions, discussion and service groups. In this way the deliberations of Assembly sessions are continued and extended.